Three Sides of Life

Open windows to three sides of life—fear sits at the other.
Girl, never blaze up like the setting sun in the evening...
You must be a glass-domed lamp, to others' whims a thrall...

Rajlakshmi Devi: 'Meye' (Girl)

Three Sides of Life

Short Stories by Bengali Women Writers

ASHAPURNA DEVI
MAHASWETA DEVI
NABANEETA DEV SEN
BANI BASU
SUCHITRA BHATTACHARYA

Edited by

Saumitra Chakravarty

With an Introduction by

Tutun Mukherjee

OXFORD
UNIVERSITY PRESS

OXFORD
UNIVERSITY PRESS

YMCA Library Building, Jai Singh Road, New Delhi 110 001

Oxford University Press is a department of the University of Oxford.
It furthers the University's objective of excellence in research, scholarship,
and education by publishing worldwide in

Oxford   New York
Auckland   Cape Town   Dar es Salaam   Hong Kong   Karachi
Kuala Lumpur   Madrid   Melbourne   Mexico City   Nairobi
New Delhi   Shanghai   Taipei   Toronto

With offices in
Argentina   Austria   Brazil   Chile   Czech Republic   France   Greece
Guatemala   Hungary   Italy   Japan   Poland   Portugal   Singapore
South Korea   Switzerland   Thailand   Turkey   Ukraine   Vietnam

Oxford is a registered trade mark of Oxford University Press
in the UK and in certain other countries.

Published in India
by Oxford University Press, New Delhi

MR. Omayal Achi MR. Arunachalam Trust was set up in 1976 to further education
and health care particularly in rural areas. The MR. AR. Educational Society was
later established by the Trust. One of the Society's activities is to sponsor Indian
literature. This translation is entirely funded by MR. AR. Educational Society

ISBN-13: 978 019568585 5
ISBN-10: 019 5685857

Typeset in Perpetua 11.5/13
by Eleven Arts, Keshav Puram, Delhi 110 035
Printed in India by De-Unique, New Delhi-110 018
Published by Oxford University Press
YMCA Library Building, Jai Singh Road, New Delhi 110 001

Dedicated to the memory of my parents

Contents

Acknowledgements

TRANSLATING A DREAM PROJECT INTO A VIABLE, BUYABLE REALITY IS NO easy task, for between the 'word' and its conversion into 'flesh' lie innumerable obstacles, which I, in my 'greenness' was unaware of. It was Prof. S. Ramaswamy, Rhodes scholar, writer, translator, who initiated me into this task, even as he has mentored me in many others and introduced me to Mini Krishnan of the Oxford University Press. To him, my gratitude knows no bounds.

The task of translating and compiling fifteen stories by five well-known women writers of Bengal today, proved formidable, for reasons both literary and practical. During the course of this daunting task, Mini has stood by me like a rock, never losing patience, steering me past the many obstacles that arose during the course of this journey. Our relationship has not ended with that between translator and publisher, she has been more than a friend and guide and helped me with many cheering words through my most despairing moments. I am immensely grateful to her and to her colleagues at the Oxford University Press, both in the offices at Chennai and New Delhi. I express my heartfelt gratitude to Dr Tutun Mukherjee for stepping in so graciously at short notice to write this scholarly introduction and for being so accommodating to our every new demand. I must acknowledge the timely help rendered by Anjum Katyal of Seagull Publishing House in making the three stories of Mahasweta Devi of my choice available to me to suit the theme of this book. I should be failing in my duty if I do not acknowledge my debt to the reviewers whose painstaking correction and suggestions have taught me much about the task of translation. I am grateful to the authors whose works are being translated in this volume, at least two of whom I have had the honour of getting to know personally during the course of this work. Finally I am profoundly thankful to my husband for his support and technical help and advice, to my son for his confidence in me throughout this venture. I am also thankful to my family in Kolkata for making available to me the material I wanted and to my friends in Bangalore for picking up much-needed books during their frequent visits to Kolkata without which this dream would not have been realized.

SAUMITRA CHAKRAVARTY

Contributors

Ashapurna Devi (1909–1995) is one of India's leading literary figures, among the first and foremost writers of Bengal, and surely one of the most prolific and popular writers of the twentieth century. A stalwart of modern Bengali literature, a path-breaking foremother in the history of women's writing, a winner of several prestigious awards including Rabindra Puraskar (1966), the Bharatiya Jnanpith (1978), Sahitya Akademi Fellowship (1994), and Honorary Doctorates from several universities, Ashapurna Devi has written over 176 novels and several volumes of short stories which explore human nature and relationships in ordinary domestic situations, with rare acuity and sensitivity.

Ashapurna Devi's will and strength to pursue her aspiration for learning Bengali was rewarded with the publication of her first poem, when she was thirteen, in a well-known children's magazine called *Shishu Sathi*. Married at the age of fifteen to Kalidas Gupta of Krishnanagar, Ashapurna retained her enchantment for literature and the dream to recreate the seething domestic microcosm through her stories. Her first book was for children, entitled *Choto Thakurer Kashi Jatra* (1938) and her first novel published six years later, was *Prem O Proyojon* (Love and necessity) (1944).

Mahasweta Devi (1926–) is not only a leading literary figure in India, she is perhaps among the most well-known and feted writers in the world today. She has received many prestigious prizes and awards, including the Sahitya Akademi Award (1979), Padmashree (1986), Bharatiya Jnanpith (1996), the Ramon Magsaysay Award (1997), and Padmavibhushan (2006) for her writing as well as for her activism for tribal welfare and the rural dispossessed.

Born in Dacca, East Bengal (modern-day Bangladesh), to Manish Ghatak, a poet and a novelist, and Dharitri Devi, a writer and a social worker, Mahasweta Devi's family was a highly talented and a creative one (for instance, her uncle is Ritwik Ghatak, one of India's best avant-garde filmmakers). She moved with her family to West Bengal as an adolescent and then studied in Vishva Bharati University, Shantiniketan, for a B.A. Honours in English. She interrupted her studies to participate in the nationalist movement and social welfare activities. An early association with 'Gananatya', a group which attempted to bring social and political theatre to rural villages in Bengal in the 1930s and 1940s also left a deep impact. Mahasweta Devi completed a Master's in English at the Calcutta University. She married Bijon Bhattacharya and had a son, Nabarun. In 1964, she started teaching in a college in Kolkata and also became a journalist. There came then a difficult time that she lived through, trying to earn a living by doing various jobs, teaching in a school, and even selling soap.

In the last forty years, Mahasweta Devi has published twenty collections of short stories and nearly a hundred novels, most of which have been translated into several national and global languages. She is also a regular contributor to journals dedicated to the cause of oppressed communities, such as *Bortika*, and is currently an editorial advisor for *Budhan: The Denotified and Nomadic Tribes Rights Action Group Newsletter*, named after Budhan Sabar who was brutally killed in March 1998.

Nabaneeta Dev Sen (1938–), the only child of the poet couple, Narendra Dev and Radharani Devi, was born on 13 January 1938 in Kolkata, and named by the poet Rabindranath Tagore. Nabaneeta seemed destined for a poetic career. She has indeed fulfilled her destiny and has achieved much more besides.

She has carved a place for herself among the best writers of Bengal and is one of the most versatile writers today. She is the recipient of many awards, including the Gouridevi Memorial Award; Mahadevi Verma Award, 1992; Celli Award from the Rockefeller Foundation, 1993; Sarat Award from Bhagalpur University, Bihar, 1994; Prasad Puraskar and Sahitya Akademi Award, 1999; Bangla Akademi's Lifetime Achievement Award, Kabir Samman, and Padmashree, 2000. She was recently nominated the J.P. Naik Distinguished Fellow at the Centre for Women's Developmental Studies, New Delhi.

She launched an illustrious career for herself as an academic when, after graduating from Presidency College and taking a Master's degree from Jadavpur University, Calcutta, she pursued further studies at Harvard University followed by research at Indiana University, USA. She continued her postdoctoral work at the University of California, Berkeley, USA, and at Newnham College, Cambridge University, UK. After a stint as UGC Senior Fellow at Delhi University, she joined the Comparative Literature Department at Jadavpur University and has recently retired as Professor of Comparative Literature after many fruitful years of service. She has travelled around the world on various assignments as an academic and a creative writer. She has delivered the prestigious Radhakrishnan Memorial Lecture Series at Oxford University and has held the Maytag Chair of Creative Writing and Comparative Literature at Colorado College, USA. She has held executive positions in national and international academic and literary bodies like The International Comparative Literature Association; The International Association of Semiotic and Structural Studies; Indian National Comparative Literature Association; Bangiya Sahitya Parishat; the theatre group 'Arshi'; and is the Founder President of 'Shoi', the Women Writers' Association of Bengal.

She has two daughters, Antara and Nandana, with former husband, economist Amartya Sen, and one foster daughter Srabasti.

Bani Basu (b. 1939) is one of Bengal's most talented and creative writers. Born on 11 March 1939 to an upper-middle-class family, Bani Basu pursued her interest in a literary career from her student days. She studied in Lady Brabourne College and Scottish Church College, took a Master's in English Literature from Calcutta University and joined Bijoy Krishna Girls College, Howrah, as a lecturer, where she has worked until her recent retirement. She has received many awards such as Tarashanker Puraskar (1991), Sahitya Setu Puraskar (1995), Susheela Devi Birla Memorial Award, Shiromoni Puraskar, and Ananda Puraskar (1997).

Suchitra Bhattacharya (b. 1950) always loved to make up stories and write them down from the time she was a little girl. She was born on 10 January 1950 in Bhagalpur, Bihar—a non-Bengali region which, by strange coincidence, produced some of the best story-tellers of Bengal, and has gifted yet another talented writer to Bengal.

Bhattacharya moved to Kolkata for higher studies and joined Lady Brabourne College to study Chemistry but discontinued her studies after her marriage. A daughter was born to her. She resumed her studies, however, and graduated with Bengali Honours. In the 1970s, she also began writing in earnest. She joined the West Bengal Civil Service but never delinked herself from creative writing. She is one of the most promising contemporary writers in Bengali literature today and has received several awards such as Nanjungud Thirumalamba Award in Bangalore for the best female writer of the year (1996); Katha Prize (1997); Tarashankar Puraskar; Sahitya Setu Puraskar; and Indu Basu Smriti Literary Prize (1997).

TUTUN MUKHERJEE

Introduction

L ITERATURE CANNOT BE CONFINED FOR LONG WITHIN BORDERS. THE HUMAN experience that the creative imagination captures as a text must cross these borders—whether of a nation or a language—to find its readers, configure a place for itself in a new cultural imaginary, and try to fulfill its potential of being able to travel through space and time.

Fiction elaborates the close links between life and imagination and perhaps that is why fictional narratives are liable to cross borders quickly. The treasure house of Indian literature, for instance, is replete with stories of all kinds, of varying taste and colour, from different regions and with different cultural affiliations. But the corpus is in its great majority, like most discourses, masculine. Till the late nineteenth century, stories were written mostly by men and formed a part of and contributed to the prevailing patriarchal normative order. Except for a few rare instances, women did not write; at least, they did not write stories to be read by the general—mostly male—readers. This, however, should not suggest that women were totally voiceless.[1] Actually, they remained unfailingly close to the oral traditions of story-telling and found hidden and subversive ways to exercise their agency even while appearing outwardly to remain within a repressive social grid. Women narrated—until they could write them down—stories which comprise a vast archive of 'subjugated knowledges'.[2] Indeed, being able to tell stories often marked the line between life and death, whether for a Scheherazade or for the anonymous woman choking with untold tales, because narrating stories made available a mode for realizing one's communal and historical identity since 'who one claims to be' often gets subliminally woven into one's stories.

Women's agency being of contextual importance here, it might be useful to quickly trace the historiography of the Indian woman crossing the proscription of the domestic and private space of articulation and activity to make her voice heard in the public domain of the printed medium. Regrettably, subtle discrimination continues to dog women who write. As has been pointed out time and again, whereas a woman who sings is called a singer, one who dances is a dancer, one who paints is a painter, one who cooks is a cook; the one who writes is invariably described as a 'woman writer'! Why should such a qualifier be used at all? Why should the act of writing be thus set apart? According to Nabaneeta Dev Sen,

This is probably because singing, dancing, cooking appeal to the senses... But the primary appeal of language is to the mind...the woman who dances, cooks, or sings is within her 'rights', but the woman who writes? She is not. She has stepped out of an area of senses and has appropriated a male gesture. Her appeal with words is to the mind and not to the senses. The power relationship has been reversed...she commits an act of transgression against the social code, has trespassed into male territory... (298).

One might very well wonder that when the stereotypes of patriarchy are so strongly persistent (prevailing to this day), how, then, was it ever possible for women to disentangle themselves from operations that immured them in limiting and confining spaces? How was the 'woman writer' born? The answer must be sought in the nineteenth century's dominating dialectics on education, literacy, and social reform—especially with regard to women—that urged self-reflexivity and introspection by creating for the first time a space for public debate[3] and thereby, an ethos that encouraged the development of a cultural critique.

It is important to bear in mind that the growth and consolidation of women's writing in India was integrally related to India's nationalist self-fashioning and the efforts through the years of the freedom struggle to revivify its social and cultural identity. Any review of the sociocultural signposts of the nineteenth century would make manifest the predominating issues of the time and, in addition to which, a genealogical study of texts by women up to 1947 would corroborate the motivations that drove the impulsion of nationalism (Seal).

Through the eighteenth and the nineteenth centuries, the inherent dichotomy in the colonial attitude to India produced contradictory readings of the country and its people as the barbaric subject of reform as well as a repository of usable Orientalist traditions (see Bearce; Kopf). But the primary consequence of the British response was the motivation to redeem the 'natives' from their 'backwardness'. Hence, the British imperialists sought as part of a 'paternalistic'[4] civilizing mission to radically alter the worldview of the Indians and their cultural orientation through the dissemination of Western ideas via English (Majumdar). There is no denying the fact that British intervention not only pushed India towards its 'tryst with destiny',[5] it also initiated profound and complex socio-cultural changes, especially in the position of women in Indian societies.

The obvious manifestation of Indian backwardness and decadence appeared to be the subjugation of Indian women. A major reformative thrust of the colonizers (supported partly by the missionary efforts and partly by 'The White Women's Burden' ideology[6]) was therefore directed towards the social upliftment, education, and cultural emancipation of Indian women. The amelioration of their ignorance and drudgery of their lives was considered possible only through education, which would inculcate in them the values of noble thinking, civilized domesticity and social progress.[7] Much collaborative energy was expended towards this altruistic cause and the ideology of reform—a central element in this configuration—was prioritized in the colonial administrative policies (Ingham; Bayly). The reforms represented the imperialist impetus for change while characterizing and legitimizing the colonial presence as altruistic, philanthropic, and morally responsible.

The British efforts were, however, abrasively ethnocentric and the sword wielded was a double-edged one—cauterizing and sanitizing at once. As a consequence, not only were religious superstitions and customs deemed primitive and barbaric, and therefore rejected, entire domains of literature, art, and performance were discredited as decadent and profane. Social and cultural initiatives and apprehensions became interlinked.

Soon matters of education and literacy became a major discourse in which women's social progress figured as a contentious issue and contributed to the formation of 'native' resistance and dissent (Basu; Kumar). The imminent threat was seen to be the unsettling of the private domestic sphere. This space which had not yet succumbed to the imperial design seemed to be the next domain for colonial conquest. There was widespread anxiety in the Indian communities. Safeguarding the hitherto unchallenged domain of patriarchal authority became crucial to the Indian male. In the light of imperialist efforts towards women's education, the reform movements, led largely by men, focused more often than not on questions relating to women who were thought of and treated rather as passive vehicles for the continuance of traditions and customs (see for corroboration, the discussions of Rammohun Roy, Radhakanta Deb, Ishwarchandra Vidyasagar, Mahesh Chunder Deb *et al* cited by Sen; Sengupta 1990). Significantly, the category of 'modernity' may be understood to have emerged out of such interaction with the colonial hegemonic system of knowledge, though it would take several more decades to impact positively upon women's condition. The 'Hindu woman' as the subject to be transformed was imbricated in the ideological struggle between imperialism and the emergent cultural self-consciousness. It is therefore hardly surprising that the image of the nation should meld with that of Indian womanhood as poignantly shackled, and demanding to be rescued from the clutches of the alien power, a condition provocative enough to become the impetus for indigenist rhetoric. For instance, one of the most influential writers of the time, Bankim Chandra Chattopadhyay deified Indian nation and womanhood as Devi Durga/Kali and importuned the release of their assimilated *sakti*. Typically, while 'Devi' (goddess) of the writer's imagination possessed immense power/*sakti*, the 'devi' (mortal woman) of the household remained severely disempowered. This, unfortunately, became the pragmatic paradigm.

That India's patriarchal societies were shaken out of their torpor was the major good that came out of the nineteenth century's sociocultural upheaval. Since much of British philanthropy was perceived as a guise for conversion into Christianity or effecting radical cultural transitions in the name of modernity, Indian communities of Hindus, Muslims, and Buddhists became agitated and perturbed enough to set up rival institutes to mediate and monitor women's education (Heimsath). Gradually, as more Indian men seemed to want educated wives, a reconceptualization of 'gender' became necessary to address the question regarding women's role and the kind of education to be imparted to women. Was it to be education in patriarchal norms or were the notions of secular womanhood to be conveyed? Interestingly, common to both the altruistic colonizers and the indigenist reformers was the view that the purpose of women's education should be to 'enlighten' the latter about the 'noble value' of their home-making role.[8] As learning for women was expected to have a different kind of structure and content, the issue became the subject of much debate. Ideally, it should have urged a rethinking of the ideological foundations of the societies. But that did not happen because, evidently, the nineteenth-century reformers wanted education to serve as an enabling (and ennobling?) process for making good mothers, wives and companions for men—not for training independent-minded or politically-aware and active participants in the process of society and nation building (the later decades would see women's cooption into the nationalist struggle though rarely on equal terms with men). When new laws were proposed, the colonial authorities readily supported the limiting parameter envisaged for the education of women.[9] Women themselves were not consulted nor were their opinions or volition regarding issues concerning their own lives considered worthy of cognizance. Caught in the crossfire of convention and modernity, restoration and innovation, social inconsistencies and contradictions, the recipients of the imperial and indigenous reformist zeal—the women of India—were reconfigured within patriarchal ideologies.

The dilemma was apparent in the way women began to regard themselves. Encouraged by a liberal faction of the society—as for instance the Brahmo view of behaviour and conduct of life and religion—the 'New Woman' emerged, one who scorned conventions and readily adopted Western education, attitude, and style of dressing, whereas the majority of Indian women remained immured in superstition and social evils like child marriage, polygamy, and the privations of widowhood. The modern emancipated New Woman figured in the writing of almost all major writers of the time who did not hesitate to parody the tendency towards excesses and the lack of moderation and depth in the behaviour and attitude in some of them. The positive result, however, was that by the second half of the nineteenth century, more women were getting educated. They began to write and give expression to their responses about the changing social conditions, including the demand to expand the scope of women's education. They wrote also to emphasize the need for change in women's conditions and philosophy of life. Given the times when they lived and the forces they had to counter, the questioning of customs, conventions, and values was of considerable significance. The spread of printing revolutionized the nature and kind of knowledge and information that could be disseminated, which in turn affected the patterns of their circulation and the consumption of texts. This was of particular importance for women because printing provided access to a public sphere hitherto denied to them. Soon, articulate women like Pandita Ramabai, Anandibai Joshi, Bhikaji Cama, Swarnakumari Devi (who wrote articles on science to popularize scientific studies among women), Saralabala Choudhurani (who created a women's self-defence group, Mahila Atmaraksha Samiti), Kadambini Ganguly (the first certified lady doctor in India), and Rani Chanda, led literacy drives to stress a modern outlook and women's social emancipation. In fact, as Mandakranta Bose declares, 'Subjected to a multitude of forces, often contradictory, the women of India—not unlike women elsewhere—began to move toward self-perception, self-expression, and self-determination, slowly, indeed, and against tradition' (215). Gradually, as education changed from being normative and religion-based to being more secular and expansive in scope, by the second decade of the twentieth century, it produced doctors and lawyers—India's first women professionals.[10]

Most of the debates and the initiatives concerning female education had involved Bengali intellectuals and social reformers and had impacted deeply upon the Bengali ethos to set in motion a subliminal turmoil. Saumitra Chakravarty, the editor of this volume, describes the upper-class woman's life in Bengal as severely constricted and governed by factors such as child marriage, early widowhood, and *sati*. Her misery was compounded by the *kulin* system introduced by Ballal Sen in the twelfth century which divided the three upper classes—Brahmins, Baidyas, and Kayasthas—into clans by tracing descent from the same putative ancestor. A kulin girl could not marry outside the clan nor could she remain unmarried after puberty. So, girls were often accorded a nominal marriage to older and much-married men, even diseased or dying grooms, to ward off the social stigma associated with spinsterhood. 'Wives' lived in parental homes and the 'husbands' visited their in-laws for a few days each year to collect their stipend. By the early years of the nineteenth century, kulin polygamy had become an established fact of the social life of Bengal. The consequent suffering that women underwent was from the rivalry of co-wives or *shotin*, sexual assaults by middle-aged men on child brides, physical and mental torture by female members of the extended household, the social taboos associated with widowhood.

By the second half of the nineteenth century, Bengali women began to write about themselves and their lives, often secretly and in pain. It was around this time that, as Tanika Sarkar writes, '...a social category was born in Bengal, along with a new word that named it: *lekhika* or the female author' (ix). Women's appropriation of the new mode of articulation marked a historical moment of freedoms of several kinds— from containment within oral and anonymous expressive modes, from forced silence within the domestic space, and from the oppression of customs and superstitions. The self-confidence with which women started to write ensured, despite many difficulties, the spread of women's literacy and social upliftment. Though many of the early women writers belonged to liberal and Brahmo families like Bamasundari Devi, Saratkumari Choudhurani, Swarnakumari Devi and her two daughters Hironmoyee Devi and Sarala Devi, Hemantakumari Choudhuri, Prasannamoyee Devi and her daughter Priyambada, Kumudini Mitra; there were also housewives from conservative homes like Kailashbashini Devi, Girindramohini Dasi and Krishbhabini Dasi and Muslim women like Begum Rokeya Sakhawat Hossain and the lesser known Khairunnissa Khatun, who wrote what they saw, heard and felt about life as women, and critically debated issues as varied as the removal of superstitions, subjugation of women, modern age and modern women, man–woman relationship and customs of marriage, women's dress and footwear, patriotism, communal amity, and so on (see for documents and discussion on the subject, Bhattacharya and Sen; Chakravarti; Dutta).[11] The noteworthy fact is that the first autobiography to be written— *Amar Jibon* (My life)—was by Rassundari Devi who was entirely and secretively self-taught. Having once breached the public–private divide, the women began to write poetry, fiction, essays, even plays. Sarkar emphasizes the 'transgressive' and 'subversive' pleasure that reading and writing made available to them and hence '...women ardently embraced the book and nurtured for it an illicit passion' (x). Of great significance at this time was the appearance of journals and little magazines, which provided the forum for women to write about topical issues for quick dissemination. Swarnakumari Devi and Mokhhodayini Mukhopadhyay also edited journals like *Bharati, Banga Mahila*, and *Bamabodhini Patrika*, which highlighted the pressing socio-economic issues relating to women.

As explained by Partha Chatterjee, the encounter of nationalism with Western modernism had initially widened the schism between the

private and the public spheres. Inhabiting the private sphere, the women
were to be the carriers of tradition and spirituality. Until education was
seen to be non-threatening to the traditional role of women, it remained
unwelcome and scorned for producing the *nabeena*/ New Woman with
her Western dress, shoes, and cosmetics, defiance of tradition, her novel-
and-poetry-reading—a 'blue-stockings' figure caricatured in the
literature of the time.[12] Education became acceptable for the new *bhadra
mahila* (gentlewomen) when it became evident that it would not alter
her role at home and would actually inculcate social discipline into her
housewifely duties and impose orderliness, economy, and hygiene.
According to Malavika Karlekar's well-researched study of the early
personal narratives of Bengali women, the general curriculum for home
education or *antahpur shiksha* contained the usual exhortatory and
normative tracts and women's access to learning was in most cases the
result of 'sustained efforts by men to make them literate' (10). Yet,
the strong desire of the women to explore, describe, and share their
experiences and find meaning in their lives, could not remain stifled for
long. Those who wrote were not many in number (estimated 400 works
between 1856 and 1910 (Karlekar 11)) and belonged to the privileged
upper class/caste or the *bhadra* samaj (with the significant exception of
the actor/courtesan Binodini Dasi. As a colonial hangover, the creative
outpouring of the women performers of ritualistic or folk forms, hailing
from the lower classes were not considered cultured or refined enough
for serious attention). The range of subject matter, style, and treatment
of the writings varied, but the concerns were the same—all dealt with
women's living conditions, their secret aspirations and the search for
their selfhood. Confined within the *antahpur* (inner courtyard) that defined
their lives, they reflected upon social inequalities, gender relations in a
stratified society, women's duties, their subjugation, and abject dependence
on the men folk.

Evidently, the 'bhadra mahila* were under-privileged vis-à-vis the *bhadra
lok* [gentlemen]' (Karlekar, 9). Life perceived from their vantage point
revealed new insights and the women expressed their views with
frankness and passion. Through their writing, Bengali women began to
discover their own reserves of strength. They explored their relationship
with the society and finally prepared to cross the threshold of the *antahpur*
and step out into the world, as it were. This momentous act has been
represented with deservedly dialectical magnitude by Rabindranath

Tagore in his novel *Ghare Baire* (1916) (*The Home and theWorld,* 1919).
Bimala, the female protagonist in Tagore's novel is escorted by her
husband through the long passage that separates the inner quarters of
the home from the outer, into the *baithak khana* (sitting room for men)—
which, for her, is an unfamiliar and fascinating space with enticing but
dangerous charms. Naïve Bimala seems to symbolize India, poised to step
into the world of complex politics, as the country's struggle for freedom
turned in a decisive direction towards nationhood.

Women's writing in Bengal grew from strength to strength in the
twentieth century and claimed a place in the literary canon. The aspects
of life that the feminine imagination embodied, made space for
countervailing narratives of recapitulation and enabled the construction
of the subjectivities of women. Though energized by the feminist ideology
of theWest, the women of Bengal fought their own battles to claim agency
to articulate their own stories. There was no genre that the women did
not choose to write in, representing the political and social upheavals
in the nation, region, and community (like Partition, Independence,
the 1942 Famine, Tebhaga, and the Naxal Movement, etc.)—but
perhaps the sociocultural conditions and the economic reasons that had
made the domestic fiction of America and England immensely popular
with both the authors and the readers, prevailed in the Indian situation
too to make narratives—both fictional and personal—the favourite
mode of writing for women. Women narrated stories about life—
of happiness and suffering, pain and death—that they had held back
for centuries. They wrote them down for others to know…and
perhaps, understand.

Explaining her motivation to anthologize women's stories, Saumitra
Chakravarty says that the feminist *agon* in Bengali society and literature
seems to centre around the creation of a *manashi* through the poet's pen
and her realization as a *manushi,* her flesh-and-blood counterpart. The
subjugation of the female, the stereotyping of women and the allotment
of set roles to her are essential prerequisites for an androcentric culture
where the male establishes himself within the family or the community
through the metaphysics of gender. He establishes the woman in a
particular niche or a frame to compensate his own shortcomings within
the family. He builds images or 'manashis' around her to suit his need of
the hour. Where, in all this, does a woman find a voice? And even more
important is the question, what is the kind of voice with which a woman

can speak out? Is it the voice of the underprivileged, seeking to define oneself in terms of loss? As Rajlakshmi Devi writes in 'Meye' (Girl):

Open windows to three sides of life—fear sits at the other.
Girl, never blaze up like the setting sun in the evening...
You must be a glass-domed lamp, to others' whims a thrall...
[Tr. Supriya Chaudhuri]

This anthology offers fifteen compelling stories by five Bengali authors that allow the manushi to find a 'voice'. They present the vicissitudes of life, in different shades, rendered with great vividness and complexity by women who have pursued long and successful careers as writers of fiction. In spite of the vagaries of publication and public taste, their works have endured—and, indeed, gained in appreciation. Their appeal is trans-generational. They speak in many voices: each distinctly different, yet each struggling to articulate a heretofore repressed and silenced female's story and voice. Gender operates as the matrix of alterity and enables marginalized and subjugated female issues to be articulated within patriarchy. These are the kind of stories that must cross borders— as they have now through translation—and defy linguistic cloisters to claim their rightful place in world literature. The renewed interest which these works have received is evidence of their contemporaneity.

The stories showcase the writers' efforts to formulate narratives that address the needs and concerns of women and offer a perspective markedly different from those of male writers. The focus is upon the domestic space and present situations of struggle and conflict, features which are always strongly evident in women's writing. The characters in the stories, the majority of which are female, address issues, emotional and psychological, that affect their lives and control their decisions. The conflicts they face are the daily, immediate living concerns: of sustaining human relationships; of dealing with a spouse (or life without a spouse); the travails of housekeeping and of saving enough money to feed, clothe, and educate children; of maintaining personal dignity in the face of routine oppression and prejudice; of being misunderstood and misrepresented; the plight of loneliness and age; the search for personal happiness. In all situations, it is through the many battles they must fight daily that the women explore their emotional, social and economic selfhood. The writers emphasize the physical boundaries and the symbolic spaces which imprison their female characters, whose life choices are severely limited, and who must conduct their quests for self-affirmation within those limitations and stereotype-driven oppressions. The themes of their poignant stories offer fewer closures, yet touch upon a broader spectrum of issues than do the work of male writers.

The careful selection of the five writers in this anthology traces the gradual shaping of the female agency in the evolving tradition of women's writing in Bengal. At once linear and circular, every step forward reveals the undertow of reflux and every gain carries with it the echoes of loss.

The story of Ashapurna Devi's life, spanning almost a century, seems like a page out of history itself and presents an amazing account of fortitude and devotion to learning. Born into a conservative family, Ashapurna Devi was not given the opportunity to attend school. She learnt the Bengali alphabet by listening to her brother read his lessons aloud. She sat near him and tried to memorize the alphabet and words as he pronounced them. Yet she was keen to read and write, know of the world outside, and speak about what she felt. She retained her enchantment for literature and the dream to explore human nature and relationships in ordinary domestic situations and recreate the seething domestic microcosm through her stories. The print medium provided her the link she sought to establish with the world beyond her home. She wrote tirelessly and fluently, in many genres, as though she had to make up single-handedly for women's late start in the narrative tradition.

A traditional and gentle person, Ashapurna Devi abided by the rules of the *antahpur* throughout her life. But she also made it her palette from which to draw hues that coloured her stories. She remained honest about her milieu, yet was gender-conscious and courageous enough to question and invite attention to its social injustices. She did not rebel against them but she certainly tried to critique them in her stories and break some moulds with her characterization. The predicament of Hymanti in 'Please Forgive Me' or Padmalata in 'Padmalata's Dream' is as poignantly real as is the repeated use of a red silk sari for a new bride after the death of the former one. Rather like Jane Austen's 'two inches of ivory', Ashapurna Devi's canvas was the mute inner world of women. Their voices resonated in her writing, their dreams, sorrows, and heartaches were etched with a fine hand, and the complexities and conflicts with the outer world of men were analysed with intensity and narrated with simple lucidity. Every narrative illustrates a perceptive delineation of a character's search for destiny in accordance with her nature. Her greatest achievement is her famous trilogy, mapping four generations—*Pratham Pratisruti* (1964) (The first promise), *Subarnalata* (1966), and *Bakulkatha* (1973) (The story of Bakul)—that both revisits the past and rediscovers it by merging the story of women's emancipation with the history of Bengal's social and cultural revolution that the imperial–Rammohun Roy–Vidyasagar reform efforts had initiated, and gestures beyond it.

　　'*Antahpur chirodin-i abahelito...*' The *antahpur* has always been neglected...is the way Ashapurna Devi introduces the narrative of Satyabati, the female protagonist of her most acclaimed work, *Pratham Pratisruti*. She explains that it is the story of an unknown woman who strove from within the ignored interior spaces of Bengal to claim a promise she had made to herself. Satyabati of the compelling parable of empowerment, is difficult to forget as it is not to acknowledge in Ashapurna Devi's literary journey the extraordinary achievement of an ordinary housewife.

　　A witness to nearly eighty years of tumultuous change, Mahasweta Devi's life has spanned the colonial period, Independence, and fifty-plus years of postcolonial turmoil. She started writing at a young age, and contributed short stories to various literary magazines. Her first novels, *Jhansir Rani* (1956) (The Queen of Jhansi) and *Nati* (1957) (Actress), reflected the early influences on her life and her feminist concerns. It also marked the beginning of a prolific literary career. Several of her early works such as *Amrita Sanchay* (1964) and *Andhanmalik* (1967) had the context of the colonial period. The Naxalite Movement that overwhelmed Bengal in the 1970s was critically important to her. She has declared that the escalating violence that overtook the movement which had begun as a peasants' revolt, made her want to document history. It was perhaps then that her writing started showing a political reflection and engagement running through it. The memorable novel (transformed into a play) on the theme is *Hazaar Churasir Maa* (The mother of 1084), also made into a film by an award-winning filmmaker.

　　Her devoted and lifelong commitment has been to tribal welfare. She lived among the so-called 'de-notified' tribes like the Santhals, Lodhas, Shabars, and Mundas and wrote about the grossly neglected, misunderstood and misrepresented indigenous people who are dispossessed of their own land by the strategies of capitalism, are exploited and treated like criminals by the non-tribal world. These concerns are expressed in works like *Aranyer Adhikar* (1977) (The rights of the forest, based on the life of a legendary tribal freedom fighter Birsa Munda), *Agnigarbha* (Womb of fire), and in unforgettable short stories like 'Rudali', 'Chatti Munda O Tar Tir', 'Draupadi', 'The Breastgiver' to mention just a few. This activism is central to Mahasweta Devi's understanding of the role of a writer in society. She likes to use her language as a weapon to speak for the oppressed and the exploited. She says, 'I think a creative writer should have a social conscience... I don't really know why I do these things. The sense of duty is an obsession. I must remain accountable to myself.'

Her writing has given Indian literature a new direction and has inspired later writers, journalists and filmmakers. The stories in this anthology represent her three major concerns: the articulation of the secret suffering of women, the reality of the self-made tensions of ordinary life, and the drama of the tribal world. Her writing is honest, incisive, and purposeful. Once Helene Cixous had remarked that language is 'a country in which scenes comparable to what is happening in the domain of the opening or the closing of borders are played out in the linguistic and poetic mode'. Instantiating a gradual shift away from *sadhu bhasha* (refined language) to colloquial idiom (*chalti bhasha*) in consonance with her themes, Mahasweta Devi's agency towards change in language use points to a significant 'opening of doors' to undiscovered domains. Her stories reflect her philosophy of life. She says,

I have always believed that the real history is made by ordinary peoples... The reason and inspiration for my writing are those people who are exploited and used, and yet do not accept defeat. For me, the endless source of ingredients for writing is in these amazingly, noble, suffering human beings. Why should I look for my raw material elsewhere, once I have started knowing them? Sometimes it seems to me that my writing is really their doing.

(*http://en.wikipedia.org/wiki/Mahasweta_Devi*).

An internationally-known poet, Nabaneeta Dev Sen is widely respected as a scholar–critic and creative writer. While the language of her academic and critical studies is English, all her creative writing is done in Bangla. She has more than sixty publications consisting of poetry, novels, short stories, travelogues, translations, memoirs, essays, and children's literature. Her first publication was a book of poems: *Pratham Pratyay* (1959) (First confidence). Her first novel, *Ami Anupam*, came much later, in 1976. Even her most scholarly essays are remarkable for the charming prose and sense of humour. Her spontaneity, unique style of expression, vast and varied experience of life is evident in her writing. Her wit and humour, an aesthetic sensibility, a sense of detachment combined with ruthless honesty, bring a nuanced womanist touch that is hard to ignore. Among her remarkable achievements are: the review of the long-neglected Chandravati 'Ramayana', a woman's rewriting of the epic; non-fictional and fictional works like *Sita Theke Shuru* (Beginning with Sita); *Bama-bodhini* (Understanding women); *Sheet Sahosik Hemantolok* (Winter-defying autumn world); and several anthologies of poems and short stories.

The three short stories in this anthology carry the hallmark of Dev Sen's humour. While 'The Kayak' and 'The Aftermath' focus on the drama of human relationships that hints at the underlying pathos, 'And the Rains Came Again' presents the pleasurable mayhem in the domestic sphere and the vain human struggle to impose order on the naturally wayward forces. Dev Sen's language reflects the rhythm of the present, contemporary style. She writes compulsively—addressing matters of women's 'voice'.

She says, 'How do I know who I am until I have written myself and read myself on a piece of paper in front of me?... Poetry has been my *kabach-kundal*—my charmed amulet, my magic armour... Every word written is the lifelong quest for that ultimate poem. Will I be able to write the poem? The lines that will live on after me?'

There does not seem to be any doubt that what Nabaneeta writes will live on...but there will be many things that must be written by her before that ultimate poem.

From the beginning of her career in the 1970s with publications in journals such as *Desh* and *Anandamela*, Bani Basu caught the attention of critics with her powerful writing style. Her first novel, *Janmabhumi– Matribhumi* (Land of birth–motherland) was published in 1987, and the first collection of short stories *Mohana* (Estuary) appeared in 1992. She has till date about sixteen novels and story collections which have been widely acclaimed and translated into many languages. Her most famous works are *Maitreyi Jatak* (Born of Maitreyee), *Gandharbi*, *Pancama Purush*

(The fifth generation), and *Ashtama garbha* (Eighth womb), which are counted among the classics of Bengali literature. These novels, which review the mythic past from a contemporary perspective, show a strong feeling for history and sociology, and display excellent sense of the craft of story-telling. Basu experiments with a stylized use of language and narrative techniques by rearranging time and space. The novels also exemplify a woman's view of the past. Her strong feminine consciousness is manifest in her popular short stories like 'Svetpathar-er Thala' (Marble platter) and 'Radhanagara' which present the dilemma of women who must choose between conformity and personal happiness.

The three short stories in this anthology from her collection 'Baro Swader Golpo' (Many-flavoured stories) presenting different flavours of life, narrate the experience of three females—Shirish, Sunanda, and Tuni. While Shirish is left desolate and lonely with her pain and sorrow, Sunanda recovers her peace of mind in solitude. Tuni's young mind learns the important distinction between emotional and material happiness. By setting her stories in contemporary society and populating them with life-like characters, Basu provides an introspective study of modern behaviour.

Basu's sensitivity to history—of recent past—prompted another remarkable novel, *Antarghaat*, drawing upon the Naxal Movement of the 1970s. Events of 1972 and 1987 are juxtaposed in the narration with apparent randomness but, as is slowly evident, actually possess an inexorable momentum towards dénouement. The decades of tremendous turmoil are described in dispassionate prose that nevertheless conveys the anguish that had led her to write the novel. The book had a period of gestation and she wrote it when the memories of the terrible decades had faded since her intention, she explains in the Afterword, was not to make the book 'a social discourse. It is a human drama, not of crime and punishment, but surely of sin and retribution'.

Whatever she writes, Bani Basu's narration never lacks the tautness of human drama.

Suchitra Bhattacharya possesses a taut and engrossing style of story-telling and has achieved sensational popularity with her powerful fiction. Focusing on the familiar world of middle-class Calcutta, Bhattacharya's fiction draws on contemporary social issues, conflicts in family relationships, and changing values. Her widely appreciated novels include

Bhangan kal, Parabas, Gabhir asukh, Hemanter Pakhi, Kachher manush, Jakhan Juddha, Raikishori and the collections of short stories are *Buker katha, Maina-tadanta, Ami Madhobi*. While making her ruthless incisions into the lesions of social evil, Bhattacharya directs attention towards women's issues that can no longer be ignored. She tells a disturbing story, for instance, in her award-winning novel, *Dahan* (The burning): 'One evening, when the city-jungle is teeming with life, Romita, a young housewife, is molested by four young men near a crowded Metro Station. No one intervenes—except Jhinuk Sarkar, a schoolteacher.' While Romita's humiliating street encounter compels her to question the fragile nature of her relationship with her husband, Jhinuk's bravery sparks off family tensions and power games with her fiancé. The two women's search for justice in a man's world relives the anguish that every woman who dares to step outside the narrow path of normative behaviour must encounter. The novel reflects contemporary society and times and raises unsettling questions about freedom, justice, and choices. Bhattacharya captures with precision and variety, the changing lifestyles of the Bengali middle class over the last few decades.

When attempts are made to categorize her (and marginalize her social protests) as 'feminist'—she prefers to describe her concerns as 'humanist'. 'But your protagonists seem empowered and scathingly critical of the patriarchal system,' they say. 'My protagonists try to protest, and ultimately because they're all alone, they lose the war. They only win the skirmishes; I don't believe we have a social system where women can win the war yet, at least not without the active support of men,' she answers.

While the short stories, 'Indir Thakurun-era,' (The Indir Thakuruns) and 'Taan' (Bonds) release sociological dialectics regarding the contemporary problems of age, loneliness, and fractured family ties, 'Madhobi' (The Testament of Madhobi) is a reissue of an ancient tale of a woman's commodification and exploitation as a sex object that does not seem out of place in the present context.

It is said that nothing remains the same forever. The problems of women seem to have disproved the axiom. They seem to move forward, yet remain at the same place in the patriarchal axis. In an interview, Bhattacharya remarks, 'Many men come up to me and tell me, "my wife loves your work, my daughter loves your work, my mother loves your work". As though I'm writing well enough to be read by women in their small worlds, but my writing is not really fit to be read by the larger world of men.'

It is to be hoped that men read Suchitra Bhattacharya's works because she has much to say that does not fail to appeal to the sense of social and human justice. When taken seriously, her writing cannot but usher in a more lasting change.

Women have opposed attempts to essentialize or categorize their writing. However, it must be admitted that the sense of being a woman, of being able to represent women's experiences and concerns, and speak in a woman's voice, do constitute important aspects of women's writing. If Swarnakumari Devi, Mokkhodayini Mukhopadhyay, Rassundari Devi, Kailashbashini, and other women of the *antahpur* epitomize the rise of feminine consciousness in Bengali literature, and if Ashapurna Devi represents the 'second wave' of women's efforts towards crossing the threshold and acquiring a 'voice', writers of the 'third wave' such as Mahasweta Devi, Nabaneeta Dev Sen, Bani Basu, and Suchitra Bhattacharya have taken women's writing confidently and strongly forward. That feminine agency has been inevitably linked to education is also evident in the stifled desire of nineteenth-century women to acquire a liberal education, to learning by mimicry, and to winning national and international recognition by the end of the century.

Yet has the woman's 'voice' become truly free? Are there really no restrictions on their speech/writing any more? According to Nabaneeta Dev Sen, a woman's writing is her gesture which, like all woman's gestures, is subject to all sorts of social codes. But such social codes are not obvious; they form a covert grid of censorship and, since the public space of printing is still largely controlled by men, a major challenge to women's writing remains the attitude of their readers and critics. Male critics ignore the dynamic vitality of women's writing and trivialize their efforts. Or, they are confined within the category of 'women writers'.[13]

As has been pointed out by Ritu Menon, 'Don't disturb the beehive' is the maxim that women are expected to follow; that is, the women who are still controlled by patriarchy and its institutions, may write about themselves and women's problems but must not disrupt the established norms and structures—of marriage, motherhood, and the control of sexuality. Perhaps not quite like aphasia, but restrictions are in place to curb the woman's tongue. As the Hindi writer Anamika once commented, 'scissors to cut with, a needle and thread to sew my lips with. If I write my subconscious, the earth will be covered with paper'.

So what should be the limit of a woman's freedom? How much can she aspire for? Urvashi Butalia refers to a story: 'Thousands of years ago it is said that Mara, the devil (and a man) came upon a *bhikshuni*/nun deep in meditation. He scoffed. What does she think she is doing, he asked. All she needs is two fingers of meditation for her work in the kitchen. The *bhikshuni* was unmoved by the comment for she knew that what she was looking for was not two or more fingers worth of peace, but for *akasha*, as she said. Nothing but the sky would suffice for her.'

Stories must be told—and in many languages; stories about women's struggles and their aspirations. Translation provides the space for negotiation, between languages and cultures, to be able to share women's stories. The Bengali stories in this anthology have been translated by several eminent translators who have pressed into service different strategies of negotiation to enable the stories to cross borders. The stories will surely find their readers and convey the aspiration of the women to embrace the expanse of the sky, aiming, as Ibsen's protagonist says,

Upwards—
Towards the peaks
Towards the stars
Towards the vast silence...

I thank Saumitra Chakravarty and Mini Krishnan for their insightful inputs to the above discussion.

Tutun Mukherjee

Professor and Head, Centre for Comparative Literature,
University of Hyderabad, Hyderabad

Notes

1. History documents writers who challenged patriarchy and sought to break the stereotypes of womanhood but they are too few. (See Tharu and Lalita.) Such poets of Bengal were: Rami (1440 approx), Chandravati (1550–1600; Anandamoyee Devi, Gangamoni Devi; Priyamvada Devi, Vyjayanti Devi

from erstwhile East Bengal; Huti Vidyalankar, Rupamanjari of Rarh; Vaishnav poets Golakmoni, Dayamoni, Ratnamoni; folk singers Jogeshwari, Mohini Dasi, Bhabani in early nineteenth century (see Gupta). The articulations of these women as 'other' were invariably a hegemony-challenging and a consciousness-raising drive urging social and cultural reformulations.

2. Foucault's notion 'subjugated knowledges' describes the archives that are rejected as being 'beneath the required level of cognition or scientificity' by the dominant 'regimes of thought' in our intellectual culture (21).

3. And quite possibly signalled the making of a bourgeoisie, the still amorphous class which would address the issues of social transformation of the time.

4. 'Paternalism' combines with 'Maternalism'. As Sangari comments, on assuming the title 'Empress of India', Queen Victoria's 'housewifeization' of England is extended to India with a 'maternal, monarchical and feudatory aura'. (2001, 189).

5. Pandit Jawaharlal Nehru's speech known as 'Tryst with Destiny' was made to the Indian Constituent Assembly on the eve of India's Independence. The speech captures the essence of the triumphant culmination of the freedom struggle. The irony of history is that the seedbed of Western ideas of freedom and democracy that provoked a rupture in traditional continuities and transformed the notions of conventional governance also engendered the spirit of resistance against Western domination, and fostered the demand for self-determination.

6. 'The White Woman's Burden'—a term used by suffragette Hester Gray (in *Common Cause*, November 27, 1914: 565–66) to emphasize the white woman's duty to help 'the less privileged women of the East' is quoted by Burton (10). The mindset of 'imperialist maternalism' on the retrogressive role of Indian women (the attempt of the 'good mother' to 'wean away' the child from the 'bad mother') (also see 4 above) was pervasive and is evident in the writing of the white women of the Raj. (For discussion, see Sarika Bose; Diver; Jayawardena.)

7. Katherine Mayo spent three months in India in the early twentieth century and wrote a scathing critique of India and the position of its women in her book *Mother India*. She argued that until the situation of Indian women remained unchanged, India was not fit for self rule.

8. Many exhortatory texts, manuals and books appeared in Indian languages, and became text books for girls' schools. They elaborated upon the 'duties' and 'dharma' of good mothers, daughters, and wives for dedicated service in the household. See Sundaram; Sangari (2001) for discussion.

9. June Purvis and Joanna Trollope discuss Victorian England's perception of women's role in the society that perpetuated the 'ministering angel' or the 'angel

in the house' concept popularized by Coventry Patmore's poem in the 1860s, and suggest that British ideas for Indian women were shaped along similar lines.

10. Initially, the *zenana* system of education was followed so that women need not step out of their home and teachers (missionaries or their trainees) would come home for tuition. The women's style of dressing had to change before they could move about freely. This was made possible by the adoption of chemise, blouse, petticoat, and shoes. The broad statistics given below indicate the gradual spread of women's education:

1881–1902: Entry of women in colleges. Two women graduated in 1883 and the enrolment in schools and colleges rose from 1.27 lakhs in 1882 to 3.93 lakhs in 1902. The importance of Secondary Education was understood, overcoming the restriction of stopping girls' education after the primary level. Primary education enrolment grew from 1.24 lakhs to 3.45 lakhs; the enrolment in secondary schools increased five times.

1902–1922: Proactive involvement of the Administration. The Freedom Movement gave further impetus. Lord Curzon supported the 1913 Resolution on Education Policy. Of historical importance was the establishment of a Women's University in Bombay in 1916 (presently, Shrimati Nathubai Damodar Thackersey Women's University). Technical and vocational schools were started and showed a record enrolment.

11. Besides the work of the writers mentioned, other relevant expositions were: Bamasundari's '*Ki ki kusanskar tirohitho hoiley ei desher sribridhhi haitey parey*' (The disappearance of which superstitions will make the nation prosper?); Kailashbashini Debi's '*Hindu mahilagan-er hinabastha*' (The abject condition of the Hindu women) and '*Janaika grihabadhur diary*' (The diary of an anonymous housewife); Rassundari Debi's *Amar Jiban* (My life); Sharodasundari Debi's *Atmakatha* (The story of my life); Mokkhodayini Mukhopadhyay's *Banglar Babu* (satirizing the desperate attempts of the Bengali *babu* to bolster his sagging vanity within the confines of his home after experiencing in the public space the daily ignomiy of a colonial subject); Binodini Dasi's autobiographies *Amar Katha* (My narrative) and *Amar Abhinoy Jibon* (My acting career).

As far as naming is concerned, the women of the higher caste / class took 'Debi/Devi' (goddess) and the others, 'Dasi' (servant).

12. Even Keshub Chandra Sen, the famous social reformer said that access to science and mathematics would 'unsex' women. When the first girls' school was set up in Barasat (Bengal) in mid-nineteenth century, people dug ditches around it to deny access to it.

13. Of critical importance for the dissemination of women's writing is the growing presence of women publishers and editors.

REFERENCES

Bandopadhyay Manabendra, Sukanta Chaudhuri and Swapan Majumdar. Eds *Voices from Bengal: Modern Bengali Poetry in English Translation*, New Delhi: Sahitya Akademi, 1997.

Basu, Aparna. *Essays on the History of Indian Education*. New Delhi: Concept Publishing House, 1982.

Bayly, C.A. *Indian Society and the Making of the British Empire*. Cambridge: Cambridge University Press, 1988.

Bearce, George D. *British Attitude towards India 1784–1858*. London: Oxford University Press, 1961.

Bhattacharya, Malini and Abhijit Sen. Eds *Talking of Power: Early Writings of Bengali Women*. Kolkata: Stree, 2003.

Bose, Mandakranta. Ed. *Faces of the Feminine in Ancient, Medieval, and Modern India*. New Delhi: Oxford University Press, 2000.

Bose, Sarika P. 'For Our Native Sisters: The Wesleyean Ladies' Auxiliary in India', in Mandakranta Bose: 215–233.

Burton, Antoinette. *Burdens of History: British Feminists, Indian Women, and Imperial Culture: 1865–1915*. Chapel Hill: University of North Carolina Press, 1994.

Butalia, Urvashi. 'The search of *akasha*', *The Hindu Folio*. 23 January 2000. np.

Chakrabarti, Sambuddha. *Andare Antare: Unish Shatake Bangali Bhadramahila/ The Bengali Bhadramahila in the Nineteenth Century*. Kolkata: Stree and Samya, 1995.

Chatterjee, Partha. *The Nation and its Fragments: Colonial and Postcolonial Histories*. New Jersey: Princeton University Press, 1993. Esp Chapters 6 and 7: 116–157.

Dev Sen, Nabaneeta. 'Eroticism and the Woman Writer in Bengali Culture', in Mandakranta Bose: 297–303.

Diver, Maud. *The Englishwoman in India*. Edinburgh: William Blackwood, 1909.

Dutta, Kalyani. *Pinjare Bashiya/Inside The Cage*. Ed. Abhijit Sen. Samaj Sanskriti Nari Series. Kolkata: Stree and Samya, 1996.

Foucault, Michel. 'Two Lectures', *Critique and Power: Recasting the Foucault/ Habermas Debate*. Ed. Michel Kelly. Cambridge: MIT Press, 1994.

Gupta, Kshetra. *Complete History of Bengali Literature*. Calcutta: Granthaniloy: 2000.

Heimsath, Charles H. *Indian Nationalism and Hindu Social Reform*. Princeton: Princeton University Press, 1964.

Ingham, Kenneth. *Reformers in India: 1793–1833*. Cambridge: Cambridge University Press, 1956.

Jayawardena, Kumari. *The White Woman's Other Burden: Western Women and South Asia during British Colonial Rule*. New York: Routledge, 1995.

Karlekar, Malavika. *Voices from Within: Early Personal Narratives of Bengali Women*. Delhi: Oxford University Press, 1993.

Kopf, David. *British Orientalism and the Bengal Renaissance*. Calcutta: Firma KL Mukhopadhyay, 1969.

Kumar, Krishna. *Political Agenda of Education: A Study of Colonist and Nationalist Ideas*. New Delhi: Sage, 1991.

Majumdar, R.C. *History of Modern Bengal, 1765 to 1905*. Calcutta: G. Bharadwaj Co, 1978.

Menon, Ritu. Inaugurating 'Women Unlimited', Hyderabad, 2004.

Raychaudhuri, Tapan. *Perceptions, Emotions, Sensibilities: Essays on India's Colonial and Post-colonial Experiences*, New Delhi: Oxford University Press, 1999.

Sangari, Kumkum and Sudesh Vaid. Eds *Recasting Women: Essays in Colonial History*. New Delhi: Kali for Women, 1989.

Sangari, Kumkum. *Politics of the Possible*. New Delhi: Tulika, 1999. 2001 rpt.

Sarkar, Tanika. Introduction to *Talking of Power*. Bhattacharya and Sen. Eds.

Seal, Anil. *The Emergence of Indian Nationalism*. Cambridge: Cambridge University Press, 1971.

Sen, Ashok. 'The Bengal Economy and Raja Ram Mohan Roy', *Raja Ram Mohan Roy and the Process of Modernization of India*. Ed. V.C. Joshi. Delhi: Vikas, 1975: 125–35.

Sengupta, Syamalendu. *A Conservative Hindu of Colonial India: Raja Radhakanta Deb and His Milieu: 1784–1867*. Delhi: Navrang Press, 1990.

Sundaram, V. 'Manual mania in 19th century Bengal', *News Today*: 2 July 2005. http://www.newstodaynet.com/2005sud/05jul/ss2.htm

Tagore, Rabindranath. *Ghare Baire* 1916. *Home and the World*. Tr. Surendranath Tagore. London: Macmillan, 1919.

Tharu, Susie and V. Lalita. Eds *Women's Writing in India: 600 B.C. to Present Day*. Vols I & II. New Delhi: Oxford University Press: 1993, 1995.

*Dhouli**

Mahasweta Devi

T HE BUS LEFT RANCHI IN THE EVENING AND REACHED TAHARR AROUND EIGHT
at night. The passengers got off in front of Parasnath's tea stall-
cum-grocery shop and went to their respective homes. To Taharr,
Parasnath's shop was Calcutta's Chowringhee or Darjeeling's Mall. The
post office was next to it. The world beyond and the wide, metalled
road ended here. Rohatgi Company's bus was the only link between Taharr
and the rest of the world. The company had about twenty buses which
plied up and down the Ranchi–Hazaribag, Ranchi–Ramgarh and Ranchi–
Patna routes. They used poor, rundown buses for poor, rundown places
like Taharr, Palani or Burudiha. The buses were crowded with adivasis on
the local market days—Mondays, Wednesdays and Fridays. On Tuesdays,
Thursdays, Saturdays and Sundays, they were empty. Empty buses didn't
make money. The service was suspended during the rainy season as
buses couldn't ply on unmetalled roads. Taharr would be completely
cut off from the rest of the world during the monsoon months.

This year, it seemed the rains would arrive early, in June. Dhouli
was standing in front of Parasnath's shop. She could hardly be seen in
the dim light of the store.

Parasnath shut his shop for the day and asked, 'Not going home?'
Dhouli turned her face away. 'Bother!' Parasnath muttered and turned

*'Dhouli' ('The Fair One') was first published in *Nainitey Megh*, a collection
of stories by Mahasweta Devi.

The first English translation, by Sarmistha Dutta Gupta, was published in
Outcast: Four Stories, Calcutta: Seagull Books, 2002.

Translation copyright © Sarmistha Dutta Gupta, 2002.

around to enter his house, behind the shop. His wife sat there smoking a *bidi*. Parasnath said, 'The girl's here again today.'

'She's had it.'

'If *deota* gets wind of it...'

'Had it.'

Then she said, 'When did Misrilal leave?'

'Nearly four months ago.'

'What does Dhouli expect? She's a *dusad* (an untouchable, did she expect a house and land?).'

'God knows! But she's finished now.'

Why?

'That contractor! The coolie lines...'

'She'll get what's coming to her. A young woman...out along at night...isn't she scared?'

'A wolf's been on the prowl since last night.'

This was true. But Dhouli couldn't seem to keep it in mind. A terrible pain in her heart. In the middle of her chest. The pain would grow and push downwards. Dhouli didn't know what to do.

She returned home in the dark. A *dibri* was burning. A *machan* on one side of the room. Their bed. Three goats under it. Her mother was lying on the bed. She didn't speak to her daughter.

Dhouli checked the pitcher. It held some water. She drank some. She shut the door and blew out the *dibri*. Then she law down beside her mother. Tears seeped from her eyes. Tears of deep despair. Her mother could hear; she understood everything. Dhouli kept crying. The night drew on, and her mother finally said, 'They'll throw us out of here.'

'Let them.'

'You are young. Where will I go?'

'You stay here.'

'You'll go?'

'Yes.'

'Where?'

'To hell.'

'Not that easy. People don't die at nineteen.'

'I will.'

'Did you go to Shanichari?'

'No' Dhouli screamed. 'Why should I? To get rid of the thorn in my womb? Never.'

'Will you see the Misras, then? Tell them, "Your son has got me pregnant, give me money for the child's upkeep?"'

'How can I? Who will listen to me?'

'They'll have to.'

'If he was here, everything would be alright.'

'What does that mean? Would he have looked after you?'

'He said he would.'

'Does he know you're carrying his child?'

'Yes.'

'Would he have brought up the child?'

'He said so.'

'They always make such promises. You're not the first *dusad* girl the Misras have ruined. *Dusad*, *ganju*, *dhobi*—who have they spared?'

'He's not like that.'

'Really? A brahman boy who knows fully well how things work here— why did he betray you?'

'He loves me.'

'Love! Is that why he's disappeared to Dhanbad for the past four months?'

'He's scared of his parents.'

'Couldn't even write a letter?'

'Can I read?'

'You fell in love, and I had to lose my cattle-grazing job. A wolf stole one of their lambs and they put the blame on me. Is that fair?'

'What can I do?'

'They were angry with you, so they punished me.'

'Throw me out then.'

'I will. Now go to sleep.'

'What did you say? You'll throw me out? Who else can you call your own?'

They quarrelled every day over this and would have done so tonight. But they heard the watchman call out, 'Arrey, Dhouli *ki ma*! We have to hear your voice all day, now all night as well? All the others in the *dusadpatty* know that the day is for yelling, the night for sleeping. Only you don't seem to realize this.'

'Okay, okay, I'll be quiet.'

'Have you let in some coolie or what?'

'May coolies enter *your* house!'

'Ram! Ram! How can you say such things?'

The watchman left. Her mother said, 'Don't I know how this place works? Everyone's waiting to see if Misrilal takes care of you after the baby is born. If he does, no one will touch you. If not, they'll tear you to pieces.'

'Your mistake. Should have left me at my in-laws' after I was widowed. Left things to fate.'

'Did they want you? And you came away yourself.'

'My elder brother-in-law wouldn't have spared me.'

'And Misrilal did?'

That hit Dhouli hard. She kept quiet. Her eyelids felt dry from crying endlessly. She shut them.

Sleep eluded her. Since the day Misrilal left. Since the day he crept off without a word, like a thief, on the early morning bus, Dhouli couldn't sleep. She could, of course, sleep forever by swallowing some of the insecticide used in the maize fields, but how could she die before seeing that traitor's face at least once more?

Traitor? No, no. Hadn't he left Taharr because his parents forced him to? Would his parents have been capable of threatening their beloved son? Hadn't the pressure applied by the head of their family, Hanuman Misra of Burudiha, scared them? Otherwise, would Misrilal have left Dhouli? How he had wept at the thought of leaving her! It broke her heart whenever she thought of it; even now she felt terrible.

Her mother tells her, 'Go get Shanichari's potion. Get rid of the thorn in your womb.'

How can she? Was this the child of Misrilal's brother Kundan and Jhalo, the *ganju* girl? Born of greed and sheer lust?

Brahman, *deota*, Dhouli had never as much as raised her eyes to look at him, while sweeping their orchard. One afternoon, as she was bathing in the waterfall while grazing the goats in the forest, Misrilal tossed a leafy twig at her. He didn't laugh or make obscene comments. He simply said, 'I'm madly in love with you. Why won't you even look at me?'

'*Deota*! Please don't say such things.'

'*Deota*? I'm your slave.'

'Oh no! Please don't!' Trembling in fear, Dhouli turned her face away.
'You say no today, but some day you'll have to respond.'

Whenever Dhouli remembers she can hear the breeze blowing through
the trees in the forest, rustling leaves, the gurgling of the waterfall. That
day, Misrilal had left it at that. How scared Dhouli felt, how scared! Misrilal
was fair-skinned, he had curly hair. Innocent and good-looking. At a glance
you would make out that he was a *deota*. And what was Dhouli? A *dusad's*
daughter. A widow. An unfortunate woman. She had no father or brother,
which was why Kundan had not let her mother till the land. Dhouli's
mother had pleaded, '*Sarkar*, I'll pay the rent; the other *dusads* will help
me till the land. I'll pay whatever rent you ask but give me the land.
Otherwise, we'll starve to death.'

'No.'

Dhouli's mother then went and prostrated herself before Kundan's
mother. 'Help us, Mataji. Or my daughter and I will die of starvation.'

The mother told her son, 'As long as her husband was alive he tilled
the land and worked as bonded labour. Is she to starve to death now
that she is a widow?'

'What can I do? I've given that land to Jhuman *dusad*.'

'Then they'll graze the goats, sweep the orchard. You'll pay for that
and give them *maroa*.'

'Whatever you say.'

Why had a son of the family on whom they had to depend for their
meagre daily bowl of *maroa* said such things to Dhouli? She knew it was
because of her tremulous eyes, her slender waist, her blossoming breasts.
Still she went to sweep the orchard, keeping herself carefully covered
with her coarse sari, bought at the local market. She never lifted her eyes
to look around at the fruit-laden trees. Took home only the guavas and
custard apples that were half-eaten by the birds and lambs. That, too,
with permission from Kundan's mother.

Dhouli went home and polished their brass plate until it shone like
gold. Then she looked at the reflection of her face. Careful not to let
her mother see. After becoming a widow, a *randi*, you were not supposed
to look into a mirror. Not supposed to look at yourself. Not supposed
to wear shellac bangles, a dot of *sindoor* on your forehead, anklets of cheap
metal. She was attractive. But a pretty face was no use to a *randi*. She
couldn't marry again, could she? Never again would the other girls call

her to sing wedding songs like *sasural chale sita maiya* or paint *rangoli*
patterns of birds and flowers on the walls of a bride's home. Yet, the
younger son of that brahman family had just told her he was her slave.
She felt scared, uneasy.

Dhouli told her mother, 'Ma. You sweep the orchard; I'll graze the
goats.'

'Why?'

'Ma, the leaves keep flying around when I'm sweeping, and I can't
run around after them.'

'Has someone said something?'

'Of course, not.'

'Don't go deep into the forest with the goats. Wolves and leopards
roam there.'

'Of course I won't, Ma! I know better than that!'

While grazing the goats in the forest, memories of long ago come
flooding back. Of going to the mela riding on her father's shoulders. Of
returning home with a mere paisa's worth of *tilua* after watching people
buy and sell goods worth lakhs of rupees. Before Dhouli left her in-laws'
place to come back to her mother, she had worked as a helping hand on
the *mahajan*'s farm. They had two broken-down rooms; her mother-in-
law would boil some corn at the end of the day. They would sit down to
eat after the men had finished their meal.

Dhouli did not remember getting married. She was too young then.
When her body blossomed, she had her *gouna* and went to live with her
husband. Her father had to borrow from the Misras for her wedding
and the *gouna*. He died repaying that loan, working for them as a bonded
labourer.

Her husband was no good. He would beat her. He died of fever. Her
mother-in-law had said, 'You'll have to work hard at your mother's. The
same as here.'

Dhouli knew that was life. Wearing coarse, dull plain black cloth, and
slaving on the *mahajan*'s farm or the *jotedar*'s fields or doing road
construction work. Barely managing one square meal before lying down
beside her mother-in-law at the end of the day. But her husband's elder
brother from Bhalatore landed up. He began eyeing her. Her mother-
in-law didn't know what to do. So Dhouli came away. She had one regret;

she hadn't got to see the *nautanki*. A troupe was to have visited their village. The *mahajan* had commissioned a performance.

After returning to Taharr, she hadn't encouraged any of the young *dusad* men. The same poverty and hunger. The same back-breaking labour. On top of that, a child, too? No, she didn't want such a life.

She thought of many such things while grazing goats in the forest. Sometimes she would lie down and rest, spreading the end of her sari on the ground. She wasn't scared of wolves or leopards. If men were afraid of animals, so were animals afraid of men. The forest was peaceful. She had almost got over the uneasiness caused by Misrilal's words. She was at peace.

But there was a *mela* at Jhujhar. While returning, Dhouli fell behind her group. She was anxiously hurrying back home. Flesh traders were known to visit such rural fairs. They always managed to smuggle out a few women.

It was on the way home that Misrilal caught up with her. He said, 'Didn't you hear me?'

'What?'

'I was calling you.'

'Why?'

'Don't you know?'

'No. *Deota*, don't say such things. I'm a *dusadin* and you are a *deota*.'

'I love you.'

'No, *deota*. Don't call it love. You're a brahman, you're a young man. You'll soon get married, your bride will come...'

'It's you I...*dusadin*, don't you understand what love means?'

'No, *deota*. Dusads and *ganjus* like us bear your children, it's not unusual, but...'

'I can't think of anything but you.'

'Please don't play with a poor woman like me, *sarkar*.'

'Play?'

'Yes, *deota*. You'll play your games and push off, but what will happen to me? Look what happened to Jhalo! And Shanichari! No *sarkar*!'

'And what if I don't let you go?'

'What can I do? Nothing. *Deotas* like you always get what you want! Go ahead, take me, dishonour me.'

'No, no, Dhouli. Forgive me, please forgive me.'

Misrilal left hastily. Dhouli was stunned. She returned home.

The day she heard that Misrilal was very ill—lovesick—Dhouli felt it deeply. Misrilal could take her whenever he wished, the Misras did it all the time, and Dhouli couldn't have resisted. But what kind of behaviour was this?

Dhouli felt confused. Then one day the village women got hold of her near the well.

'*Randi*,* fortune's smiling on you.'

'Can a *randi* ever be lucky?'

'*Deota*'s younger son is crazy for you.'

'Lies.'

'We all know about it.'

'Don't lie.'

'Why should we? Everyone knows now.'

'No, no!'

A distracted Dhouli fetched water and came away, then went into the forest with the goats. What would happen to her now?

The whole village knew. Would they spare her? Why did *deota* have to lose his head?

She was too scared to go anywhere near the Misra household. Her mother told her he was being treated. A doctor had come from Bhalatore. Dhouli couldn't make out whether her mother knew what the women at the well knew. One day she told her mother, 'Let's go to Bhalatore, Ma. We'll work as coolies.'

'Are you crazy?'

Then she heard that Misrilal was better. He would be getting married soon. They were on the lookout for a good-looking girl. For his elder brother Kundan, the family had not sought a pretty match. This time it seems they were looking for a beauty.

She was very relieved. At the same time it hurt somewhere. And yet, a sense of triumph. She, Dhouli a *dusad* girl, had driven a brahman's son crazy.

It was with an easy mind that she went into the forest and bathed herself under the waterfall. She spread her sari to dry on a rock, then wrapped

---

*Randi: Ironically used for both a widow and a prostitute.

it around her, still damp. It was ragged with use. Dhouli would have to buy another the next time her mother got paid. Ma would have been livid had she seen Dhouli in a wet blouse and damp sari. She would have said, 'Are you a widow or a street-roaming *randi*? Showing off your body?'

That was when Misrilal came up to her, saying, 'I don't want to get married, Dhouli. I want only you.'

In the forest bordering their village, the afternoons were primordial, langourous. Dhouli's mind and body were caught off guard. Misrilal's eyes were helpless and pleading, his voice aching with despair. Dhouli could no longer refuse him.

The next two months were like an enchanted dream. The forest was their meeting place, the afternoons their appointed hour. All caution was swept away in a flood of passion. Nineteen and twenty-three. Each time, Dhouli would tremble in fear. What will happen?

'Happen to what?'

'You'll get married.'

'To you.'

'Don't say that, *deota*.'

'I don't care about things like caste and untouchability. Besides, Taharr is not the only place on earth. And the government law too sanctions our marriage.'

'Don't say that, *sarkar*. You're still young, immature. What will your father and Hanumanji say to all this? They'll drive us out of the village.'

'It's not that easy. The law of the land is with us.'

'Not for us, it isn't.'

'You don't know.'

Misrilal would avow such daring plans in the privacy of the secluded forest and his words, interwoven with the fables and fairytales of the forest, would take on an unreal, magical aura.

Time could have stopped for them. But it did not. Dhouli realized that she was pregnant.

Strangely, Misrilal was very happy. He said, 'I'm as illiterate as you are. I have no interest in owning these lands and orchards. We'll go to Dhanbad via Bhalatore and from there to Patna. We'll open a shop and earn our living.'

But the day Hanuman Misra came to Taharr, Misrilal was unable to utter a word before him.

Kundan said, 'We'll kill them both, mother and daughter, and get rid of the bodies.'

'No.'

Hanuman Misra said, 'First, clean up your own house. The garbage outside will automatically vanish.'

'We'll kill them.'

'Fool!'

'Her mother, that bitch, raised a hue and cry saying a wolf had stolen the lamb. How come they have three goats in their hut? They used to have two.'

Misraji was furious. 'You silly ass. It's better to talk to your wife than to you.'

'Forgive me, please.'

'Don't bother murdering them, deny them food instead. Sack them. And remember, your brother has brought shame to the entire family. People are laughing at us. First, restore our honour. How does it matter if we have one less goat? You big goat, you! Look, first send your brother away.'

Misrilal said, 'I'm not going anywhere.'

'If you don't go, we'll make sure your corpse leaves the village. Men like you are a stigma to our name.'

Later, in desperation, Misrilal told his mother, 'Ma, Dhouli is carrying my child.'

'So what? The men of our family have planted their seed in so many *dusad* and *ganju* girls. You're a hot-blooded young man. Even Jhalo has three sons by Kundan.'

'What will she do?'

'She has sinned. She'll suffer for it. They'll both starve to death, mother and daughter.'

'How is she to blame, Ma?'

'It's always the fault of the woman. For not considering a brahman's honour, she's even more to blame.'

'Ma, you love me, don't you?'

'Aren't you my baby boy?'

'Swear by me.'

'Why?'

'Please.'

'Okay.'

'I'll obey you all, I'll go away. But promise me that you'll ensure she doesn't starve to death.'

'I...promise.'

'And that no one will harass her.'

'Alright.'

'If you don't keep your promise Ma...you know me, I may not be able to speak up in front of *Deota* but you know how stubborn I can be. I swear I'll never return or get married if you fail to keep your word.'

'No, no. Don't say that, please. I'll look after the *dusadin* and...provide for them.'

Dhouli found out about it. It never occurred to her to protest. This was not the first time that a brahman's son had ruined a *dusad's* daughter. Their village society held Dhouli solely responsible. Her kinsfolk rejected her because she had fallen in love. She had kept aloof from the men of her community. That was alright. If Misrilal had used force, they would not have spurned her. There were several illegitimate Misra children growing up in the *dusad–ganju–dhobi* quarters. But Dhouli had been willing. An unforgivable offence. The *dusad–ganju* lads and the contractor's coolies were watching closely to see how the situation developed. Sometimes, the Misras looked after the mothers of their illegitimate children by giving them work or money or food. Such women and their children were treated well by the villagers. Otherwise, the Misras would be offended. And if that happened no one would be spared. They thought, if the Misras provided for Dhouli, they would forget about the entire episode. Otherwise, they would see to it that Dhouli, the *randi,* the widow, was forced into prostitution.

Dhouli was aware of all this and knew what would happen. Fear and sorrow overwhelmed her. Suddenly, the forest lost all its charm; the trees were ghostly sentries; even the rocks seemed to watch her. She waited in vain near the waterfall. Misrilal didn't come.

Finally he came. When Dhouli was exhausted and drained from waiting for him. Misrilal appeared. She looked at him and read her death sentence. Dhouli buried her face in Misrilal's chest and wept inconsolably. He too wept, his face in her hair. The scent of soap. Misrilal used to bring her soap and fragrant oil. Bought her two saris as well. They were printed saris, so Dhouli never wore them. A strange emptiness filled Misrilal.

'Dhouli, my beloved, why were you born a *dusadin?*'
'Don't say that, *deota*. Please don't. I can't take it any more.'
'Listen. Crying won't help you now.'
'I have a whole lifetime to cry.'
'This time I have to leave. I've had to accept all their conditions.'
'Why did you talk of love?'
'I still love you.'
'*Sarkar*, your Dhouli is dead now. Please don't laugh at the dead, *sarkar*.'
'Listen to me, you silly girl.'

Misrilal made her sit on a rock. He lifted her face up and said, 'I'll stay quiet for a month. I won't be pressured into marriage, I've told them that and they've agreed.'

'You'll forget me.'

'Of course, not. Listen, I'll return in a month's time. By then I'll have decided where to go and what to do. I am not an educated guy. I don't want a good job. Nor do I want all the land and property like my elder brother. I'll settle somewhere and open a shop. These things have to be arranged, after all.'

'What should I do?'

'You stay here.'

'How will we survive? Your brother called Ma a thief and sacked her.'

'My mother has sworn that she'll look after you and your needs. Besides...'

Misrilal tied five ten-rupee notes to the end of Dhouli's sari. He told her, 'Be brave for a month.'

Then he left. After caressing her and reassuring her. She returned home after a while. Mother and daughter talked things over, then put the notes in a jar and buried it under the floor.

Misrilal left the village. After a couple of days Dhouli's mother went to the Misra house. Without a word, the mistress of the house doled out a kilogram of *maroa*, careful to avoid touching her. She told Dhouli's mother, 'Come back after three days.'

On her next visit, the quantity of *maroa* was halved but the three-day frequency remained unchanged. The third time Misrilal's mother grimly told her, 'Since you were here last I haven't been able to find the *lota* for storing milk.'

'But Maiya I never...'

'No, my elder son has asked me not to let you in the house. Stay near the door and call me.'

Without a word of protest Dhouli's mother left the place. But when she stood outside and called on her next visit, she was told that Maiya had left for Burudiha. From Hanuman Misra's house, Dhouli's mother returned home furious and beat her daughter mercilessly. Dhouli did not utter a word. After her mother finally gave up, Dhouli handed her a sickle. She said, 'Here, use this. Your hands must be tired. Besides, just one stroke will do the trick. It's very sharp.'

Mother and daughter held each other and began to weep. Then the mother said, 'I'm telling you for your own good. Ask Shanichari to give you a potion.'

'Why?'

'Get rid of the thorn in your womb.'

'No, Ma.'

'He's not going to come back. Too immature. He may have thought he could keep his word but he won't be able to. It's not possible.'

'I'll poison myself if he doesn't return.'

'Will you?'

'Yes.'

Her mother kept quiet for some time. Then she sighed and said, 'Let me go to that contractor, the forest contractor. He once asked me to cook for him.'

'Shall I go?'

'No, no, I'm old now, I'll go. Even if he doesn't pay he'll give me food. And I'll bring at home.'

'You go then.'

'You graze the goats.'

That's how they worked things out. Dhouli's mother didn't get a cook's job but she worked as a helper. The day she got something to eat, she brought it home. The *dusads* kept a close watch on the mother and daughter. So did the coolies. They felled trees. Got paid in cash. But she's Kundan's brother's kept woman, that's the problem. They were keen to see what would happen ultimately. Felling trees and transporting the wood to cities would go on for a long time. Waiting was not a problem for them. Rather, it held a kind of excitement. Since Dhouli had been involved with a brahman's son, her attraction seemed to have doubled.

One month, two months, four months passed. Every day, Dhouli would return home after waiting for the bus. Today, lying on the *machan*, she relived everything. Every little detail. Then she shut her eyes. Put her hand on her belly. The baby kicked. Strange *sensation*. Misrilal had said if it was a boy he would name it Murari. But somehow Misrilal and his love were beginning to seem as unreal as a fairytale.

Dhouli's son was born at the end of Ashwin. Shanichari was the midwife. She cut the cord. She said, 'It's Dhouli's* child, that's why he's so fair.'

Earlier, Dhouli's mother had spoken to Shanichari. Dhouli had to be given a potion to make her infertile. Shanichari gave her something. She said, 'It's very bitter but it will do you a lot of good.'

Dhouli's mother asked, 'She won't die, will she?'

'No, no. I gave the same medicine to Kundan Misra's wife. She didn't die, did she?'

'It won't harm her?'

'No.'

'I hope so.'

'What are you going to do now?'

'Leave it to God.'

'Misrilal is getting married.'

'Shshhh…Dhouli will hear you.'

'What next?'

'Whatever is to happen will happen.'

'They'll stone your door.'

'I know.'

'Misrilal will be sent to Dhanbad after the wedding. They've set up a cycle shop for him there.'

'I had warned Dhouli.'

'I told you earlier that if the *deotas* don't provide for Dhouli, I'll send the forest overseer to your place.'

'Let's not discuss this now.'

Shanichari was the village gossip and medicine woman, so the Misras left her alone. She was somehow moved by Dhouli's plight and, in her typical manner, decided to raise public opinion in the girl's favour.

*Dhouli: Literally, 'one who is fair'.

She went to treat Misrilal's mother for rheumatic pain and told her, 'Dhouli's had a son.'

'So?'

'Looks exactly like your son.'

'Says who? That's a lie.'

'Come now. We all know that your son was in love with her. So many of your offspring are born to our women, does anyone sit in judgement?'

'Since you've brought it up...'

'Yes?'

'Can you make them leave this place?'

'Where will they go?'

'Anywhere. Misrilal's would-be in-laws are a renowned family, and the bride's not all that young. If they get to hear of this, they'll be annoyed.'

'Part with some money and they'll leave.'

'How much?'

'A thousand.'

'Let me see. I'll talk to my elder son.'

'You didn't support her, didn't provide for her. That really gave you a bad name. Haven't your husband and elder son fooled around with *ganju* girls? They've always been provided for. What happened this time to make you turn your face away and act so pious?'

'Dhouli's mother stole a *lota*...'

'That's not true, Maiya.'

'So what should I do now?'

Misra's wife tolerated Shanichari because of her potions, which helped keep her old and promiscuous husband under control.

'Do something for them.'

'Let me speak to my elder son.'

Her elder son Kundan said, 'Forget it. She's just had a son. Soon she'll start taking in clients, the slut. I'll take care of things at this end—even when Misrilal gets married, he won't come to the village.'

His mother was most relieved to hear this and forgot all about Dhouli.

But Hanumanji objected, 'That won't do. After the marriage, the bride must first come home and then they can leave for Dhanbad together. Why shouldn't they come to the village? For fear of that *dusad* woman? What can she do?'

Dhouli heard all the news. She sat at home with her son, thinking things over. Her mother could lose her job any day. Dhouli and the infant were dependent on her. They could perhaps sell off the goats, one by one. But could they live off that? For how long? And after that? After that?

The very thought of Misrilal made her mind go numb. Did all that love, all those words, mean nothing? No, it couldn't be. The forest and the waterfall had always been the source of numerous legends. A fairy was apparently seen there on full moon nights. The famous *daroga* Mukkhan Singh was said to have gone mad at the sight of her. It seemed so unreal, so magical, that tale. The *ganju* girl Jhulni had fallen in love with her brother-in-law and the panchayat had driven both of them to suicide—they had gone into the forest and swallowed the poisonous seeds of the *kolke* flower. Dhouli had known them both, yet the whole story seemed unreal to her, the stuff of legend. In that very forest, near the same waterfall, once upon a time, had a brahman boy whispered sweet nothings to a *dusad* girl, murmuring 'You are my *koyeli*, my beautiful dark bride?' Had they lain wrapped in each other's arms on a bed of red flowers strewn on that forest floor? Had it really happened? Had a *deota* really kissed the feet of a *dusadin* after extracting a thorn from it one day? No, it couldn't have been. It was all a fantasy! Only the child sleeping in her lap was real.

So Misrilal couldn't honour his word. Dhouli had nothing to say. But what was she to do now? Would Misrilal feel compassion on seeing his child? Would he give her some land to till?

The Misras had done so before, hadn't they?

Dhouli's mind said no.

Would clients then start knocking at her door and after saying 'no' to them a few times, would she ultimately succumb to hunger and let them in? For the sake of a sari from someone, a few coins from someone else, some *maroa* from a third?

Dhouli's mind said no.

How could Dhouli even fetch water from the well? All the women would be busy talking about Misrilal's *baraat* and wedding. When the *baraat* enters the village, even *dusad* girls sing and dance at a distance. They are given *laddoo*, *chira*, *chhatu* as well as money at the Misra house. But how could Dhouli take part in the dance? How could she sing, *Mai nachaot mai gawat baraat aiyo rey?*

What will Dhouli do?

After giving the mistress of the Misra family a piece of her mind, Shanichari went off to the *dusad* neighbourhood. She told them, '*Deota*'s son brought shame on Dhouli. And all of you looked the other way. What's to become of the girl?'

'No one's brought shame on Dhouli. She was in love. And she spurned the men of her own caste. We are not interested in what happens to her. Let her do what she can.'

'What is she to do?'

'Let's wait and see what her beloved *deota* does for her, how well he looks after her!'

Misrilal did nothing. He didn't even raise his head as he entered the village, leading the *baraat*. No lamps were lit at Dhouli's home. New clothes, sweets, liquor were freely distributed in the *dusad*, *ganju* and *dhobi* neighbourhoods. The village had never seen such an ostentatious wedding before. Dhouli sat near the waterfall in the forest, waiting and waiting. In vain. Misrilal never turned up.

Dhouli fell at Shanichari's feet.

Shanichari came back from the Misra house and said, 'He's very upset.'

'Why?'

'You refused to accept the arrangements his mother made for both of you.'

'Did he say so?'

'Yes.'

'Then you'd better tell him to come here. Say that if he doesn't, I'll take his son and go to his wife. Even if the chief *deota* kills me for it.'

Misrilal arrived. Spoke not a word. Even full of questions. Dhouli knew. He was still attracted to her. It felt good. Sometimes, a sense of triumph could make one merciless and force out the bitter truth.

'Did you tell Shanichari that we refused the dole your mother was handing out?'

'That's what my mother told me.'

'*Thuu*! I spit on such lies! Your mother handed out something like two kilos of *maroa*, that too once in ten days. Then she called my mother a thief and chased her away.'

'I didn't know.'

'Why did you ruin my life?'

'I love you...'

'*Thuu*! To hell with your love! If you had taken me by force, I could have got an acre of land. But you're not even a man! Your brother's a man! He gave Jhalo sons and he also gave her a house and land. What did you do for me?'

'Whatever I did was against my wishes.'

'You can get married, get a shop set up for you, all to please others! But to please yourself it seems you can only ruin the poor! My people too have turned against me now all because of you!'

'I'll give you...'

'Money? How much? Give me what I need to bring up your son.'

'I'll send it to you from the shop.'

'You're lying.'

'I will, I promise.'

'We'll see.'

'For now...'

'Hand it over.'

Dhouli tied the hundred rupee note to the end of her sari. Then she said, 'A hundred rupees won't go far even in Taharr these days. I was doomed the day I got involved with you. If you don't send me money, I'll go to Dhanbad and leave your son with you.'

'Go on. I'll have to accept whatever you say.'

'You've ruined my life, *deota*. Does it hurt to hear a few home truths? Or are all rich people like you so thin-skinned?'

Dhouli came away. Told her mother, 'Go to Bhalatore and speak to Mausi. We'll shift there and if necessary, I'll sell myself there.'

'Bold words.'

'Yes. If I have to disgrace myself, I'll do it there. Not here.'

'Will you get more money there?'

'How should I know?'

The next day Misrilal left for Dhanbad with his wife. While they were boarding the bus, his wife's brother asked, 'Who's that girl?'

'Where?'

'That one there with the baby. Staring at you.'

Dhouli. With her son in her arms.

'A *dusad* woman.'

'So attractive?'

'Maybe. I didn't notice.'

The bus began its journey.

Some people live to see most of their dreams come true. But Dhouli's life held no hope. Such lives never do. Her aunt offered no encouragement. The hundred rupees that Misrilal had given Dhouli were soon spent on food. Only nine rupees were left. He sent no word, nor any money. Although they later heard that he had once sent twenty rupees through a truck driver who pocketed it. Dhouli's mother lost a goat. She had to sell the other two and as always, because the seller was needy, it went cheap.

Dhouli realized that her community, the Misra family and the contractor's labourers, would watch her keenly now. They could see that her son was growing up on scraps and scrapings. They knew that her mother searched for roots and tubers in the forest. They were aware that Shanichari visited them sometimes with *makai* tied to her waistcloth. Seeing all this they realized that Misrilal had washed his hands off the whole thing.

One night Dhouli could hear someone pelting stones at her door.

'Whoever you are, I sleep with a *baloa* beside me,' Dhouli screamed. Someone whistled and left.

More stones. Dhouli pretended not to hear. Again.

'Fuck your mother and sisters,' she shouted.

Her mother mumbled, 'How long will you keep them away?'

'As long as I can.'

'I can't take it any longer.'

'Nor can I, Ma.'

'What shall we do?'

'Can't we move to a city and take to begging?'

'Who'll give us alms? And the men will be after you there, too.'

'Do I still look like something men will want?'

'Why else the stones?'

'For the sake of the child...'

'I can't bear it any more. You and your son. Else, I would have gone to Shanichari long ago.'

'I'll do something tomorrow.'

'What?'

'Work as a field hand.'

'People do it every day. How much will you get? Almost nothing.'
'Let me see.'

Next morning Dhouli went to Parasnath's shop and said, 'At least let me earn something by sweeping this place. We are starving to death!'

Parasnath told her, 'Here's some *maroa*. Take it and leave. I don't need a helping hand. If I give you a job, the *deota* will be annoyed with me.'

'Why? What have I done to him?'

'Because of his brother.'

Dhouli tied the *maroa* to the end of her sari and sat in the shade of a tree. If Kundan Misra didn't kill her physically, he would finish her off by denying her food. That was her punishment for loving his brother. How long would this *maroa* last? Even if cooked as a watery gruel?

Her mother didn't say a word when she saw Dhouli return with the *maroa*. But when it was time to eat, she served them and said, 'You and your beloved son can have it. I'm leaving. I'll go where the road takes me. Can't starve to death like this.'

'Won't you eat?'

'No. Wretched female, if you can't do anything else, why don't you kill yourself!'

'Yes. I will.'

Dhouli tried that, too. Tried drowning herself under that very same waterfall. If she died, the community would look after her mother. As for the child, if Dhouli's mother was able to take care of him, he would live. Or else he'd die, too.

But she couldn't do it. That man in a printed lungi and shirt—the head coolie—took her by the hand. He said, 'So? Where's your *baloa*?'

Dhouli looked him straight in the eye. Fearlessly.

'Let go.'

He let go of her hand.

'You came to my door?'

'Yes.'

The man made an obscene gesture. Dhouli realized that this was her fate. She paused, sighed, and then said, 'Alright.'

'Will you let me in?'

'Yes. And...'

'Yes?'

'Bring some money.'

'Money?'

'Yes. And some *makai*, too. If I'm setting up shop, I might as well charge.'

Dhouli returned home. Told her mother, 'Go and sleep with Shanichari from tonight. Take the baby with you.'

'Why?'

'They'll come. I'll let them in.'

Dhouli's mother might have started to cry, but Dhouli spoke impatiently, 'Don't raise a hue and cry. Come back quietly before dawn.'

That night Dhouli inaugurated one of the printed saris that Misrilal had given her. She borrowed some oil from Shanichari and rubbed it into her scalp. Took a bath, groomed her hair. What else ought she to do? There must be more.

That night there was a rap on their door. The man bought *makai*, dal, salt and a rupee. Dhouli gave him his money's worth and said, 'Never come empty-handed.'

'Don't let anyone else in.'

'Whoever is ready to pay can come.'

There were many ready to pay. They kept coming. Dhouli and her mother wore proper clothes again. Ate two square meals a day. Dhouli felt very sleepy these days, after her clients left. How simple to sell one's body in a loveless exchange for salt, corn, *maroa*. If she had known it was that easy, she would have done it much earlier. Her son too would have been well fed, healthy. Dhouli thought she had really been too naïve.

There was somebody else watching all this. Kundan. He realized it was a case of the survival of the fittest. Dhouli had learnt to survive, had bested his attempt at vengeance. Kundan was burning with rage. That *dusadin* had become such a coveted female.

One day, seeing Dhouli fetch water from the well, Kundan told Shanichari, 'You drink water from the same well she uses?'

'Who?'

'That Dhouli.'

'What is it to you, *deota*? Everyone frequents her these days. We've accepted her...'

'Why?'

'Why not? How is she at fault?'

'She's become a *randi*.'

'She was a widow. But your brother forced her to become a prostitute. If she hadn't, would your brother's son have survived? Everyone seems to be happy now. Even your friend, the contractor. His coolies no longer wander off here and there for a bit of fun.'

'Your tongue is getting sharper by the day!'

'That's enough. If it wasn't for me, your mother and wife wouldn't be alive today.'

Kundan realized that he had been defeated. He went home without saying a word. Shanichari was indispensable to the village. People depended on her medicines.

Kundan went to Dhanbad and threatened his younger brother. Either give her some land, or some money. Because of you we now have a whore in the village.'

'What.'

Misrilal paled. Kundan was secretly delighted. His brother still had a soft spot for that female! And Kundan had succeeded in rubbing salt in his wound! *Shabash!* This brother of his was not man enough! He was not even proud to be a brahman! A man should be a man! If Kundan had been the younger brother, would he have given up his woman on the say-so of Hanuman Misra? But this one had done just that! He had to be made into a man! Untouchables must always be kept totally under control; at times one could take pity on them but one must be a man! Otherwise, how would Kundan manage it all? So many fields, orchards, illegitimate offspring, sexy, low-caste females! Such bliss! How else would he manage his empire?

'Want to know why? That sweetheart of yours, that damned *dusad* woman! Fell in love with a brahman and became the mother of a son! And now,' he made an obscene gesture 'the door through which the lion entered is being visited by rats and swine!'

'No. Never!'

'Yes. And everyone's laughing at us brahmans!'

'Can't be.'

'A hundred times yes! Sissy! Coward! Why couldn't you tell Hanumanji to his face that you wanted her as your kept woman? Jhalo's my mistress! Hanumanji didn't want me to give her land or a house. Did I listen to him? *Thuu!* To hell with your love! Falling for a *dusad* girl! You should have fun and at the same time keep everyone under your control, from the panchayat to the *prajas*. Sissy! Faggot! You've brought shame on all us brahmans!'

'I must see it with my own eyes. Only then will I believe you! If it's a lie...'

Kundan smiled a sly, triumphant smile. 'Kill me! I got you a gun license, didn't I?'

Misrilal came to Taharr burning with rage and venom. There was no Dhouli waiting for him at the bus stop, she didn't see him arrive.

He knocked on Dhouli's door that evening and, draped in a red sari with green bangles, hair smoothly oiled and braided, Dhouli opened the door to him.

At the sight of Misrilal, her face went pale. But instantly she grew hard and composed. In a cold voice she said, '*Deota! Sarkar!* Do you wish to come in?'

Misrilal came in. A lantern instead of a *dibri*. A fresh rug and pillow on the *machan*. Stored under it, a sack of *maroa* and a container of oil.

'You've become a whore?'

'Of course.'

'Why?'

'You left after you'd had your fun. Your elder brother tried to kill us by denying us food. I had to save your son and myself.'

'Why didn't you die instead!'

'I tried to kill myself. But then I thought, why should I? You can get married, run a shop, see movies with your wife, and I have to kill myself? Why? Why? Why?'

'I'll kill you!'

'Do it.'

'A brahman's son to be brought up by *acchuts*.' Untouchables! I'll kill you!'

'You aren't man enough!'

'Don't say that, Dhouli, don't call me a sissy! My elder brother said the same thing! Don't you start! I'll show you that I'm both a man and a brahman's son, too!'

Misrilal, Kundan and Hanumanji summoned a panchayat meeting within a few days. People were not asked their opinion at the meeting.

Hanumanji announced, 'Dhouli cannot practise prostitution in this village. She can go to some town, to Ranchi, and do her whoring there. If not, her house will be set on fire and mother, daughter, child will be burned to death. Such sinful activities cannot continue in the heart of this village. This village still has brahmans living in it. Puja is still done in their homes every day.'

Dhouli asked, 'Why didn't the brahmans pay for the upkeep of one of their own offspring?'

Hanuman Misra took off his shoe and flung it at her, saying, 'Shut up, *randi*!'

Misrilal said, 'Now you know that I'm a man and that I'm also a brahman's son!'

The *dusads*, *ganjus* and others didn't challenge the verdict. But where was Ranchi? How would Dhouli get there?

Kundan said, 'My contractor will take her there. Tomorrow.'

Early next morning, Dhouli and the contractor took a bus. A bundle in Dhouli's hand. Dry tearless eyes. Totally shattered. As if her mind had stopped functioning. Mechanical movements. A puppet. Controlled by the will of others.

Her mother stood there with the baby in her arms, weeping inconsolably. The child stretched out his little arms to his mother. Dhouli said softly, 'Keep some *gur* with you. If he cries at night, put some into his mouth.'

Her mother let out a cry. 'It would have been better if you had just stayed with your brother-in-law!' Dhouli's face broke into an inscrutable, pitying smile. If that had been the case, she would have been a *randi* in her private life. But now she was about to become a professional *randi*. When you are a kept woman, you're all alone. But now she would be part of a community. The collective strength of that society was far more powerful than an individual's strength. And those who had forced her to be a whore were the ones who controlled society. They were the most powerful! Her mother wouldn't understand all this, but Dhouli did. Which is why she could smile and say, 'Keep some *gur* for him. And leave a lamp lit, he's scared of the dark.'

The bus driver working for Rohatgi Company couldn't look Dhouli in the face. He blew the horn and started the bus. Dhouli refused to look back because if she did, she would see the brass trident atop the temple of the Misras.

Kundan's contractor couldn't face Dhouli either. Eyes averted, he said, 'Rest a little. Ranchi is a long way off.'

The bus picked up speed. The distance between Ranchi and Dhouli was gradually being bridged. The sun shone brightly. The sky looked blue and the trees as green as always been. She realized that nature was unaffected by the upheaval in her life. This painful thought made her weep. Wasn't everything supposed to change from today? Everything? The day Dhouli was to finally enter the marketplace? Or, is it that, for girls like Dhouli, nature accepted such a fate as only natural? The nature which, after all, was not created by the Misras—or, had the sky, the trees and the earth sold out to the Misras as well?

Translated by Sarmistha Dutta Gupta

The Divorce*

Mahasweta Devi

FTER HER MARRIAGE, KULSUM HAD ASKED HER FATHER, YOU CHOSE *HIM*? No property, no poultry, nothing. Felt like adopting someone? But later Kulsum realized that Arshad was a very even-tempered man. He knew how to live in peace. He had told Kulsum, 'With the money given by your father, how about raising poultry? We'll sell eggs. Should be enough for us.'

Kulsum's father had given her some money; with it they bought chicken and ducks. All the money they earned from selling eggs came to Kulsum. Arshad could slog like a horse. He would go to Diamond Harbour to sell the chicken and eggs, and hand over the entire earnings to his wife.

And so, Kulsum was no longer unhappy. True, they did not have a betel plantation like her elder sister, or a three-plough stretch of land like her younger one.** But they had peace and contentment.

Arshad never asked Kulsum to go out and collect dung or firewood. Never did Kulsum have to fetch groceries from the shops. Everyone was rather jealous of her. Her father, Gonu, who would often spend a day or two with her, would say, 'Very peaceful out here. Phuli–Duli have money, but no peace of mind.'

---

*'Talaq' (The Divorce) was first published in 1973. The first English translation, by Vikram Iyengar, was published as part of *Till Death Do Us Part: Five Stories*, by Mahasweta Devi, Calcutta: Seagull Books, 2001.

Translation copyright © Seagull Books, 2001.

**Three-plough is an indication of a large area of land. Small plot holders usually borrowed ploughs from the large landholders.

For a number of years peace reigned. Kulsum's son finished school, found a job with a shipping company, got married. He now lived in Khidirpur. Everyone used to say, 'Gonu married off his three daughters to three types of men. But Kuli has been the most happy. Even her son has done so well for himself. And why not? His father would drop him to school and bring him home every day. He was uneducated himself, but he would light the lantern and roll out the mat every evening, and make sure that his son sat down to study. Kuli is very fortunate.'

People said Kuli was lucky. She stored the money her son sent her in a brass container buried underground. The money she earned from selling eggs was what she used for their daily expenses. Kuli planned to build a new house and move into it before the next monsoon. But suddenly, all her dreams were shattered.

Shattered the day Arshad uttered the three *talaqs** before the entire neighbourhood.

The same Arshad had often told her, 'Can't you ever hold your peace? Always have to say something? Brothers kill each other over a single thoughtless sentence. A single matchstick is enough to spark off a devastating fire—don't you know that?'

When his grandson fell ill, this same Arshad raised a veritable storm against Kuli over whether the child should be taken to the local homoeopath or to a doctor in the city.

Kuli suggested, 'Since they're here, let Nitai *daktar* take a look at him. They can take him to some other doctor once they return to Calcutta.'

Kuli's daughter-in-law was the daughter of Arshad's cousin. Her father asked, 'Why? When you can afford better, why take him to Nitai *daktai?*'

Arshad replied, 'Let that woman say what she likes. He's my own flesh and blood. I'll take him to Diamond Harbour.'

Kuli rejoined. 'You seem to be flush with money suddenly!'

'Who have you buried all that money for?' asked Arshad.

'I've told you I'm going to buy a cow to give milk for your grandson!'

'Get him alive and well before you arrange milk for him.'

*Three *talaqs*: Muslims believe that if the husband utters the word *talaq* three times, his wife gets instantly divorced from him.

'Go take him to the doctor if you have the money.'

'It's your money—is that why you're getting so uptight?'

'And what if I am, you blockhead?'

Blind with rage, Arshad began to shout at the top of his voice. Kuli, too, began to scream hysterically. The neighbours gathered to see what the commotion was about. In their presence, Arshad sneered, alright, then. Let it be *talaq* between us.'

'*Talaq?*'

'Yes.'

Arshad shouted, '*Talaq! Talaq! Talaq!*'

'Oh my god, what have you done?'

Kuli crumpled to the floor, unconscious.

When she came to her senses, she was smarting with injured pride. 'Keep everything', she exclaimed. Taking 400 rupees from the brass container, she tied her gold bangles and silver girdle together in a bundle, and marched off to her elder sister Phuli's house in Dhabdhobi. 'I'll leave as soon as I can. Let his son take care of him. Never want to see that brute's face again', she told them.

Phuli said, 'You're 50 now, he must be nearly 60. Where will you go? Stay here. You have money on you, what're you worried about?'

Kuli replied, 'Ever seen such a traitor? You're night-blind, can't see well, I stand at the door with a lantern so you can find your way home at night. You love soft *kanthas*, I make them for you from cloth that doesn't have a single tear in it. You can't have a meal without green chillies. I grow them and make sure they're served with your food. I have a new pair of glasses made for you. You go and lose them on a train. I would have got you another pair! But you said *talaq*? Why? Because of your grandson? Didn't our son ever get a cough when he was young? Didn't he ever have fever? If Nitai *daktar* could cure me when I had typhoid, why can't he deal with Balai's illness?'

'Don't think about all that now.'

Phuli went about her own chores, secretly very happy with the situation. Her husband had two other wives, and she regularly quarrelled with him. Phuli had always been envious of Kuli's marital bliss. Lighthearted and happy, she called her youngest son, 'Go and cast the fishing rod. She loves fish. And listen, stick close to her. When you get the chance, ask her if she'll buy you an umbrella.'

While she was with her sister, Kuli heard that Arshad's paternal cousin had come to stay with him. A new intimacy had sprung up between them. They regularly ate chicken with their meals. Kuli's son had not yet taken leave and come home.

Phuli said, 'You were so deeply attached to your family! Look what's happened now. You must have unknowingly committed some terrible sin. Otherwise, why would Allah punish you so?'

Kuli reacted by giving Phuli a piece of her mind and storming off to her younger sister's place. Duli said, 'Settle down here. You have money with you, so that's not a problem. Buy some poultry, build your house here.'

'I've turned my back on all that, I can't do it again', said Kuli, stone-faced. She felt as if the embers of a fire were glowing within her heart. Could she ever go back to what she had left behind—the home that she had nurtured with such care and affection? Could she be the same again? Could she feed the birds and go out into the gathering dusk to round up the ducks and chicken for the night?

Her son arrived one day and said, 'Come home, Ma. Everything seems to have suddenly gone haywire.'

'Expect me to live with a stranger? Your father isn't my husband any more, you know.'

'He says...'

'What?'

'Says, "What's happened has happened." There is a way out. Besides...'

'What?'

'Refuses to eat anything. He spends the whole day crying over what he has done.'

Kuli felt a strange sense of joy.

'What else does he say?'

'Says, "I said *talaq* to the one person I live for." My wife's grandfather says there's a way out of this.'

'What's that?'

'Her son shifted from foot to foot. They'll tell you about it', he said.

They came to Duli's house. At Kuli's expense they had tea, biscuits and *paan*. Her daughter-in-law's grandfather was a primary school teacher—elderly and knowledgeable. Everyone had a great deal of respect for him.

Kuli listened to the entire proceedings from inside. The old man cleared his throat and began, 'So, Hara, does your mother want her family and husband back?'

Kuli's eyes filled with tears. Hara said, 'Of course.'

'Then there's not much of a problem. You'll just have to spend a little money, that's all.'

'Let Kulsum get married again', they suggested. 'Irfan Mondal was ready for the *nikah*. After a few days he would divorce Kulsum, and then she would be free to marry Arshad again.'

Kuli was shocked. In all thirty-five years of marriage, she had never so much as looked at another man. Even when her male relations came to visit, she would serve them through her son. And today, at this age, with a twenty-seven-year-old son, how could she possibly do such a thing?

'Well then, go to hell!' they said angrily and left.

Arshad came crying to Duli the next day: 'Please make her understand, Duli. If we don't do it this way, it'll be a sin. Otherwise, do you think I would have agreed to such a thing?'

'What can I do? She doesn't listen to anyone.'

'Tell her I'll kill myself. I'll take *folidol*.'

Kuli shot back from inside the house, 'Tell him Duli, he would never allow me to go down to the shops to buy a thing. I couldn't even leave the house alone. How could that same man ask me to do something like this?'

Weeping uncontrollably, Arshad went away.

A few days later they heard that Arshad had sold off all his possessions and had decided to become a fakir. Nitai *daktar* had bought everything—the poultry, the house—for 500 rupees.

Kuli was quiet the whole day. Then she said, 'I left behind my bracelets, girdles, everything, Duli. I had buried it all for safekeeping. Let me go and get it all.'

'While Hara's father is still around?'

'I'll be back in a jiffy. After all, I can't go there when it belongs to Nitai *daktar*.'

Duli and her husband glanced at each other and smiled. They would surely get a slice of the pie now, if not all of it.

'You'll go alone?'

'I'm old now. There's nothing to be afraid of.'

Kuli walked five miles to her own home in the middle of the night.

There was complete silence all around. Arshad lay stretched out on a mat. She went up to him and tapped her foot on the floor.

'Is that my wife?'

'Be quiet, you fool. I'm not your wife any more. Listen, I've got all my money and jewellery tied up in this bundle. I've given Duli the slip and come away. Come on, let's go away while it's still dark.'

'How?'

'By train. Don't you remember, we made a trip once? We'll go to Calcutta, find a place to live. In Beckbagan. You can stay at one end of the room and I'll stay in the other. We can find some work, can't we? You can roll *bidis*. I'll put the pot of rice on the fire to cook and you can take it off when it's done. That way we won't be committing any sins.'

'But we'll be in the same room.'

'It's better than asking me to live with that asthmatic Irfan, isn't it?'

'What will Hara say?'

'Let him say what he likes. We'll tell him, we're not living as husband and wife any more. After all these years, it's more like a habit. And we can't do without each other. If you want to call it a sin, then do so.'

'And what about the others?'

'Let them say what they like. Come on, get up.'

Like thieves they crept through the night towards the railway station. The next day, the whole village would come to know what they had done. The whole village would accuse them. None of this bothered Kuli.

Arshad said, 'I can't see. Give me your hand.'

'Hold one end of your stick, I'll hold the other. I can't hold your hand any longer! Come along, carefully now. Otherwise you'll trip.'

Bengali original: 'Talaq'
Translated by Vikram Iyengar

Love Story *

Mahasweta Devi

FTER THIRTY YEARS, EVERYBODY SUDDENLY REMEMBERED KUSUM. This was unexpected. The people who watched theatre these days, who set up clubs in every little lane of every locality, did not know her. Unless a name crops up frequently for some reason or the other, people have difficulty in remembering even great heroes, let alone Kusum.

Nevertheless, they were made to think of her.

There was, of course, a particular reason—it was in the context of staging an opera. Perhaps, the playwright had not been talented enough, or perhaps he had not been able to foresee what the future held in store. Either way, he had written a sum total of just four or five plays and then stopped. Why he stopped writing, why he chose instead to eke out a miserable living by taking up odd jobs here and there, why for the past four years he had not been seen, as was his wont, walking the lanes of Ballygunge after ten at night—no one had bothered to find out all this while he was alive. Though his closest friend did say, 'Oh, it was an old habit of his. He loved to take long walks at night.' With a wave of his hand, he continued, 'Yes, my friend was addicted to walking late at night.' And he wiped his glasses and looked through them. He could have avoided the word 'addicted'. Particularly in relation to his friend who had just recently passed away, a friend who everybody knew got addicted to everything he did, became easily attached to everything. This had proved

* 'Bhālobāsha' (Love Story) was first published in 1963. The first English translation, by Vikram Iyengar, was published in *Till Death Do Us Part: Five Stories* by Mahasweta Devi, Calcutta, Seagull Books, 2001.

Translation copyright © Seagull Books, 2001.

to be fatal for him. Gravely, his best friend said. 'He was a man who loved life. He found joy in the most insignificant of things.'

He spoke at length after that. They had known each other very long, they were childhood friends. Fired with romantic imagination, engrossed in conversation, they would walk from Potoldanga to Deshbandhu Park and back. One of them would fail to notice that they had walked past the boarding house where he lived, the other would forget that he lived in his uncle's house, and the front gates of that house were locked at nine p.m.

He spoke about many things, but never once did he mention why, after he was well-established, he had failed to think of his friend these past ten years. Some time ago his friend had come to him. 'Can you do something about my plays?' the playwright had asked. It wasn't that there was a lack of inclination on his part. But things did not materialize, they never do. To forget is the norm. And he had told the playwright not so long ago, 'Look, you never did have any practical sense, did you? You don't need to do much, things are so much easier these days. Just present your case to the right person…your record isn't bad at all.'

He had said as much to the playwright's son-in-law. And it struck him then that there were actually many advantages to growing old. Elderly people who had tried to achieve something in their youth had, in one way or the other, come in contact with the powers that be, as a result of which they were indispensable in this day and age. The playwright had known all this, and yet he had taken no steps to secure his own future. At a time when there had been no hope of any immediate reward or recognition, he had single-handedly taken on so much. He ran a press, he wrote plays, he published books—all of which was highly acclaimed at that time. But when the time came for him to accept honours long overdue, he gradually receded into the background.

'Can you tell me why?' he asked the playwright's son-in-law.

With a frown, the son-in-law replied, 'Please don't ask me anything. I got married only because people entreated me that I live with my wife and son. But I've never talked about my father-in-law anywhere. Even at home, it's forbidden. No one talks about him.'

After which, of course, he put forth his own request. He said, 'Leela told me to come to you. She said you would definitely see me if I mentioned her father's name.'

The playwright's friend helped out as asked. This obvious contradiction in human nature amused him. The son-in-law had no qualms in approaching his father-in-law's friend for a favour, but was too ashamed to even mention the man's name.

But hadn't he, too, experienced some hesitation in this regard? Hadn't he always made excuses to evade this topic while his friend was alive? It was all because of Kusum.

Their final meeting was not something he liked to remember. Wrapped in a shawl, his friend had come to him one night asking for help. Without a word, he had given the playwright some money. Then, with folded hands, he had apologized and said that he could do no more.

His friend had not picked up the few notes offered to him. He stared into space for a while and then asked softly. 'I hear that Leela's husband came to you.'

'Don't you know how much Leela wants you to stay with her?'

'I know why', his voice grew softer still—it was barely audible. He shifted his tender and humble gaze towards the window, reminding one of the soft leaves of the deodar tree.

And then the misty grey haze was replaced for a moment by the person he remembered from long ago, 'Why? They took all I had. I'm not giving them this house, too.'

'Come on, why are you angry with your daughter? She was just a child then.'

Angry! The playwright laughed, a strange laugh that made his friend feel distinctly uncomfortable, a laugh he could not quite comprehend. The playwright said, 'I'm not angry. But you do know that they've never asked after me. My daughter got married but her mother never thought it necessary to inform me. And now both my daughter and son-in-law are too ashamed to even refer to me.'

The man looked directly at his friend, silently, and then said, 'Tell them, as long as Kusum is alive, that house belongs to her. I've taken so much from her, and never been able to give anything in return.'

The playwright rose, and his friend, relieved, asked, 'How's Kusum?'

'She's fine. She talks about you. She was so happy when she heard I was coming to see you. "You can be sure he won't turn you away," she said again and again. Actually she doesn't understand that times have changed.

She thinks you are still the person you used to be. The two of us used to visit her so often, remember?'

Without another word, the playwright had walked out. Recalling the incident made his friend feel rather discomfited. They had not only visited Kusum regularly in the past, they had taken money from her, had meals at her house, spent innumerable nights in her living room. All because of his friend, the playwright. How else would he have had such frequent access to Kusum? The playwright had been well-known then, while he had had hardly any identity of his own.

Conveniently forgetting all this, he had turned the playwright away that night. He had not even tried to arrange a government pension for Kusum. But now he felt he would be able to do something for her.

'Why don't you perform one of his plays? They were very popular at one time.'

But this was where the problem lay. The people who had come to him were not to be ignored. They wanted to present a play in memory of the playwright. They were ready to spend a lot of money, and whatever funds they raised would go towards preserving the memory of the playwright. But where were the plays? He had written only four or five in all, which are staged everywhere.

A round-faced youth with cropped hair, sporting a colourful shirt and tight-fitting trousers, had so long been silently blowing smoke rings into the air. From his appearance and manner of speech, it was quite natural to assume that he was a rogue of the first order, perhaps a thief or a professional wrestler. But strangely enough, his knotted and cracked fingers had an intimate connection with the fine arts. He said in a deep rasping voice, 'We'll do his opera.'

'Who'll sing?'

As soon as he heard this question, the playwright's friend seemed to suddenly brighten up. 'Why don't you go to Shefali?'

'Shefali?'

'Kusum. I'm sure you've heard of Kusum.'

They all looked at one another. An elderly gentleman with a shawl thrown over his shoulder looked extremely dissatisfied with the suggestion. Knitting his brows together, he asked, 'Would she agree? And would it be right to approach her at a time like this?'

'Oh, I'll come along with you to meet her if necessary. And even if I don't, I'll give you a letter of introduction. She will definitely agree. She was the one who used to sing in that opera. Gradually, people identified her as Kusum and not by her real name. She even cut a few records in that name.'

The young man said, 'That wouldn't be a bad idea at all. At least we'll get a lot of publicity. If she sings for a play in his memory...she can still sing, can't she?'

'Of course! She doesn't get invited to programmes, and she has her pride. She won't go around asking anybody. But take it from me, one doesn't get to hear a voice like hers these days.'

He wrote out the letter for them. When they left, he accompanied them right up to the gate of his house. Full of enthusiasm he said, 'I'll come, too.'

'Yes, of course. You're the president, after all.'

A big grin on his face, with folded hands, the master of the house stood at the gate and watched them leave.

Kusum was quite surprised at first.

Her eyes filled with tears as she looked at the playwright's photograph. 'See, they've come', she said soundlessly. 'They haven't forgotten you, and they've remembered me, too.'

She told the maid, 'Sit them down and offer them some tea.'

Then she twirled her matted hair between her fingers distractedly as she wondered which sari to wear, whether to put on slippers or not. Eleven days of mourning, eleven days since she was struck dumb with sorrow—she had no tears to shed, all her tears had been wrung dry. Confounded with grief the day the playwright died, she had arranged flowers around his body and poured essence onto it. Let him stay a little longer. Let me look at him for some more time, she had begged. Suddenly she heard someone say, 'We'll have to hurry up. His daughter is waiting at the cremation ground.' Kusum felt as if someone had slapped her. His daughter! Waiting at the cremation ground! But she had never once come to visit her father in these thirty years! Only Kusum knew how they had survived the last four years. Where were all these well-wishers then? Today, his friends were arriving in droves with large garlands and wreaths. All so expensive. The money spent on one of them would have paid for a day's medication for him. He had been ailing for the last four years. Only Kusum and her maid knew how they had lived through those times.

She ran her eyes over the room. It had been a room tastefully decorated with furniture acquired over many years—large almirahs, a dressing table and a gramophone cabinet. They had had to dispose off all of them, one by one. The other part of the house had been let out, otherwise they would never have been able to manage. And finally, her *benarasi* saris, her jewellery—she had been able to keep nothing. But no one bothered to find out how they had survived. They carried him out for the funeral as she watched silently, burning in anguish. The maid had asked, 'Ma, won't you go with them?' She had said, No. She tried to convince herself that it was only a lifeless body, a discarded garment. After all, for thirty years she had had the real person all to herself. Where were all these devoted friends, his daughter and son-in-law, at that time? If, without a moment's thought, they could take the body away, dismissing all her claims, she would accept it stoically.

She chided herself for having shown her grief so openly. She did not want to invite further ridicule by going to the cremation ground. Suppose, the daughter decided to insult her?

But she could swear that she had never thought of her as an outsider. They would always find out about her from mutual acquaintances, she would ask how Leela was, how big she had grown, what her marriage had been like. She had often comforted Kusum's father by saying, 'You've tried all you can. When she refuses to acknowledge that, what's the point of brooding over it?' He had laughed and replied, 'I'm not the one who's brooding.'

She had not gone to the cremation ground. And people had had so much to say about it—that she was unfeeling, that she was heartless, who would imagine that they had shared such a long relationship. The news that Leela was delivering great speeches about her father also reached Kusum. She suffered silently. Who could she turn to, to put right this injustice? Everybody else seemed entitled to speak about the playwright except her. People began remembering him at great length now—someone who had studied with him in college, someone else who had once accompanied him to Benaras, and even his daughter who hadn't seen her father since she was a child, spoke eloquently at a memorial meeting.

All this added insult to injury. Kusum knew she had been observing all the rules to be followed by a Hindu widow. There wasn't a single one that she had overlooked. But she had no tears to shed. The maid said her tears had been scorched dry in burning anguish. Perhaps they had.

But these people had come to meet her, after all.

She wore a white *dhakai* sari and adjusted the end of the sari to cover the frayed portion. She had no cotton slippers that would suit the occasion; leather ones were forbidden. Kusum drew the sari over her head and went downstairs.

The very fact that they had come to meet her regarding the playwright moved her deeply. Her eyes began to smart as she read his friend's letter. Waves of contradictory feelings dashed against her heart, making Kusum quite unaware that they were all observing her with great curiosity. She said, 'These days no one stages this opera.'

She was reminded of a soft, gentle and tired voice. So often, at odd times in the day, he would say to her, 'Nobody comes to see me anymore. They must have forgotten all about me.' And she would reply, 'That's not true! They'll come, they'll all come.' She would have to console him thus ever so often. Whenever he read the newspaper he would come across this one, that one, so many familiar names. Immediately he would cover his face with his hand and sit quietly. She was choked with emotion as she recalled that posture of his. Kusum had ultimately stopped subscribing to any paper. Her eyes filled with tears, she bit her lip to control herself and then lifted her eyes to meet theirs. What wonderful people they were, with such sensitive minds. But where had they been all this time? If, in his lifetime, he had got just a bit of the attention that people were now showering on him, the playwright would have known that he was not forgotten and forsaken. He would have been able to spend his last days in peace.

The youth asked, 'You will sing for the opera, won't you?'

Kusum nodded affirmatively.

Her eyes lit up. How was Kusum to make them understand that she hadn't forgotten a single song, how many lonely mornings and evenings she had spent singing those songs for him. They had first met through this opera. Kusum had been a much-sought-after actress at that time. Any song she sang would be an instant hit; she had even had saris named after her. Kusum had gone against the wishes of the theatre owner to take part in the opera.

But not as the heroine—she was the supporting actress. She would make her entry singing, and then take leave of the hero and heroine to appear again only in the final scene. After her exit, the audience would be reluctant to watch the rest of the show. She would receive a number of bouquets from well-known personalities, all singing her praises. One evening, the playwright himself had come to the green room. She used to have a dressing room of her own, and he had come to meet her along with the theatre owner. There was something in the way he looked at her.

Singing those songs had made her famous as Kusum. How could she forget them?

'Yes, I will sing', she said.

The youth continued, 'You'll also be asked to say a few words.'

'That's what I'm waiting for.'

She did not realize how cheap and contrived she sounded to them. As they departed, Kusum stood at the door. Things had begun to look up at last. She went through the newspapers on the table. She had been keeping a record of all the pieces published about the playwright over the past few days. So many people had said so many things, but nobody had once mentioned Kusum. As if she had never existed in his life! But there was no reason to think of all that now. People would again get to see his opera, hear the songs composed by him. Kusum would find her voice again in front of so many people. This was no small consolation.

She closed the door and went upstairs. It did not strike her even for a moment how urgently she needed money, that there was now nothing worth selling in the house. He had been ill for four years and his room was littered with empty medicine bottles, cotton wool, his bed linen, and all the other paraphernalia of sickness. It was astonishing how, as soon as the person in question had passed away, all intentions to clean out his room had also vanished. Besides, there were so many other things to be done. All the rooms had to be cleared out and the furniture arranged in a single room. Every other room would have to be rented out, otherwise she would just not be able to manage. None of this occurred to her now.

She opened the chest of drawers and felt about in it. Yes, it was all there. Kusum had never used costumes hired by the theatre company.

She had always carried her own. She pulled out a sari from the cardboard box, draped it around herself and looked into the mirror. She had retained her complexion and figure, she still had long hair. But her face was now furrowed with age, and there were dark circles beneath her eyes.

Kusum sighed deeply. Her appearance had undergone this drastic change looking after the very person who had always been so eager to see her happy. But it didn't matter. If she applied thick make-up, none of this would be noticeable on stage. She took out her silk-bound notebook of songs from a casing suffused with the scent of naphthalene and camphor. The maid stood at the door and stared at her in amazement. She said, 'What are you settling down to now, Ma? This is the only time of her day when you eat a little, you've completely stopped having a meal at night. If you don't eat regularly, how do you expect your body to cope?'

These few words of concern were enough for Kusum. She picked a clean sari off the Wardrobe to change into.

'What's the point of brooding so much, Ma? You'll have to accept this now. Since you've lost your husband, there's nothing to look forward to but sorrow.'

Kusum was overcome with emotion when she heard this. She changed her clothes and examined the *dhakai* sari carefully. She would have to darn the frayed portion. Otherwise, what else could she wear on the day of the show? She felt somewhat proud that she had never let the playwright know how bad things were. Kusum had always appeared before him in sparklingly clean saris, she had somehow managed to buy flowers to brighten up his room. A number of times she had gone without meals, had *paan* instead and was forced to glibly tell lies as she sat beside him. It was good that he died when he did. It would have become very difficult to keep the truth from him for much longer, and it would have been impossible to save themselves from total destitution.

'Do come and eat, Ma!' the maid sounded tired.

'Coming!' As she left the room, Kusum glanced at the playwright's photograph. She drew her sari over her head as a matter of habit. As she stepped out, she decided to buy a large wreath for him on the day of the programme. Perhaps, the organizers would give her some flowers. He had a fondness for beautiful things. Flowers on the window sill, incense sticks in the incense holder, new books on the table, her fresh and clean saris—everything had to be just right, absolutely perfect. And he himself loved to wear freshly starched and ironed clothes.

She dusted the photograph with the end of her sari and left the room. Nine at night.

In the dressing room, Kusum was vigorously scrubbing her face and neck with a towel. Her arms, weighed down by the garland, felt as if they would slip off her body. In her childhood, she had once bought a clay fish and a silver-coloured sheep from a fair and hung them in her room. Within a few days, the clay fish had softened and slipped off on its own.

She was burning with rage at having trusted them. Everyone had come to the programme, all his friends. Everyone spoke at length about their association with the playwright. Not once did they mention Kusum, even though she had been sitting right there. Nobody brought up the fact that, even before they had met each other, the playwright had written all his plays in the hope that Kusum would act in them. And the opera! That had been for her, too, just for her. She still had all his letters. And that special friend of his! Kusum's lips twitched as she remembered him all the while brushing her hair vigorously. At one time that man used to spend all his time in their sitting room. He had written long paeans after watching her performances.

How that man spoke about his relationship with the playwright! Relationship! Not one of them had kept in touch with him. Not one of them had bothered to find out how he was, while he was alive. He had had a genuine relationship with only one person. But they didn't have the courage to say so in public! Nobody had requested her to say a single word about the playwright. She sang beautifully and there was a thunderous applause in response. That was it. Had Kusum come all the way just to hear that applause?

She came out of the dressing room. There were flowers everywhere—lotuses, roses, tuberoses…she had a vacant look in her eyes. No one was waiting to meet her. They had all left. Unknowingly, she sighed deeply. Kusum felt very tired and old. The fact that she had ignored all societal norms to be with him all these years did not count—she was being treated with utter disregard, given to understand that everybody had the right to talk about the playwright but her.

The young organizer was waiting downstairs along with a few others. He was saying something to them, looking highly amused.

'No, no. No question of grief. She jumped at the chance as soon as we broached the subject. It felt odd even then. But look at his daughter, she refused to come at any cost. Actually, these relationships hardly last. After all, she's...'

Every word reached her ears, even as he stopped short on seeing Kusum.

Quickly, one of the others said, 'Your programme went off quite well. I heard you've managed to collect three thousand rupees.'

Flashing a toothpaste-advertisement smile, the young lad replied, 'Yes, the publicity was rather good.' He looked at Kusum with eyes full of contempt. He harboured a grave distrust and dislike for anything that represented a bygone era. He and many others of his generation believed that Kusum and the playwright belonged to an era of impulsive, passionate hedonism. He would not credit the strong bond that the playwright and Kusum had shared. His gaze now mocked her, as if to say, I was the only one who was able to know you for what you are. And there was something else in that gaze that upset her, that made her want to look away. Kusum realized that the entire programme had been nothing more than a publicity stunt, and that she had been merely used.

She got into the big car.

It was a station wagon. There were the three of them and her. They began a conversation ignoring her completely. 'The hall rent has gone up ridiculously, it isn't possible to organize such shows any more. And the way Kalyan behaved was shocking. Not only was he irresponsible, he was petty to boot. Really!'

Kusum became a bit restless. She felt really tired. In the morning she had done her *habishya** and she was hardly eating a meal in the evening these days. She didn't want to think of going home, with its room full of empty medicine bottles and piles of things dumped here and there. The streetlights flashed before her eyes as the car sped ahead. As the night advanced, the next morning seemed nearer. Another day meant attending to the pending medical bills, the fruitseller's dues, returning the oxygen cylinder which was on hire... There was no end to her liabilities. She felt inundated with debts.

---

habishya: food cooked without oil or spices, prepared by the chief mourners for consumption during a bereavement in the family, before the *shraddha* or memorial service is held.

A splitting headache tortured her. The others were still talking, and their words seemed to slam into her like a sledgehammer. She clapped her hands over her ears as the car blew its horn.

Actually, everything seemed meaningless. It was all false. She felt a kind of rage welling up against the playwright, a hatred. While alive, he had driven Kusum to destitution, now that he was dead, he was being widely lauded with garlands and applause. And what was Kusum left with? Nothing, nothing at all.

These people had deceived her, too. Her house was drawing near. Throwing all caution to the winds, she suddenly said, 'Excuse me, please.'

Perhaps, she would have said something indiscreet, but at that moment the car screeched to a halt. The young man got off and held the door open. Kusum alighted from the car without so much as a glance at the others.

'You must be very tired…', he mumbled something else and thrust a stiff piece of paper into her hands. A cheque. Had they assumed that since they had not shown her due recognition, she was about to brazenly ask for money? Kusum felt terribly ashamed thinking about it. But that was not what was on her mind! She wasn't asking for money. If they had shown her a little commiseration, a little respect, would she have thought of money at all?

But, on the other hand, how was she supposed to make ends meet without money? She looked at the cheque. Held it up for a closer look. A mere two-digit amount! Even though they had ostensibly collected so much money! Could there be any greater insult?

She slumped on the steps of her house. In that dark lane, in the dusty light of a lone lamp-post, she pressed the end of her sari to her mouth and tried to stifle a sob. Only an old dog heard her. She cried for herself because it had only just dawned on her that she was now alone, absolutely alone. She realized that perhaps her love of thirty years wasn't as honest as she had believed. That ultimately we love ourselves more than anyone else. She would have to live alone now, and she knew how merciless that experience would be. So Kusum wept for herself. This was the first time that she had cried since the playwright's death. Not once did Kusum think of him. Her tears were too precious to waste.

Bengali original: 'Bhālobāsha'
Translated by Vikram Iyengar

The Kayak

Nabaneeta Dev Sen

KAUSHIKI WAS ON THE BALCONY, WATCHING BOATS GO BY. THE VERY moment they had arrived here, day before yesterday, Tukudi's mother had burst out:

'There! There! Look! Kaushiki, so many boats pass by this way! I never seem to get my fill of them!'

Tukudi's mother is a bit of a yearning type. Can't get enough of watching boats! Really! She's not exactly young, you know.

Tukudi goes to college here. This was Kaushiki's first visit to America, but everything seemed so familiar—she seemed to have seen all there was to see in films. Of course, there is the slight discomfort of having so many white people on the streets. Strangely, Ma looks so dark here— but she isn't really, even if she isn't as fair as Kaushiki. But then, compared to the westerners, Kaushiki herself might be considered dark. Who knows. She can't see herself on the streets, can she?

Quite a country, this. People on the streets always walk on the pavements, cross at the zebra crossing, even the dogs seem to know the traffic signals. There was this dog waiting at the traffic lights yesterday. Here, they have traffic lights for people, too—the red signal says 'DON'T WALK' then a white signal says 'WALK'. The dog had a blind gentleman with him, he had a white stick and dark glasses. The dog walked him across the street like it was the easiest thing on earth! Kaushiki liked that far better than these silly boats.

Right at this moment, Tukudi's mother let out a cry: 'Look Kaushiki! Look at them rowing away on the rowboat!'

Kaushiki looked over her shoulder and shook her head: 'That's not a rowboat. That's a kayak.'

Tukudi's mother's eyes almost popped out. 'Kayak? What kayak? Isn't that what Eskimos have?'

Kaushiki continued to lecture her gravely:

'A kayak is just for one person. A canoe can have more than one person but not more than four. A rowboat usually has six to eight people rowing.' Of course, Kaushiki wasn't entirely sure about this knowledge she was imparting, but this was her belief and she generously passed it on to Tukudi's mother. Tukudi's mother may be a professor like Kaushiki's mom, but she didn't seem to know all this. 'Really?' she said, her eyes big and wide. 'Gosh! You kids know so much these days—why, when we were your age, we didn't even have half your knowledge!'

'You don't, even at this age,' said Kaushiki to herself. But she wouldn't say it aloud. She just smiled.

Where's Ma gone now? Must be making tea. Ma excels at overdoing things. Why does she need to make tea in someone else's house? And not just tea. She charged into the kitchen yesterday, insisting on washing the dishes. Tukudi's mother laughed and said, 'Don't worry, the machine will do all that. There's a dishwasher.'

Kaushiki was so curious to see how the dishwasher washes dishes. Wouldn't the crockery be smashed to bits in there? How will it clean the cups and dishes? Does it have a brush inside it? And a scrubber, too? Does it have two hands tucked away inside it as well? But Kaushiki won't ever ask these questions, never mind her curiosity. She's not the desirous type like Tukudi's mother.

But Kaushiki's mum spoke up: 'I can never figure out how a dishwasher washes dishes. I can still understand clothes being washed in a washing machine, but crockery...?'

'Oh it's simple, here...' Tukudi's mother opened the machine to demonstrate how the dishes need to be lined up inside. Then she poured in the soap and shut it. You couldn't see a thing after that. Only heard the loud gush-gush of the machine. Just to prove that it was working, obviously. No big revelation, this. She still didn't know how it worked. But what she did know was that you had to clean up the dishes and wash off the remnants of food with hot water before putting it into the machine. Pretty pointless, this exercise. If you are fiddling to such an extent with dirty dishes and hot water, may as well just clean them with soap, too, while you're at it. What's the point of such a machine?

Kaushiki is on holiday here. Well, not exactly a holiday. She has come to stay with her father. In a week they will leave for Canada. That's where they'll live. Baba had come to Canada two years ago. Ma has finally managed to wrap things up back home and so they are now joining Baba. Grandma had to be put in a decent old people's home, you see. Their house was sold off before they left. It wouldn't be a good idea to bring grandma to this country, at her age. She has her *pooja* for her gods, she has her beliefs and habits. Cleanliness and worship are her passions. Here, people eat beef and pork. (As if they don't back home! What about the ham Kaushiki's had? Or the *kebab* rolls? But grandma doesn't know.)

They brought their tea out onto the balcony. Tukudi's mother had made lovely, hot fish cakes, just like home. It was slightly smelly, though since she had used tuna. And she has also made a lovely crunchy mixture, trying to approximate the *daalmoot* back home. With puffed rice cereal, tiny savoury biscuits, peanuts, cashews, raisins, salt, turmeric, chilli powder, fired mustard seeds—quite delicious! Ma's got some classy Darjeeling tea from India. They'll have their own little tea party.

Kaushiki doesn't like tea. Although it's not forbidden—after all she's old enough, at 13. Many of her friends drink tea. But she prefers cold milk with cocoa—chilled, it's just like chocolate milk shake. The *daalmoot* was nice. It reminded her of grandma. Grandma loves *daalmoot*. Because she can't chew very well now, Ma brought her mixtures that were easier on the teeth. Grandma ate it when she got it from the big shops. Wonder who's going to get her that now in the old people's home.

'It really is a beautiful balcony.' said Ma. 'Can't believe we are indoors—boats on the river, people strolling on the river-bank...'

What nonsense, thought Kaushiki. Where does Ma see people strolling? Everyone's running. Ever since their arrival, Kaushiki has been on the balcony, scrutinizing her surroundings. Not a single person is strolling, or even walking. In Calcutta, people walk around the lakes, people sit on the benches near the water. Here, everyone runs. Continuously. At first she thought they were practising for a race. Then she realized that the runners were endless. So, she was forced to ask Tukudi's mother—who else? She said, 'They are jogging. People here are very concerned about their health. They are obsessed with their bodies, never mind whether they are youngsters of 16 or old people of 76. And oh, you can't call them old people, you know that, don't you? Like you can't call the blind "blind" or the lame "lame". Careful, don't ever refer to a deaf–mute as that, okay? All that is over. Doesn't work at all now. It's very politically incorrect, see? You have to call old people "senior citizens". The mute is now "speech impaired", the deaf "hearing impaired"'.

So, you can't call the blind that? So, what will they call the Blind School? Kaushiki was astounded. What a strange country! Well, everyone knows that you don't call the deaf 'deaf' and the blind 'blind' to their face. It's rude. But how can you do away with the words altogether? Just delete them from the dictionary?

Huffing and puffing away by the riverside to keep fit. Huh! Such a lovely river, and not a single person sparing half a glance towards it! Just exercising in clean air, is that what all this beauty is about? Really!

So many styles of hurtling about. Most are running on their own feet. Some have tied wheels to their feet. Some stand on a wooden board with wheels and rush around. They even zip across the street on that! The very sight of it terrified Kaushiki. What if they trip and fall? And some have tied to their feet strange narrow strips on which they have stuck wheels—four small ones on each in a row—and zoom off balancing on these. Strange name, too: roller-blades. Kaushiki had seen roller-skates in India, with their sturdy wheels they looked like foot-size trucks. This was very different. All the wheels were in one single row. But what speed! Gosh, they reminded Kaushiki of the robbers of the past—dacoits who ran on stilts and robbed villages long ago. These people would make great snatchers on these roller-blades. The riverside was pretty deserted in the evenings.

Evenings. Tell me another. The day seems to drag on forever in this country. The sun doesn't set before seven in the evening. The twilight carries on till nine-thirty or ten. Even at ten at night it looks like six-thirty in the evening. Come to think of it, what seemed like dusk yesterday to Kaushiki must have been actually pretty late at night. Naturally, there weren't too many people at the riverside. Well. It does take time to understand things, of course. It's a new place, a new country.

Kaushiki will go to school in Canada. It's not difficult to get enrolled in school there. Not like back home. In India, if you merely managed to get admission in a school you were in seventh heaven! (This is such a bad thought. Why would we need to be in heaven? Is heaven the best place? It's not such a great idea to go to heaven either. It's clearly not a wonderful holiday destination. In Bengal we are quite obsessed with this heaven thing. As if that's the ultimate in destinations. But nobody really wants to pack off their dear ones to heaven, right? Strange language habits.)

Grandma's face flashed in Kaushiki's mind. Ever since grandpa went to heaven, grandma has been obsessed with her gods and super-finicky about cleanliness. And what else could she do anyway? She had no other work—her whole life revolved around grandpa.

Kaushiki's parents were busy professionals, but Bindudi was so efficient. Bharati used to come twice a day to clean the floors, wash the clothes and do the dishes. Bindudi cooked, served, tidied things about the house, organized the wardrobes, got clothes ironed, packed lunch for Kaushiki, looked after Ma's needs as well. Bindudi has now gone to work for some other household. Kaushiki's family doesn't even have a house in Calcutta, let alone a household.

Kaushiki had gone with Ma to drop grandma off at the old people's home. It was full of old ladies. They met quite a few of them. A lot of them have sons and daughters in the US or Canada. They send money regularly, so their mothers are looked after well. Some even take their mothers over to Canada or the US for a holiday at times.

Kaushiki's mom wants to bring grandma over to Canada, too, if possible, once they have settled down. You see, Ma hasn't ever been to these countries either! First, she has to understand the situation, then decide. What if grandma doesn't fit in? Baba doesn't understand anything. He just goes on saying, 'No, it's absolutely impossible for Ma to live in this country.'

But Kaushiki's mom doesn't agree. She believes that once grandma is here, she will change. She won't weep for grandpa secretly all day, as she does now. Ma didn't want to keep grandma in an old people's home. Baba insisted. 'That's the best option,' he explained. 'It has doctors and nurses, people to look after her when she's sick. She will have a room and bathroom of her own, she could spend all her time at her *pooja*, with her gods. It also has a kitchenette, but the management supplies the food. You can eat in the dining room, chatting with others, or in your own room, alone. Excellent arrangement all round.'

Somehow, Kaushiki still felt that those who lived there were not that happy. They had had to make a deposit at the home for grandma's admission there, out of the money they got from selling the house. But then the house was grandma's—they couldn't sell it without her signature. So baba flew down and got it all sorted out before bringing them here.

Around this time every evening, when the sun goes down, grandma goes into her pooja room for her evening prayers. God alone knows what she does in that little room for hours on end three times a day! Yet, she's such a cheerful person otherwise. Even when Kaushiki was leaving, she didn't break down. Her smile stuck on, as sweet as ever.

Kaushiki's mom was telling Tukudi's mother, 'My mother-in-law is very strong. She might break but won't ever be forced to bend. Her only son, her only grandchild, everyone was leaving for a distant land, but she didn't shed a single tear!'

Tukudi's mother said, 'Really? Must say she has a lot of self-control. Can't be that she doesn't feel the pain.'

Kaushiki knows that grandma is always saying. 'We are women, see? Our hearts might shatter but our mouths won't open. Careful, don't chatter away so much. It's very bad for you if everyone knows your mind.'

But Kaushiki still chatters on. Not that grandma doesn't but maybe, she doesn't let out the words she holds closest to her heart. Like when they left, grandma wanted to stay in her house alone with Bindudi. Baba put his foot down. It was not safe. How could two women—and one of them so old—stay all alone? Okay, so she is physically fit today. What if she is unwell tomorrow? Can't depend on Bindudi to take care of her, right? And grandma's brothers are even older. Who would look after her? So...

'Kushi, what are you thinking? Your cold milk is getting warm.' Ma nudged Kaushiki out of her thoughts. She gulped down the chocolate milk in one go.

Grandma loved chocolates. Then someone joked that chocolates had egg in them. That was it. She wouldn't touch a chocolate after that. She is a pure vegetarian, naturally, being a widow. Ma kept saying chocolates didn't have anything to do with eggs, but would grandma listen?

'Watching the leaves change colour, are you, Kaushiki? Really, it's so amazing! The leaves take on so many colours, red, orange, golden, isn't it just like a tree in full blossom?' Tukudi's mother's words focused Kaushiki's eyes on the trees in front. Yes, indeed! The trees were blazing with red and golden leaves, just a few leaves remained green. And the ground beneath was literally covered with fallen leaves. She hadn't noticed this before. In all the three days that she had been here. The first day, of course, she was half-asleep. Yesterday and today were better, but she still didn't feel entirely fit. Can't sleep at night, and she feels sleepy all day. Tukudi's mother said, 'Jet lag. Everyone has it. The time difference is too much to ignore. When it's night here, it's day back home, so you can't sleep properly. You'll get used to it. It's always like this the first few days.'

Does grandma nod off at odd times because she wakes up so early in the morning? Is that a kind of jet lag, too? Does everyone have this when they get old? Will Kaushiki have it, too? When she is old?

It suddenly occurred to Kaushiki that once upon a time, grandma too was 13. Did they have old people's homes then? And when Kaushiki is old, what will they have?

The river was alive with boats slicing through the water, the surf fanning out behind each. Kaushiki saw someone sitting on a bench on the riverside, among all these running people. From the back, she could just make out the shock of white hair and the overcoat. All those running around had shorts and T-shirts on, with big, fat running shoes and socks. She couldn't make out this person's face. But there were birds fluttering about the seated figure. The person dug into his overcoat pocket and threw some stuff at the birds. They pecked at it excitedly. Next to this figure on the bench sat a big fluffy white dog. Very serious. Not trying to scare off the birds or anything. The birds too seemed quite unconcerned by this dog watching them gravely.

He must be an old person. He must have come for a walk by the river.

Not for a jog, or for exercise. So there still are people here who go for walks just for the heck of it? People who think of birds?

Every afternoon after lunch, grandma used to go up to the terrace and scatter a handful of rice for the crows. Oh, the number of crows that would come to her then! What do those crows do now? Does grandma feed the birds in the old people's home as well? They would allow it, surely, wouldn't they?

Even Kaushiki herself has never stayed in a boarding school. Obviously, grandma had not. She was married when she was 17, now she is 69. It must have been sad for her to leave the house she had stayed in for so long—for her whole life—and move into a boarding house. But she hadn't said anything. She accepted Baba's decision. What if one day Kaushiki puts Baba in an old people's home and moves to Venezuela?

'Is the fish cake okay, Kaushiki?'

'It's delicious. The *daalmoot* is very nice, too.'

'What about some more chocolate milk? With some ice-cream in it?' Tukudi's mother tried to entice her.

'No milk. But I wouldn't mind some ice-cream on its own.' Kaushiki was a smart girl.

Sipping her tea, Tukudi's mother said, 'Let's go, Kaushiki. Before your father turns up, let's go to my friend Ruth's house. Ruth has written several books for children.'

Kaushiki loved the idea. It would be great to meet a children's author.

'Shall we go, Ma?' She asked. Her mother gave a quick nod, clearly she was as eager to meet this writer as Kaushiki herself. My god! Just dropping in on a neighbour, and even for that they have to call and seek permission beforehand! Tukudi's mother called up and asked Ruth if it was a convenient time to come over. They seem to have such rules here. Nobody materializes at another's doorstep without notice. They need prior permission. And in Calcutta? Everyone drops in day and night. They never, ever ask. At times, it really creates problems for Ma and Baba. But they never say that to anybody.

Ruth answered the doorbell. Closely cropped red hair, glasses, blue jeans and T-shirt. Difficult to tell whether she's a man or a woman at first glance. But yes, she had some lipstick on. 'Hi Shamita! Come on in!' Ruth welcomed them cheerfully and led them into her home. 'My mother's here.' The words seem to spit out enormous irritation. 'Please don't mind if she bores you. She's driving me up the wall!'

Kaushiki was shocked. How could anyone talk about one's mother like this? She looked at her own mother, trying to figure out what she was thinking. That was impossible. Ma had that smiley politeness pasted on her face. Even Kaushiki could never figure out what she thought behind that mask.

There was an old lady knitting away in Ruth's living room. The moment she saw them she chirped: 'Oh, your Indian neighbours, are they, Ruth? Come in, come in!'

'Uh, Mother, do have patience. I'll introduce them to you,' said Ruth. 'This is my mother. She was in Florida, but now I have brought her near us.'

'I am Shamita,' said Tukudi's mother, 'this is my friend Rupashri, and this is her daughter Kaushiki.'

'I never remember names,' said Ruth's mother. 'And your names are too complicated!'

'What nonsense!' snapped Ruth. 'You think their names are too complicated? Or have you lost your memory altogether? This is Shamita, and this is...what was it...Rup...Rup...' 'Rupa is fine,' said Kaushiki's mother hastily, 'and this is Kushi.'

Ruth stared at her mother and hissed: 'Rupa. Kushi. Complicated names, you think? Maybe, you should pay some attention, for a change.'

Ruth's mother seemed genuinely surprised now: 'Rupa? Kushi? I thought I heard long and complex names. Really, never hear anything right these days.'

Kaushiki's heart went out to her. 'You heard right,' she explained quickly, 'First, we did give you long and complex names. Ma's name is Ru-pa-shri. The shorter version of that is Rupa. I am Kau-shi-ki. Kushi, for short.'

'You see, we are Bengalis,' Tukudi's mother laughed. 'We have two names each, a complicated one and an easy one.'

At that, Ruth's mother laughed, too. 'See, I was right! First, you gave me the tough one, didn't you?'

'Just stick to your own business, will you?' snapped Ruth again. 'There is no need for such research on their names.'

Kaushiki was stunned. What a way to speak to one's own mother! Will Ma ever speak to her mother like that?

'Let's go to the other room. Mother will chatter away if we stay here.'

Even Tukudi's mother was surprised at that. 'So what?' she said. 'Let her. That will be very nice.'

'Mother talks too much these days. Naturally, she doesn't like that colony for senior citizens where she is now. Why would she? People mind their own business there. She hates it.'

'Of course, I hate it. I have spent 20 years in sunny Florida, everyone is friendly there, we know each other. I wanted to stay on after your father's death, with my neighbours and friends, but you insisted...'

'It's impossible for me to keep running to Florida to look after you. It's possible if you are nearby. Besides, the colony where I have placed you is one of the very best.'

'It better be. It's so expensive. Not that you don't have the money— you made quite a killing from selling my house in Florida. How long will I last, anyway? I am in my nineties...'

'And I am 62 don't forget. I am a granny, too!'

What, 62? A granny? Kaushiki couldn't believe it. She had taken Ruth to be about the same age as Ma. No, definitely a weird country. Can't even tell one's age here.

Ruth's mother was exactly like her own grandmother, but Ruth was not like her mom. Ruth was not like anyone she knew. Huh, Ruth! Ruthless would have been a better name for her. So does 'Ruth' mean mercy? Kindness? Benevolence? Sympathy? God knows.

Ruth's mother was silent. Tukudi's mother tried to change the topic: 'What's that you're knitting? A cardigan, is it?'

'No, it's a scarf,' she replied.

'It's lovely! Who is it for?'

'Thanks,' said Ruth's mother, flashing the sweetest smile. 'Let's see who I give it to.' She looked at Ruth.

'Must be for her darling grand-daughter.' Ruth almost spat out.

'Who else can I give it to, other than your daughter? She's such a treasure—loves me very much. She sends me so many photographs...'

'Doesn't ever think of visiting you though!'

'She did come to see me, just the other day...'

'That's because she wanted a holiday at Cape Cod. Not because she wanted to see you.'

Ruth's mother fell silent at that. She looked depressed. What kind of talk was this, thought Kaushiki. What was wrong with Ruth—why was she saying hurtful things to her mother? If her mother loves Ruth's daughter, shouldn't she be happy? Then why did Kaushiki detect a dash of envy in her words? Kaushiki looked at her mother. Ma was staring at the floor.

How can this insensitive woman write for children? Is it possible to be cruel to the elderly and yet love children? One who doesn't love one's own mother and daughter, can she make other children happy? And Kaushiki and her parents will live in a country like this.

While her mind strayed, Kaushiki's hands picked up an album of photographs lying in front of her. Ruth's mother perked up immediately: 'My grand-daughter gave that to me. Look, look, that's her! It has all her pictures—of her college, her camping, her boyfriend. You see, I lived in Florida, so she sent me photographs all the time. She wrote to me giving all her news, she called me every week! She does that even now.'

Kaushiki noticed how Ruth's mother's voice had changed, how her face was lit up with joy. Yes, Kaushiki understood her, never mind Ruth. 'What a beautiful album!' whispered the old lady, 'it has her whole life sketched out just for me. That's her graduating from high school. That's her in college. Let me show you something else...' Her voice dipped conspiratorially as she turned to open a drawer from the small table next to her and brought out a red notebook. 'And she's given me this. She's said, whenever I feel like talking to her, I should write down whatever I want to tell her, in this. So that when she's here, she doesn't miss a single thought of mine. Isn't it wonderful how much she loves me?'

'Yes,' Kaushiki looked Ruth's mother in the eye.

Ruth thinks her mother talks too much. And her daughter does not want a single thought of her grandmother to be lost. With such lack of basic understanding, how does Ruth write?

'Must get home,' Ma spoke Kaushiki's mind.

'What, already? Have something to drink, won't you?'

But they left for home. Baba and Tukudi's father should have come back by now.

Once out of Ruth's door, Kaushiki blurted out: 'How can you be friends with Ruth? She treats her mother so badly. She loves neither her mother nor her daughter. How can she write for children?'

'This is hardly bad,' said Tukudi's mother softly. 'Ruth is far better than many. She kept her mother in a holiday home at Cape Cod for the summer. She's busy arranging her mother's woollens for the winter already. Of course, her mother is convinced that she will not last the freezing winters here. Poor woman. People retire and go to spend their last days in Florida. It's so nice and warm there. Instead, at age 90, she has had to move here from Florida after her husband died. Ruth does go and visit her mother often. She cooks things for her mother. She doesn't really treat her badly at all. You should see some of the others. They hardly ever see their parents once they have deposited them in the old people's home. Just send them cards off and on. Flowers on their birthdays. Chocolates at Christmas. And greeting cards for Mother's Day or Father's Day. That's it. Just the fact that one is arranging for a summer holiday home for one's mother means she is being cared for especially well. This is a tough country. Their ways are very different from ours.'

Not that different, thought Kaushiki. Grandma is in an old people's home. How many times will Baba and Ma go to visit her from Canada? They'll do just what people here do:

they'll write letters. No flowers, no chocolates, just letters. Picture postcards. One day, grandma too will say to strangers, 'Isn't it wonderful how much my grand-daughter loves me? See, she's sent me so many photographs...'

There was a lump in Kaushiki's throat. She wanted to dash off to Calcutta. She didn't want to stay here. The moment she grew up, grew up enough to live by herself, she would go straight back home. She'd live in Calcutta like grown-ups did, just herself and grandma.

Kaushiki's eyes drifted over the river. There was a boat there. A steamer. Its lights danced on the ripples in the water. This was a steamer, thought Kaushiki, this house of Tukudi's. The house they lived in back home was a row-boat. It had grandpa, grandma, Baba, Ma, Kaushiki and Bindudi. Six people. Now? Kaushiki, Baba and Ma will live together in Canada, that will be a canoe. And grandma is alone. In a kayak.

Kaushiki saw a mountain stream gushing through the rocks, just like she had seen in films so many times. And in that white frothy water was a kayak, with grandma rowing hard as she ducked the rocks and sped off, carried away by the mountain current into the distance, alone.

Bengali original: 'Kayak'
Translated by TLM

The Aftermath

Nabaneeta Dev Sen

R AMCHANDRA AND LAKSHMAN RETURNED HOME. SITADEVI HAD BEEN rescued, the conquest of Lanka was complete. The city of Ayodhya rejoiced in unrestrained celebrations. After fourteen years, Kaushalya smiled again. After fourteen years, Kaikeyi dried her tears. After fourteen years, Urmila woke up. Bharat laid down the royal sceptre at Ram's feet. Ayodhya exploded into festivities. Brightly coloured silk pennants lined the avenues. Festoons of oranges and grapes decorated the archways. Marching bands criss-crossed the roads. Musicians and dancers performed at street corners. Young and old, beautifully attired to suit the occasion, took to the streets. Resplendent in their finest jewelry and perfumes, women walked around the city. Men, wearing flowers and *tilaks* instead of weapons, joined in the merriment.

Every corner stall offered sweets piled high on silver trays, *badam sharbat* in white marble goblets, fruit in wicker baskets and fruit juice in cups made from leaves. All this was for free, for everyone. Music was in the air. The people were ecstatic and full of hope. They were looking forward to an era of perfect contentment. They would be the halcyon days:

Ramrajya. A reign where sorrow, sin and sickness would disappear, hunger would be a thing of the past, resentment and greed, distant memories. Already, the trees were heavy with fruit, the harvest bountiful. The rivers and lakes were full. Happy homes resounded with the laughter of children. This was an exhilarating, enchanting Ayodhya—a veritable paradise.

On a royal chariot drawn by fourteen horses, the four brothers, Ram, Lakshman, Bharat and Shatrughna, joined the parade in full regalia. After his long absence, the people were seeing King Ram for the first time. They cheered the four princes and showered flowers on them. While they were driving down a road, a delightful and fascinating aroma assailed their senses. Ram and Lakshman felt a tingling sensation in their bodies. Ramchandra called out to Sumantra. 'Sumantra, what is this heavenly smell?' he asked. Immediately, Sumantra cracked his whip and speeded up. '*Chhi, chhi,* Your Highness!' he exclaimed, 'What are you saying? How could you compare it to the heavens? This is not a delightful smell at all. This area is peopled by infidels. And that smell is coming from their kitchens. A mere whiff is enough to pollute the soul.'

Bharat explained the situation to Ram and Lakshman. During their fourteen-year exile, the economy had undergone substantial changes. Business and commerce had grown. Merchants from various countries had followed the trade routes into the territory. They were a peaceful lot. Their only interest was trade and business. Thanks to them, the market had been flooded with new things. New clothes, new appliances, even new architectural styles. Everything about these traders was fine, except their religion—a new faith. The rituals were different, they prayed five times a day instead of three. Their food habits were different. That smell was that of onions and garlic, which were absolutely forbidden in the kitchens of the Ikhshwaku dynasty. In fact, even the smell was to be avoided at all costs. *Ghranena ardhabhojanam*—smelling, as they say, was almost like eating. And eating the food would be sacrilege.

'How appalling!' cried Ram. 'Sumantra, let's get out of here. Pass on my blessings to my heathen subjects.'

In time, everyone forgot about the heavenly aroma, except Lakshman. It had him hypnotized. Every time he remembered, he salivated. He knew he would have to taste the forbidden food. He had endured fourteen years of inadequate food and sleep—enough austerity for a lifetime. Ram's kingdom was in place. Ramchandra had what he wanted. Now it was Lakshman's turn. He walked down to the heathen neighbourhood. He tracked the aroma down to a white bungalow and knocked at its blue door. A distinguished old gentleman in silk pyjamas and a robe opened the door. His beard was fragrant with *attar*, his flaming hair tinted with *mehndi*. He recognized Lakshman immediately and, with an appropriate *salaam aleikum*, invited him into the living room. Quickly, he went to the kitchen and ordered some *sharbat* for his guest. His wife was cooking meat and the aroma had already started tickling Lakshman's palate. So, without further delay, Lakshman made his intentions very clear, much to the delight of his hosts.

The courteous couple served Lakshman *parathas* and an assortment of *kababs*. Never in his life had Lakshman tasted such wondrous fare. 'There is nothing half as delicious as the flesh of a young calf,' explained the hostess. Lakshman burst into applause. 'Now I know why the sages of the Vedic era killed calves to entertain guests. And that's why another name for *atithi*—the guest—is *goghna*. A-*titbir*: someone who has no fixed time of arrival. And *go-ghna*: someone who kills cows. Finally, I understand the true significance of the words.' He thought for a moment and added as an afterthought, 'But that word, *goghna*, is best avoided. These days, Hindus are forbidden beef at the table. Strange, that a social ritual practised by our ancestors is now considered a sacrilege. Another incomprehensible puzzle from history.' But as he spoke, Lakshman's expression changed, his voice became urgent. He jumped up. 'Oh, no! That means I too have just lost my faith, huh?'

The distinguished old gentleman was aghast. 'What a dreadful thought, my prince,' he exclaimed. 'Losing one's faith is not so easy. Entertaining a guest can never be a sin. If it were so, Lord Buddha would never have accepted meat offered by his disciples. No, no, don't concern yourself with these complicated theories of religion. They are beyond our understanding. Instead, have this *meetha paan* now. And here's another— have it as you amble back to the palace. Just don't tell anyone about all this. As long as no one knows, it's okay.'

But Lakshman, unlike Ram, could not conceal his thoughts. He always spoke his mind and could never keep a secret. He expressed his admiration for heathen recipes to all and sundry. And he meticulously explained the meaning of *goghna* to Urmila. A terrified, trembling Urmila clasped her palms together. 'Aryaputra, it seems that you have had beef. Hindus become godless if they eat beef. So you are now godless. I cannot bear to be the wife of an infidel, my lord. Please let me leave,' she pleaded, burying her face in the *anchal* of her sari.

Lakshman laughed at her. 'Stupid girl. Here I am, back after fourteen years, and can't wait to have some fun together, and you're bickering about faith and religion! You stayed a chaste wife through fourteen years for this? Bah! If I have become an infidel, you, my better half, have become half an infidel, too, right? So instead of whining about leaving, go to Faridabibi and learn the art of cooking *gosht*. I'll tell Sumantra to drive you there.'

Urmila rushed to her mother-in-law Sumitra for permission. The three queens, Kaushalya, Kaikeyi and Sumitra were thunderstruck when they heard the news. They had heard rumours, but Kaushalya had always dismissed them. But now, what should they tell Urmila?

In the fourteen years since Dasarath's death, the three queens had had to put up with a lot—Ram's banishment to the forest, Bharat's strange reverence for Ram's sandals, Lakshman's adulation of Ram. The trio had found comfort in prayer and meditation. In fact, Kaikeyi had almost become an ascetic. Kaushalya was the one who looked after the household. Sumitra had become pernickety about cleanliness, and very finicky. She flared up the moment she heard Urmila, 'That son of mine is forever a pain in the neck. Bless Shatrughna, such a nice boy. But I can do without this Lakshman. He goes and eats forbidden meat, and is he ashamed? No shame, no regrets, no attempt at getting a priest for penance and purification with *gobar–gangajal*. To the contrary, he has the nerve to send his wife to that heathen's home for beef recipes! Enough is enough; I'll deal with the brat right away. Call the royal guru, Vashistha.'

When Ram returned to the palace from his court, it was absolute mayhem. And things would get worse—he had no doubt about that. Sumitra had summoned the royal priest, Vashishtha, and formally disowned Lakshman. This was no great surprise. Lakshman was no longer a proper Hindu. He had, of his own accord, eaten beef with the heathens. Ram sank into depression. After all, Lakshman was his most devoted follower—and thus his favourite person. When the *shaktishel* had struck Lakshman down, Ram had realized how much he loved his brother. But Ram was now king. This was his *Ramrajya*. Just when the going was good, Lakshman had to go and eat beef and screw it all up. And then Ma Sumitra made it worse. With some delicate handling, Lakshman could have been forced into the proper purification rituals and the whole incident hushed up. Now, it was too late. And Lakshman, being seriously pig-headed, would certainly leave home if he heard of his mother's decision. There would be no stopping him.

Sita said, 'Really! Ma Sumitra shouldn't have taken such a drastic step. She should have just scolded Lakshman in private. No one would have known, tongues wouldn't have wagged. After all, this is Ramrajya. People don't bitch, they don't speak ill of others. Nor do they care about what others eat or where they go.'

Ram looked a little embarrassed. 'Well, not exactly,' he said. 'A couple of days back, the dhobi was bitching about you to his wife. One of my spies reported it.'

Sita made a face. 'What nonsense.' she said. 'Why do your spies eavesdrop on bedroom conversations? And remember Ma Kaushalya's reaction to the whole thing? Didn't she say that we were never to pay attention to commoners? Why bother about a dhobi's opinion? You haven't turned me out, have you? Don't pay any attention to slander. Remember Ma Kaushalya's advice: "When you are all set for big achievements, ignore small talk."'

'But Ma Kaushalya couldn't stop Ma Sumitra, could she?' sighed Ram.

'Whatever!' replied Sita. 'But Ma Sumitra shouldn't have gone overboard with this thing. She disowned Lakshman without a thought for my sister Urmila, who's five months pregnant.' Sita glanced at her own tummy. She was into her sixth month.

Ramchandra was deeply disturbed. If he was to maintain his Ramrajya, he too would have to disown Lakshman and turn him out of the palace. Otherwise, he would lose control over his subjects. Loyalty is a very fragile virtue.

And so, Ramchandra told Lakshman and Urmila about his decision. They were to leave Ayodhya and set up a new kingdom in the adjoining province of Karupath. Of course, a small army would accompany them, and they would have substantial funds and a large retinue of servants.

Lakshman's coronation was performed with suitable pomp and fanfare in his new kingdom. The name of the province was changed to Lakshmanavati. The capital city was referred to as Lucknow. Lakshman became Nawab Lachhmanullah; Urmila's name was changed to Umrao Begum. In time, Urmila gave birth to bonny twins, Hassan and Hussein. Sita and Ram had also been blessed with twins—Lav and Kush.

But by Sumitra's decree, there was no contact between the two kingdoms. Ram and Lakshman were not to communicate with each other. So they brooded in private while spies provided updates on the children.

After their sixteenth birthday, Lav and Kush decided to go on a deer hunt, a princely sport. On an auspicious day, armed with bows, arrows, swords and spears, the two brothers rode off on their chestnut steeds. Sita gave them a packed lunch—a picnic basket stuffed with goodies—though she was not particularly in favour of sending the boys off on a deer hunt.

A huge forest separated Ayodhya from Lakshmanavati. In the olden days, during Ratnakar's time, it had been a hideout of thugs and brigands. But after *Ramrajya* was established, the thugs made way for animals and birds. And in Ram's kingdom, all creatures lived in happiness. The river Sarayu flowed through the jungle. This was where the deer came for water and the tiger came for deer. The tigers waited in ambush, camouflaged by the reeds in the shallows. And people conveniently interpreted this as:

'Tigers and deer drink together from the same pool in *Ramrajya*.'

Meanwhile, in Lucknow, Hassan and Hussein were growing up as well. They were sixteen, too. And they decided to go on a tiger hunt. They wanted to be *Sher Bahadurs*. Armed with bows, arrows, swords and spears, they rode off into the forest on their white horses. Urmila gave them a lunch basket full of yummies.

Deep in the forest, hidden by the bushes on the banks of the river Sarayu, Lav–Kush and Hassan–Hussein waited for their quarry. Two pairs of eyes sought a deer, another two pairs looked for a tiger. When the deer came to drink, the tiger sprang forth for the kill. Instantly, a cloud of arrows flew across the sky. The tiger lay dead. So did the deer. Lav–Kush and Hassan–Hussein emerged from their hideouts to claim their trophies. But there was a problem—although both the tiger and the deer were very much dead, it was obvious that Lav–Kush's arrows had killed the tiger and Hassan–Hussein's had killed the deer. There was some confusion. Had the arrows been on target, or had they missed? Was this a proper, successful hunt, or a failure? True, both animals had been brought down, but not by the correct arrows. Technically, Lav–Kush had failed to kill their deer, and neither had Hassan–Hussein been able to bag their tiger. Even as the creatures lay there, the four boys stood around disappointment writ large on their faces.

'We are Lav and Kush, sons of Ram. We live in Ayodhya,' said Lav–Kush. 'We wanted to hunt a deer. Everyone knows we have come on a deer hunt. If we go home with the tiger, people will say it was a fluke.'

'We are Hassan and Hussein, sons of Lakshman, from the city of Lucknow,' replied Hassan–Hussein. 'We had come to kill a tiger. If we go back with the deer, people will laugh at us as well.' Then simultaneously, all four cried out. 'But why don't we swap? You guys take what you came for, we'll take what we want and we'll all be better off.'

This was such an agreeable solution that the four brothers embraced each other in absolute joy.

At exactly the same moment, unfortunately, Narad, with his *veena* under his arm, was soaring above the forest on his flying *dhenki*, humming to himself. He saw the cool, shaded banks of the Sarayu and decided to rest awhile. As he landed, he saw the four princes embrace each other as they sealed the barter.

Narad, as was his wont, quickly made himself invisible and eavesdropped. He saw Lav–Kush and Hassan–Hussein picnicking. The lads had spread the contents of their baskets out on a large, colourful rug, and were merrily sharing their food. Narad was scandalized. Hassan–Hussein freaked out on the sweets, *puris* and *payasam* from Lav–Kush's basket. And Lav–Kush were floored by the *kababs*, *tandoori rotis* and *biryani* offered by Hassan–Hussein. But Narad, not bound by mortal frailties, watched the proceedings calmly. It seemed that the four brothers had been created from the same mould—each appeared to be a reflection of the other. Even the young princes noticed the amazing similarity. It was the beginning of a beautiful friendship.

After the meal, the four brothers swore never to tell anyone about the meeting. They also agreed to meet on every full moon night, at the same spot, with their picnic hampers. Then they rode off—Lav–Kush with the deer, Hassan–Hussein with the tiger.

When Sita saw Lav and Kush returning with the deer, she heaved a sigh of relief. She had had a strange, uncomfortable feeling about this 'deer hunt'. She had learned her lesson the hard way. Lesser mothers would have confined themselves to their prayer rooms. But Sita was Lakshmi incarnate. She didn't have that option. Ram was happy to see his sons back from the *mrigaya* as well, though he didn't say so. Public display of affection was not quite his style.

Celebrations had started in Lakshmanavati, too. The two young princes had returned with a huge Royal Bengal tiger. Urmila had locked herself in her *puja* chamber. She was only half an infidel; the other half was still Hindu. The people of Lakshmanavati were allowed to follow their own faiths; Nawab Lachhmanullah had no problems with that. Urmila breathed easy. Thanks to Bonbibi, the Goddess of the Forests, her sons hadn't fallen prey to the tiger.

Meanwhile, Narad was terribly distressed. The celebrations had no meaning, the boys were frauds. They were getting kudos for what they hadn't done. Besides, there was an issue about the food they had shared— that had to be set right. Narad couldn't bear it any more. His first stop was Lakshmanavati.

Lachhmanullah was in a meeting with his ministers and viziers. He was thrilled to see Narad walk in, twanging his *veena*. That diamond on the Nawab's turban seems familiar, thought Narad. Was it the Koh-i-Noor? With an elaborate *salaam*, Lachhmanullah invited Narad in. 'Please do come in. It is our privilege that you grace us with your presence on such an auspicious occasion.'

'Actually, it's a disgraceful occasion for you, Nawab Lachhman,' replied Narad. '*Kya sharam ki baat hai*—your sons are cheats. They killed a deer and claimed they had killed a tiger. Are they fit to be tiger hunters? Liars! The tiger was killed by Ramchandra's sons.'

Lakshman, of course, was no Ram. He had a very short fuse. 'What? How dare you?' he thundered as he proceeded to eject Narad from his court. 'You come in here and implicate my sons, in *my* palace? And you claim that my nephews have killed the tiger just to create a rift between my brother Ram and me? Think we don't know your evil ways? Cut the crap and get lost. I'm not waiting for a place in your heaven—I have my seat reserved in *behesht*. I changed my religion, remember? Your curses can't touch me, so just hit the road, mister.'

Lakshman's tirade left an incensed Narad speechless. Furious, he knocked thrice on his *veena*, cracked his knuckles and cursed Lakshman. 'Just because you've become Lachhmanullah, Mister Lakshman, doesn't mean you're immune to my curse! If I can't break you, there's always your brother. Narayan, Narayan!' His eyes became two fiery pits, he breathed fire; Narad looked exactly like a dragon. He jumped on his flying *dhenki* and swooshed away over the forest towards Ayodhya.

Flying high and chanting 'Narayan, Narayan' helped Narad control his rage. By the time he landed in Ram's court, his usual smile was back on his lips. Ramchandra wasn't as pleased to see him as Lakshman had been. He knew that Narad did not always bring good tidings. All the same, he got up and greeted Narad with great respect. After all, he was a divine sage. Narad blessed Ram and came straight to the point. 'What's happening. Maharaj Ramchandra? Heard that the princes have bagged a deer?'

Ram smiled broadly and nodded. 'Oh yes, Your Reverence. A big *sambar*. At least eighty to a hundred kilos of meat.' Ram was so proud of his sons.

A grim-faced Narad said, 'Your Highness, there was a tiger. And there was a deer. Raja Ramchandra's sons would slay the deer but not the tiger? Is that what you think?'

Ram didn't know what to think. He wasn't sure what exactly was happening. With his palms still joined in greeting, he started contemplating. 'A deer? Or a tiger? A tiger? Or a deer? What is this? A deer hunt is *mrigaya*. So is a tiger hunt. If the kids killed a tiger, why would they bring home a deer? Of course, killing either was a punishable offence.' He turned to Narad apologetically, 'I understand, my Lord. The tiger is a protected species. And the *sambar* has recently been admitted to the same category as well. Hunting of both is strictly prohibited. My boys have broken the law. I shall fine them.'

'Oh, pooh!' cried Narad. He had lost his patience. 'What is this piffle about legalities and fines? Up in our heavenly abode, we don't care about your earthly laws. Let me tell you what actually happened. Your sons didn't kill the deer. They killed a tiger. I saw it with my own eyes.' Ram stared at him blankly.

'A tiger? But where did the deer come from, then?'

'Maybe, you should ask your sons.'

The two princes were summoned. When Ram asked them what had happened, Lav–Kush hung their heads in shame. Ramchandra was visibly upset.

'How stupid can you get? Is this what they teach at Valmiki's boarding school? And what were those other two lads doing in the forest? They tricked you and disappeared with the tiger?' Lav and Kush protested:

'There was no trickery, father. The four of us discussed the matter and arrived at a solution. It was the best arrangement. Everyone got what he had come for. So where's the problem? Yes, we are at fault for concealing the truth. Please forgive us.'

An elated Ramchandra immediately pardoned his sons. They had solved the problem brilliantly. Lav–Kush explained further: 'Those boys are the princes of Lakshmanavati, Hassan and Hussein.'

Overcome with affection, Ram became downright maudlin. 'Well done, well done,' he gushed. 'What use is a tiger anyway? Now, the deer— that will be quite a feast.'

Narad was seriously irritated. 'What was all that about, Your Highness? You are a wise king; you can't be blinded by affection. Will you allow these kids to advise you on governance? What will your subjects say? Send an emissary to Lakshmanavati immediately: tell them to return the tiger.'

With utmost humility Ram said, 'Lord, please give me a couple of minutes to think this over.' In those two minutes he held a closed-doors meeting with his ministers. The ministers split into two camps. 'Tell them to return the tiger!' demanded one group. The other group said, 'Why get into needless hassles?' And Ram thought, 'Well, it's my Lakshman's kids who have the tiger, let them keep it.' Suddenly, the discussion was disturbed by a huge ruckus outside. Guards rushed into the room. 'The people have surrounded the palace,' they said. 'They are yelling, "Don't want the deer, we want the tiger. Don't want the deer, we want the tiger."'

At this point, the plinkety-plonk of Narad's *veena* was heard. He walked into the conference room and drew Ram aside. 'Listen, Ramchandra, I've only informed them about the exchange. There is still that bit about Lav and Kush sharing the *biryani* and *kababs*. The merry sharing of each other's food, of drinking water out of shared tumblers. I haven't told the mob…yet. But if you don't ask for that tiger, I'll be forced to spill the beans. And you'll have to disown your sons then, of course.'

Just then, the palace gates collapsed. The crowd surged in. Ramchandra rushed to meet them.

What happened then? Then Ram's army met Lakshman's army. A dead deer lay on one side, a dead tiger on the other. A fierce battle ensued. Two pairs of distraught boys, Hassan–Hussein on their white horses and Lav–Kush on their chestnut steeds, rushed into the battlefield, arms raised, pleading, 'Stop this! Please, stop!'

But no one heard their cries. Millions of arrows whizzed through the air. In an instant, four unarmed, peace-loving boys lay dead. As the blood of the innocent tainted the waters of the Sarayu, it gushed forth in a fierce surge. Mad with grief, Ramchandra and Lachhmanullah threw themselves into the swirling, boiling, raging, bloody waters. And the river Sarayu, unable to bear the pain, instantly turned into a dry bed of sand.

Still, the carnage continued. The blazing rage and blood turned trees into lifeless blocks of stone, blades of grass wilted away and became specks of sand. The once verdant forest is now a harsh desert. But the bloodshed hasn't stopped. On his flying *dhenki*, Narad still patrols the skies, grinning thirty-three times a minute as he watches the continuing destruction. The world has accepted him as a UFO.

And Pavanputra Hanuman, the heroic Hanumanji—disconsolate, deathless, with no alternative—beats his chest in anguish as he rides the winds, shattering the silence of the skies with his wails:

'*Ha* Hassan! *Ha* Hussein! *Hai re* Lav! *Hai re* Kush!'

Bengali original: 'Uttarakanda'
Translated by Ahitagni Chakraborty and TLM

And the Rains Came Again

Nabaneeta Dev Sen

'FOR HEAVEN'S SAKE! HOW ON EARTH DID YOU MANAGE TO TURN THIS gorgeous sitting room into a third class waiting-room at a railway station?'—Dadamoni froze at the doorway and stared. It was perhaps just this kind of traumatized, mesmerized look that Rabindranath had once described as 'a stilled gaze'. It was a look that grazed every object in the room like a probing searchlight in the grip of a police sergeant—while, from head to foot (Sanskrit would have it 'from foot to head') I gradually became weighted down with shame. Following my dear elder brother's piercing glance I saw the room, as it were, anew. The luminous Italian marble floor bordered with black marble and mother-of-pearl—a space that ought to be, and usually was, adorned with carpet and sofa and couch—how was it embellished now?

(1) Piles of blankets and mattresses trussed up in bedspreads, with soiled mosquito nets oozing out of every gap and slit.

(2) Three enormous bundles of old clothes set aside for Mother Teresa, the Ramakrishna Mission and Bharat Sevasram.

(3) Bare drawers piled up next to a dismembered secretariat writing desk. Teetering on them, bolsters, cushions, six or seven box files. The desktop leaning against the bookshelf. Hanging from it, a shirt, and atop that, the cat asleep, in comfort.

(4) A huge round wooden container on the floor holding cans of distemper, a turpentine-soaked brush, a bottle, sandpaper, a mound of putty.

(5) Dotting the floor, seven or eight large plastic shopping baskets overflowing with important documents, toys, letters, snapshots.

(6) A wicker basket full of jars and bottles (empty).

(7) A hamper of white wheat.

(8) A twenty-litre jerrycan of kerosene.

(9) The bed, now bereft of mattresses, totally dismantled and all its wooden slats and shafts propped up against the far wall. Wet towels dangling from them.

(10) On the floor, the harmonium case. On it, the T.V. and on that, two chunky beli garlands in a glass bowl, perfuming the air with their fragrance.

(11) The telephone, now out of order, ensconced on the carpet like a queen, and grovelling at its foot like a flattering courtier, our Bhutanese bitch Kutul. The carpet, by the way, was the wrong side up.

(12) The contents of partially emptied bookshelves in tottering towers on the floor, surmounted by casually piled on Jamini Roy, Gopal Ghosh, Sunil Madhav Sen and Debiprasad paintings, all surrounded by innumerable gramophone discs.

(13) Two gigantic stereo speakers squatting side by side on the floor. On them, some empty tea cups and water bottles. Casually thrust to one side, the record player and on that, two mangoes. A plate of salted crisps.

'Disgraceful! Absolutely disgraceful!' Dadamoni could hardly speak for shame and grief. 'How on earth did you manage this? It looks like a relief camp for flood-ravaged people.' Like a demonstrator wielding a pointer, he gestured with his umbrella towards a corner. 'What is this? Have you even stopped sweeping and cleaning the rooms?'

Balls of Kutul's white fur twirled here and there. Sand and mortar everywhere—dislodged from walls and ceiling. Grimy dirt swirls wafted across the room like butterflies on the wing.

'Honestly, if I hadn't seen it with my own eyes, I wouldn't have believed that such a room could look like this.' That it could be made to look like this.' I sat with my head bowed in shame.

'No! I don't think you'll ever be a lady, Khuku.You'll never be house-proud. Didn't you see the Begum of Oudh's picture in the papers? How she's running her household like a queen, sitting on the platform of New Delhi railway station? With her waiters, and cook, and sons and daughters, four hunting dogs, flower pots, her Persian carpet, Chinese vases, everything? A real queen can turn even a platform into a palace. And a plebeian can turn a palace into a railway platform. Bah!' I slowly digested Dadamoni's diatribe. Then I flared up.

'Can't you see? That there are workmen all over the place? No sofas in this room—only all the junk from the bedrooms, the store, the study, all cluttered up in here? Everything on the floor? Beds, tables, all opened out? Everything in bundles? Do you really think I live like this? Only this room's usable—every other room has been taken over by the men. How will I keep things tidy, what's the use of tidying up anyway? They've all got to go back to their proper places. This is only temporary.'

'All the other rooms taken over? Why have they been taken over? They can only do it if you let them do it? Why did you let them do it?'

'They simply started off in every room all at once.'

'I tell you, whoever heard of workmen starting off in every room all at once? Why did you let them in? They should finish one room at a time, rearrange everything neatly, then move on to the next room. What sort of crazy work is going on here?'

'What am I supposed to do? I gave the contract to Rahman. He's doing things his way. He's working in two or three rooms all at the same time. I can't keep clearing up after him. Bit by bit, things have moved in here. The store, the bedrooms, the study, they're all out of my hands.'

'All the rooms are being done up at the same time?'

'The work's all finished, actually. But none of the lights and fans are working, you see. So we can't sleep there. Only this room is alright.'

'None of the lights and fans are working, you see! And why not, pray?'

'I haven't a clue. All I know is, they aren't. Rahman says that with all the moving around it's normal for this to happen.'

'Not at all! He's just making an ass of you! Don't you people have a local electrician you know?'

'I did give him a call. He said he can't fix the fan without a cross-wrench. But he doesn't have it with him. They're working somewhere else and it's there.'

'Do you mean to tell me no other electrician has a cross-wrench?'

'That's just it, all the other are ladder-owning types. A ladder won't do.'

'So, where do all of you sleep? Right here? That bed's taken apart. This mattress on the floor won't take more than one person—at a pinch, two—'

'Another one takes that folding cot. And in that corner over there, one more on the Dunlopillo mattress spread out on a mat. Mercifully, the room's quite large.'

'But how do you sleep on the floor with all this dirt and dust? Why don't you sweep it out? Don't you possess a broom?'

'Why shouldn't we possess a broom? We don't have a maid. She quit the job.'

'Of course, she would, with the house at sixes and sevens like this. She'd go crazy trying to clean it.'

'She said she wouldn't come back till the workmen left. That's why the place is not cleaned regularly. I've been giving those men a couple of rupees to wipe the floors. But they're fasting for Ramzan and don't want to do extra work every day. They didn't wipe yesterday. Yesterday, they left early. Today is Id, you see. Today they're on leave.'

'Today's both Id and Rathayatra. There's bound to be some mayhem somewhere. You can look forward to a couple of good horror stories at least.' From the far corner, where he was lounging on the only chair reading a newspaper, came Dipu's smug voice—cigarette ash, used matches, spent butts, empty packets, all littering the floor at his feet. An arm's-length away the neglected ashtray gleamed, as if amused. Dadamoni looked. And bellowed.

'Get up, you wretched hippy! Pick up those butts. Can't you use the ashtray? When it's right next to you?'

With a wearily philosophical look on his face as though all is but illusion, the ash as well as the ashtray, Dipu began to push the pieces together with his toes. Dadamoni appeared to be satisfied. The very next moment his brows knit together. He pricked up his ears and listened. From somewhere came the raucous sound of scraping—scrape, scrape, scrape. Without a break.

'Great background music you've arranged? What's that noise?'

'The floor polisher. He's polishing the bathroom floor.'

'Po-lish?' Dadamoni burst out laughing. 'With the house in this squalid mess, you're getting the floor polished?'

'No, no, the repair and paint job in the bathroom is absolutely complete. All that's left to do is to polish the floor. Ponchu turned up today, he has nothing to do with Id.'

All of a sudden, without any warning, an ear-splitting cacophony broke out just above our heads. The most terrific din. The house shuddered.

'Good Lord!' Dadamoni was visibly rattled. 'What's that? What's that clanking? Some iron thing being banged?'

'Oh, that's nothing. Probably just breaking up the water tank.'

'That's nothing? Breaking up the water tank? What tank? Who's breaking it up? With whose permission?' Dadamoni looked patently agitated.

'Well, that old overhead water tank was full of holes, you see. We're replacing it. A scrap dealer we know has bought it. He's just come to cut it up and take it away.'

'I see. Well, whatever you say, Khuku, you've really turned this house into a railway station. How can any decent person live here with all this noise? Do you realize how much you are vexing Kakima? It's just as well that she can't come down the stairs any more—she'd die of a heart attack for sure if she saw this room or maybe a stroke. I'm quite sure her life span's being cut short by this horrendous din—if this isn't noise pollution, I don't know what is—' As he spoke his eyes fell on another corner of the room. 'Good grief! Jamini Roy, Sunil Madhav, everything on the floor? Pick them up, pick them up, put them away properly. I can see you're determined to destroy Kakababu's cherished art collection.' He gathered up the paintings even as he spoke. 'Have you any idea what these pictures are worth in the United States today?' Right next to them stood a triple-decker Rathayatra chariot, partly festooned with paper streamers. The remaining streamers were strewn on the floor, along with scissors, glue and pieces of coloured paper. The artisans appeared to have been drawn away from the task by some other mischief. Candles, cymbals, all were laid out. 'Oh, of course. Today's Rathayatra. Bound to rain. The sky is darkening already. I'm still indoors, there'll be trouble if it rains. Start off with your tidying—I want to see everything spick and span when I get back around four or five in the evening. You can give me a hot cup of tea then—' Dadamoni vanished as abruptly as he had appeared. He'd been transferred to Durgapur—this visit was after three months.

I got to work the minute Dadamoni left, attacking dirt and rubble and fur with duster and broom. The Gopal Ghoshes and Jamini Roys were hoisted up on the two speakers. Cups and saucers and jars and bottles were carted out on trays. Other trays were marshalled in to clear away innumerable odds and ends as best as possible. Shoes and slippers were whisked out of sight. There seemed to be no option but to send the hamper of wheat and the jerrycan of kerosene back to the kitchen—but before that, the windows needed to be shuttered, the rain was already coming down in torrents. I hoped Dadamoni wouldn't get soaked. And how were the children to pull the rath, the chariot, in this deluge? Of course, the heavy rain suited me very well—the terrace had been repaired again at so much expense—I could now check out whether the leaky ceiling of the study had been properly fixed or not. The study had become practically unusable with the rainwater constantly trickling in. According to Rahman I could now look forward to at least thirty years without so much as a drip, he'd made such a splendid job of it.

After closing the windows I looked carefully around the room, only to discover that, despite all my efforts, it still hadn't graduated from a third-class waiting-room to even a second-class one. All those huge shapeless bundles wrapped in the bedspreads, those piles of books, the dismantled bedstead, the dismantled desk, the dismantled stereo system, the two wicker baskets, where was I to put them all? And the T.V. on the harmonium case? And the two garlands on the T.V.? Oh, just let them all be. I couldn't do more.

All my promised contributions to the special Puja journals still remained to be completed. With no workmen around, this seemed the ideal opportunity to flop down on the mattress and set to work with pen and paper. One long story was just halfway through. Outside, the steady drumming of the rain. A lightning-strike somewhere, a peal of thunder. This was the first big downpour of the season. The pattering sound enchanted the mind. The scrap-iron man had left off banging the tank and gone down from the open terrace. Ponchu was still scraping away—but that noise was drowned out by the thrumming of the rain. What one really needed right now was a cup of tea.

'Jharna? How about a cup of tea? Jharna?'

As though brought to life by the touch of a magic wand, the drowsing Dipu leapt up at the sound of the word 'tea' and began to yell—'Jharna! Jharna! Tea! Tea!'

Jharna's face appeared at the top of the stairs. With a huge smile she declared. 'Can't make tea! Kitchin's one big mess.' The ever-smiling Jharna showed us her thumb.

'Why?'

'Water's fallen, water! Kitchin's full of water—rice, flour, oil, sugar's all one mess!' Jharna indicates the extent of the mess with uplifted, circling arms.

'No! How did it happen?'

'How'd I know how't happened? Not getting time t' move things even,—putting bowl here, water falling there...putting plate there...water dropping here—we just running in circles, putting plate–bowl here–there...putting and mopping, putting and mopping—made fools of us all, it did! No tea now or anything! First I got to put things right!'

'So where are you setting anything right? You're only giving us a long lecture.' This from Dipu.

'Ma'd said t' make *kijri* today, rainy day, and now God's mixed everything up and made kijri in the kitchin all by itself. Go see fo' yourself.'

Dipu said—'That's a load of rubbish. There were no leaks in the kitchen. It's the study that was leaking.'

'That room's bone-dry. This's got to be a new hole—wasn't there befo'.'

'Well, what's making some tea got to do with water coming in? Your logic's amazing.' Dipu's attempts to persuade Jharna only earned him another blast.

'All th' demons of Lanka let loose in the kitchin, and he says what's tea got to do with it? Go see how you make tea in there!'

'Why don't you go, Dipu: just go and see what the matter is.'

'Okay okay. For Pete's sake, you can't even ask for a cup of tea. You're immediately put to some household work.' And Dipu swung his feet up on the T.V., looked out of the window, and exclaimed—'Oh, didi—it's so beautiful outside—', and then broke out into a wistful tune— 'In the shadow of the cloud, in the rain-drenched breeze'. No sign at all of his proceeding upstairs.

But truly, wasn't the scene outside absolutely magical? Raindrops glinting like jewels on the nearby *kadam* tree, its lustrous green shimmering in the cloud-shadowed half-light: whoever said our beloved Kolkata was a dying city?

'Mummy! Mummy! What fun! What fun! Come and see the river in Dimma's balcony—'Tumpa comes dancing in, clutching a paper boat fashioned out of the cover of a 'Span'.

'So much water in the river—more than ankle-deep, nearly knee-deep for me. Didi's floating boats as well, this is the seventh one— Granny called them the seven galleons.'

'They'll all go and clog the drain outlet. Boats won't float in so much rain, only when it's over.'

'Where do you see so much rain? It's only drizzling. The boats are floating alright.' Tumpa's voice, nasal and defensive, floated down as she raced up to the second floor, boat in hand. The very next moment, a shout of joy.

'Mummy, mummy, come and see the fun. Dimma's room is full of water—like a flood.'

And then, a heart-rending wail from Ma's attendant Putul—'Didi! Kanai! What shall we do? The water's coming into the room. Get a broom! Where's the broom?'

'All this is because you were sailing boats.'

Like one devoid of the *rasas*, I bounded up the stairs, a plunging snarling tigress. And dived into the inundated balcony, flailing a broom. Kanai, too, was not one to ignore Putul's emotional plea. Another broom in hand, his pants rolled up to his knees, he charged at Tumpa's rampaging river.

Together, we attacked the blocked-up drain. Surely this was the handiwork of those workmen. They'd stuffed all their rubbish down this drain. The soggy carcasses of several paper boats were exhumed. Pico and Tumpa stood around with wan faces, while their grandmother kept on consoling them— 'The seven decked "Madhukari" always sinks, but always comes up again, my dears.' But they were listening. From the storied depths of the jammed gutter Kanai was excavating pebbles, matchsticks, slivers of brick, withered garlands, and similar treasures, one by one. Gradually, the level of the dammed-up water decreased. Relieved, I relinquished the broom and turned to inspect the chaos in the kitchen. Rainwater was cascading in through cracks in the centre of the ceiling. A freshly-laundered saree of mine was swathed on the floor, performing the function of blotting paper. Rows of bowls and dishes, cups and saucers, were lined up around it to catch the drips. Sitting under my favourite Japanese umbrella stuck with a flourish on the kitchen cupboard, Jharna was vigorously grinding spices to the accompaniment of volleys of choicest abuse directed at the workmen and all their ancestors. The gas burner had been surreptitiously lowered beneath its designated counter and the cooking was furtively in progress. Feeling too intimidated even to bring up the subject of tea, I tiptoed out, judging discretion to be the better part of valour—at least, this situation was under control. The thing to do now was to go downstairs and get back to the writing.

As I entered the room below, it seemed to me that my feet encountered something like water. Now hold on a minute, how could there be water in this room? Did one of the water bottles break? A closer look revealed a racing river staining the polished frame of the dismantled bed. Now where could that have come from? Weren't both the windows shut? Didn't the books on the window sills look dry? Then it couldn't be through the windows. Rainwater could have entered earlier through the cracked window panes, but all the broken ones have just been replaced—so, then? There came the stream, rippling from under the book racks. There it went dribbling around the bundles. Kutul jumped on to the mattress from the sodden carpet—the telephone, unable to move, sat in a pool of water. This was disastrous! Just where was so much water coming from?

Honestly, Kutul should have at least barked a warning when she moved away from the water. But then, why should she? Water was neither a thief nor a bandit that a dog should bark at it. Water was an intruder which was out of syllabus as far as a dog's curriculum was concerned. But there hadn't been any water here a while ago. Hadn't I just gone up to clear the balcony—how could this have happened so fast? The rain had almost stopped. And what about Dipu? Surely, he could not be sitting quietly in the middle of all this? Not noticing a thing?

'Dipu!' My thunderous roar rivalled a Tantric ascetic's howl. But where was Dipu? The chair was empty. No doubt about it, with no chance of tea at home, he had slipped out to the neighbouring tea stall. What an odd boy! Let the whole house go to rack and ruin but he couldn't care less, as long as he got his tea and cigarettes.

'Piccolo! Tumpa! Kanai! Jharna! Putul! Come down at once! At once! The sitting room's flooded—' I tried to mobilize my entire manpower. Without every hand on board it would be impossible to tackle this calamity.

'Water? In the sitting room? Oh-my! Isn't that great!'

'Where? Where? Where? Are you sure?'

Bubbling with excitement, my two young princesses cavorted in, their grins a mile wide. I felt like giving them two tight smacks. Don't they realize what a crisis this is? They think it's fun? That all our earthly possessions sitting on the floor—books, records, everything—risk getting water-logged and destroyed at a moment's notice:

that this room was under siege from the seething water:

they didn't seem to understand it at all, these stupid children. Tracing the path of the water, I followed it to the next room—from between the bed and the steel wardrobe swaddled in drapes, from below the bamboo scaffolding, irresistibly soaking the bottoms of newspaper-draped trunks and suitcases and dressing-table, a swelling tide gushed towards me, caressing my feet, greeting me with gurgling glee. Its source—the drain. Through the drain outlet in the corner the entire raging contents of the rainwater pipe outside were tumbling into the first floor bedroom with ease. From the balcony above, I could still hear Kanai thrashing away at the trapped water with leonine vigour in some kind of cathartic frenzy.

It was clear to me in a trice. All the accumulated water that we were thrusting down the upstairs outlet was taking shelter in my bedroom below. For some reason or the other, it was unable to flow freely down. So the first thing to do was to stop the water from being pushed down that conduit from upstairs.

'Kanai! Hey, Kanai! Stop clearing the water! Stop clearing it, I say!' But my desperate entreaties served only to whet Kanai's frenzy. Naturally, he knew nothing about the catastrophe down there. So, the more I thunder— 'Stop that work!', the louder he yelled back— 'I'm not in the least bit tired ma'am:

just give me a little more time, and we'll be high and dry.' He wouldn't be dissuaded, he'd vowed to make the balcony water-free.

'Hey, Putul! Hey, Jharna! Stop Kanai! Let the water be, don't push it down—let it be, let it be—block up that outlet again—stuff it up with rags—' Kanai must have thought I'd gone out of my mind. Ignoring my pleas, he started flailing around with renewed gusto. Putul and Jharna, equally disbelieving, came down to check for themselves, only to beat a hasty retreat to the kitchen—this was no longer a matter for mops and buckets—this was an unmitigated cataclysm—capable of being tackled only on a war-footing. People began piling in from all over the house clutching whatever vessels they could grab. Even Tumpa and Pico joined the battalion armed with serving bowls and worked to scoop the water into pails and pots—Kutul suddenly opened an eye, took in the scene, and begun to howl without a break—the pandemonium brought Ponchu the polishman in at a run to deliver his verdict:

the strainer covering the mouth of the outlet pipe must be broken open to allow the water to move out. And he produced an iron rod and proceeded to hammer at it with mighty whacks. I was now vainly attempting to drag the heavy mattress aside—thank heavens the discs were not in the path of the flood, they were on the other side of the room—now trying to shift the bundles of pallets and quilts—but to no avail—Putul was brandishing a broomstick with both hands like a cricket bat and taking enormous swipes at the water to head it away from the mattresses and towards the open doorway—each one had taken up his or her strategic position. Jharna was by the door—using both hands and feet, she was sloshing water on to Dipu's jeans curved into an arc like a tongue-scraper and then tossing the water down the stairwell.

By this time Kanai, too, had come downstairs. And had immediately lifted the damp and heavy bundles and bedclothes on to the bedstead in the next room. He put the two stereo speakers on the mattress, and moved the suitcases from under the bed to higher and drier spots, grumbling all the while— 'The covers are left on top while the water is down below, and look at the state of these "phoren" boxes.'

Without warning, in the middle of scooping up the water, Tumpa let out a wail— 'Oh my rath! My chariot! It's dripping wet! My rath!'; while Pico screamed— 'Mummy! Mummy! The stereo! The stereo!'

But what could Mummy do about the stereo? Kanai had heaved that huge object up with both hands, only to discover, like Lakshman holding the fruit in the myth, that there was no place to put it down—stooping under their weight like the Vindhya mountains, Kanai appeared to have congealed into a posture of eternal anticipation. And all of us were shouting, all of us were peppering each other with commands and advice, while my poor mother upstairs was ringing her little bell continuously like a tocsin gone berserk, and calling desperately— 'Hey there! Where are all of you? Why isn't there anyone up here? The balcony is still full of water!'

The fact is that each of us downstairs was in the situation of Casablanca who could not leave his station on the burning deck and poor Ma had no inkling of this.

Amid this uproar...three long and urgent trills on the front door bell below. Nobody responded. In the meantime, Panchu had compounded the calamity by shattering the outlet cover. 'The foaming waters swoop and swell and roar around in rolling rage.'

Freed of that flimsy barrier, the water rushed in without let or hindrance. Then the door bell rang again! And again! This time Putul with her broom and Piccolo with her tin plate peered out. Two impatient, indignant gentlemen in impeccable attire. The residents from our ground floor.

'Your water's getting into our rooms. Unless you do something about it—'

'Why don't you come up and see for yourselves what we are doing about it,' the answer shot out from upstairs.

They were probably intending to do that anyway, but the over-enthusiastic Jharna had by now already propelled another torrent down the stairs. A murky Niagara swoops down and swirls around their knees. It was this water that was seeping into their room from under the doorway—the consequence of not having a raised threshold.

'Stop the cracks under your door with a couple of gunny bags,' I yelled. 'They're under the stairs.'

The gentlemen from downstairs were both courteous and intelligent. In a flash they sized up the gravity of the situation and plunged in to join the rescue party. That was to say, they charged out into the courtyard oblivious of the rain, and proceeded to inspect the offending rainwater pipe, poking and prodding and peeping up it in a variety of acrobatic postures. Their diagnosis:

'Totally jammed. Blocked a long way up. Hard as concrete. The workmen must have emptied their spare cement into it—the pipe's filled up and the water's getting into your rooms.' And they began trying to crack open the pipe. That rang a bell—hey, where's that scrap iron chap who was cutting up the water tank? He's bound to have the right tools.

The ironmonger was sitting on the stoop of the house opposite, smoking a bidi. The prospect of appropriating the hat as well as the head—the blocked-up rainwater pipe as well as the cast-off water tank—brought stars into his eyes, and he was at it in a jiffy with hammer and wrench, *clang, clang, clang*. But before he could make any headway, young Ponchu's demoniac assault on the crumbling fifty-year-old iron joint a floor up had its desired effect. How much more aggression could it bear, anyway? Convinced that the blockage was somewhere there, Ponchu had been jabbing away remorselessly:

all of a sudden the rusty iron disintegrates, and the filthy accumulated water, thundering down in two torrential shafts bearing shards and pebbles and stone chips and iron slivers, crashed with unbridled energy on to the exposed heads of the two well-meaning gentlemen as well as of the ironmonger hard at work in the courtyard. I froze with fear. How terrible—what a thing to happen! But human nature never ceases to astonish. The cheers that arise from those bedraggled human beings could have rivalled the combined hurrahs of a stadium—full of people applauding a sixer by Ravi Shastri—and indeed, Ponchu's victorious stance could well have given Shastri a run for his money.

So the water had stopped gushing in. Now relaxed, we, the water warriors of the first floor, were engaged in mopping up puddles in the rooms, balcony, stairs, wherever. My sari was hoisted up to my knees. I gripped a coconut-branch broom and worked with complete concentration. From being a campaign waged on war footing, the whole enterprise had taken on a mundane, domestic colour. Abruptly, the frenzied tocsin rings out and my bed-ridden mother hollers,—'Holla! I can smell the rice burning! Isn't there anybody up here?'

Hugely embarrassed by her oversight, Jharna rushed up. Then unexpectedly, at my ear—'Didi!'

'Who's there?' I was startled. Two boys.

'We're from the "Madhukaitav"—your contribution for our Puja number—'

'Please, could we leave it for today—I'm terribly busy—'

'Just one love poem—this will be a special issue only on love poetry—'

'Not today, please, some other time, okay? I can't even think now, you can see for yourselves—'

'Did water get into that room? How did it get in?'

'I'll tell you all about it another day—you could come back on Sunday morning—'

I carried on clearing out puddles. The two boys left. A love poem indeed!

'Didi!'

'Not again!'

'This is Shauqat. Id Mubarak!'

'Oh—'

Shauqat, in sparkling festive garb, was holding out a cardboard box. Looked like snacks of some sort. Sweet, *kebabs*? Well, whatever it might be—was it an appropriate time for a visit?

'Id Mubarak, Shauqat. Sorry, I'm a little—'

'Just take this, Didi. Some pastries for Pico and Tumpa.'

'How'll I take it? I'm holding a broom. Have you seen the state of the house?'

Why shouldn't he have seen it? But Shauqat was an extremely decorous young man. Came from an aristocratic family. He would never draw attention to anybody's discomfiture. He'd behave as though this was perfectly normal—these water-logged stairs, this receiving visitors with exposed knees and a broom. As though nothing had happened. As though everything was fine. There's surely some similarity between British decorum and the graciousness associated with Lucknow.

As though drawn by the aroma of pastries, the two girls suddenly materialized. One in sodden jeans rolled up to her knees, the other in a limp wet dress. Each one was bearing aloft an aluminium dish of dirty water like a flower offering. Tumpa, the greedier of the two, took in the box of pastries with shining eyes and chirped—'Hello there. Uncle Shauqat! What's in that box?'

Looking relieved, Shauqat held out the box—'Nothing much. Just some pastries. Here, pop them in your mouths—'

Tumpa promptly tilted her neck, thrust forward her curly head, and opened her mouth wide enough to gulp down the whole universe—'Here.'

Shauqat was expected to put a pastry in her mouth. That was not the done thing. Pico said courteously—'Please put the box on that table. That's a dry, spot. We'll eat later. Maybe, you can sit on that chair. I think it's dry too. Such commotion we've been through today! My God!'

'You and I...locked up in the same room...' Warbling a line of the Hindi song, at the top of his voice, Dipu entered, satiated with tea. The warbling modulated to a yelp. 'What's this? Why's there so much water on the stairs? Kanai! Kanai! Get the bucket and the mop at once! How could so much water get in——' He mounted the stairs and stopped, his eyes rounded like saucers.

'We're ruined! The books? The records? All soaked? The stereo? The T.V.? I hope you put them all away!'

'They're all gone...the whole lot! Why don't you get back to your tea shop, you! Couldn't you call us when the water started coming in? When you were sitting right here?'

'Did...did I know anything that I'd call? Nothing was coming in earlier. When did it come? Honestly! What a mess you've made!'

'I? I made the mess?'

'No, no, what I meant is, just look at the mess.'

'Do you think you've seen anything at all of the mess?'

By this time Jharna and Putul were wiping the rooms and Kanai mopping the stairs, having mixed disinfectant with the flood water. They looked almost happy——the damage was less than we had feared. Suppose, this had happened at night? When everyone was asleep? Curtains, towels, dresses, panties, whatever had come to hand had been used for the laudable purpose of soaking up the water. With great concentration. Kanai was right now swabbing the stairs with Dipu's pajamas. Dipu saw but did not recognize it.

'What's that? What's that? Blast——', he sprang forward and snatched up a sopping wet pack of cigarettes 'Jee...eez.' He caressed the now worthless packet as though it were a lifeless fledgling fallen from its nest, before tossing it away.

The rain had stopped. A soft shy sunlight filtered in. Putul had settled down to deal with the dripping bundles. Masses of wet, torn, discarded garments and bedclothes were draped around the rooms, to the accompaniment of shouted admonitions from my mother——'What's going on, who's put wet things on the bedstead? Take them up! Take them up! You shouldn't put water on polished wood——.' If only Ma knew about the water-logged bed downstairs. The moist books have to be spread out on the floor. 'Turn on the fan.' The fan did not move. A power cut. Id as well as Rathayatra, and even then, load-shedding? Oh, by the way! Shauqat was still waiting downstairs.

'Pico, give Shauqat tea and sweets.'

'Jharna-di, give Uncle Shauqat tea and sweets.'

The instruction was relayed on as though by the drum-bearing harbingers of the Lord of the Forest. But neither am I the Lord of the Forest, nor was Jharna my serf. So she made no bones about her stand.

'Can't give tea and sweets to anyone now, baba! Have to change first, don't I? Whole body's one wet rag? Sopping wet! Give tea, indeed!'

'It's alright, it's alright, Didi. I'm not in the mood for tea—I think I'll be off today—I'll drop in again some other time—' Shauqat got up. At this moment, his old-world courtesy seemed out of place in this house.

Suddenly discovering a suitable role for himself, Dipu came forward. 'Come, come, Shauqat, we'd better go down to Dhiren's shop for some special Id tea—methinks it behoves us to abandon this house apace— Good luck, Didi. Id Mubarak.'

Even the amicable Shauqat could not resist a smile as he stepped out.

The soggy carpet had been hung out on the balcony. Wet things were strung out everywhere. All the debris had been washed away. In clean dry clothes and neatly brushed hair, we were all relaxing and chatting over cups of tea laced with ginger. The electricity had been restored. The fan was whirring. The books were drying out. Nevertheless, that terrible thudding in my chest hadn't eased. My heart was still thumping away, as during an emergency. It was difficult to forget that very recent scene of our rooms inundated by a swirling mass of water.

The door bell chimed. In freshly pressed pajamas, snow white vest and carefully slicked hair, Monsieur Kanai opened the door, humming a tune.

'Whew, what rain! What horrendous rain! Didn't get anything done.' Dadamoni's voice came up the stairs. Entering the sitting room, he called out— 'Hi there! Finished decorating your chariot?'

Squatting on the now dry floor, Tumpa was still stripping damp paper from her chariot, while Pico was making a new set of paper chains with fresh paper, scissors and glue.

Dadamoni looked around the room with enormous approbation—

'Wonderful! This is magical! Just a while ago I saw cobwebs and dust and debris, and this room has already had a face-lift. Just look at this gleaming floor—you've scrubbed everything, from the stairs to the rooms. Bravo! Who says Khuku is not a fantastic home-maker.' And in his elation, Dadamoni plunked himself down on a couple of drenched discarded blouses draped out to dry on the nearest chair.

Bengali original: 'Abar Eschhe Ashadh'
Translated by Krishna Sen

Please Forgive Me

Ashapurna Devi

THE STRING OF PALACES LAY ON THE BRINK OF RUIN, SCATTERED AT RANDOM across half the village, like the torn pages of history. Even today, they evoked reverence in the minds of the villagers—reverence tinged with compassion. They bore silent witness to the departed glory of the Majumdars, supposedly honoured with the title of 'raja' in the past.

This mansion was once abuzz with its innumerable chambers—its *kutcherry*, its courtroom, its outer chambers and *andar-mahal*, its sanctum sanctorum for the family deity, its courtyard for the annual Durga Puja, its vast dining halls and kitchens. Today, these were just epithets for a pile of broken bricks...bricks that carried the hazy memories of yesteryears. One's head automatically bowed in reverence before it. It was reverence and nostalgia for the tumult and grandeur of the past, and wonder at the drama of birth and death, laughter and tears, joy and sorrow lived out by its inhabitants within these walls. Trapped within their crevices, you could still hear the sighs of long dead souls, hungry for the countless ingredients of desire they had left unsatisfied behind them. And in the months of Chaitra and Baisakh, when the broken windows flapped in the evening gusts, one could almost hear the anguished lamentations, the pent-up sighs of these long-lost souls. One could hardly expect anything other than bats and pigeons to survive within these ruins. And ghosts! That was certainly possible. Yet, there was such a presence. Perhaps, only because she was left with no other choice.

She occupied one of the chambers that had somehow managed to remain intact within the 'andar mahal'. She was 'Nutan Ginni', the third wife of Nawadwip Majumdar. She was a bent and broken crone of seventy, with faded vision, though her voice remained loud as ever. Stumbling and tripping at least fifty times a day, she managed to fend for herself, showering curses liberally upon all, her own fourteen generations up and down and upon bird, animal, insect, god or demon alike. She seemed to harbour a strange, deadly anger at everything in this whole wide world—as if given a chance she would grind it all to pulp between her teeth.

Frustrated with the vain effort to straighten her broken back in the sweltering heat of summer, she would look up at the sky, hands on hips and rail shrilly at the sun,

'Pouring out fire from your furnace to scorch the earth, you inauspicious one? I curse you, curse you in the full noontide! Burn yourself out! Roast yourself to ashes in your own fire!'

Whether the fiery curses of a Brahmin's daughter had their effect on the sun-god or not, it is difficult to say, but certainly the old crone was relentless in her consumptive fury.

On a monsoon day, you could hear her discontent brimming over at the rain-god, her voice overriding the monotonous drumming of the rain,

'Oh, this intolerable whining of yours! Why, who's flogging you with the broom? Or, has Yama got you in his clutches?'

Crow or kite, cockroach or rat, no adversary was ever spared those verbal missiles.

At this point Shyama happened to fall within her line of vision on the courtyard, a bunch of drumsticks in one hand, a ripe wood apple in the other, a few lemons tied up in her saree at her waist. Caught red-handed, the girl could only smile in embarrassment at Nutan Ginni. She hated coming up close against her. The old woman's anger boiled over:

'Here, you wandering beggar, off to rummage for scraps first thing in the morning? Aren't you ashamed of yourself, Shami, begging at every door? And all for that one wretched stomach of yours, not even a whole household to feed, just one greedy stomach! Set it on fire, burn it up! Shame on you! If I were you, I would have hung myself!'

Whether Shyama had any real claim on the Majumdars, any tenuous link of kinship other than the universal one of the destitute, it was difficult to say! The ruined mansion stifled her, so she wandered around the village all day, giving service wherever required and begging for whatever could be had under the veneer of respectability.

There was one other resident, Hymanti, who shone like a golden lamp in that dark, haunted dungeon. Perhaps, that would be the most befitting comparison, if indeed lamps do shine in dungeons. She was the wife of

Samudranarayan, the last descendant of that dynasty, chosen by them with great care, tested on the touchstone of her beauty and her auspiciousness. The unfortunate events of her life, however, denied the validity of that test.

Years ago, when this girl from a poor family had stepped across the threshold of this mansion as a bride, the last traces of aristocracy still clung wistfully to it like the dying strains of a melody. Her grandfather-in-law, Bishwaranjon, dressed in the raiments of bygone splendour, the richly embroidered shawl, the paisley-bordered Shantipuri *dhoti*, had blessed her with 5 gold Akbari *mohurs* on a silver plate.

Hymanti was a girl from western India. Coming from a poor family, she had not brought with her, sumptuous wealth. What she did bring, however, was her flawless beauty and her incomparable gift of melody. In this aristocratic zamindar family where women were literally shrouded in gold from nose-ring to anklet, Hymanti was a phenomenon indeed!

Her husband Samudra had accorded her the respect she deserved. In a household fenced in with a hundred taboos, he had granted her a widened horizon and the light of freedom. But it was too sweet to last. Like the spluttering lamps of the ceremonial chandelier, the light of those golden days was soon gone from her life.

It was a moonlit night, the air heady with the strong scent of the *champaka*. Hymanti sat on the steps of their private pond, her sitar in her hand. Moonlight glistened on her form, clad in a *neelambari* saree. Her husband Samudranarayan lay sprawled out at her feet.

'I don't feel like playing tonight,' she cried, 'there is a sense of foreboding within me. I feel as if...'

'What is it, tell me, my dear!'

'I feel as if this bliss is too sweet to last. This uneasy feeling in my breast...as if the end is near!'

Her words were lost within the close circle of his embrace,

'Frightened, my love?' He smiled. 'Even within the warm circle of my arms? Frightened of what? Why Hyma, it must be the touch of the southern breeze. That's what poets call an intoxicating breeze... Come, play for me that tune you had strummed the other night on the roof.'

Hymanti slowly picked up the sitar, but her fingers on the strings remained listless, inert, the music out of tune.

'I can't play tonight,' she pleaded pitifully, 'just hold me close, my dearest...closer...'

'Closer still?' Samudra laughed, but before the strains of his laughter could die away, they were abruptly interrupted by the maid, Khiroda, running towards them for dear life,

'Dadababu,...something terrible has happened,' she gasped.

'What's the matter, Khiroda?'

'Apparently Indir Dadababu was involved in some scandalous affair in the Bagdi colony, and the whole pack has come running after him, armed with lathis.'

In a moment anger swelled in Samudra's veins. Again? How many times would he have to be humiliated like this? Just the other day, he had been forced to lower his dignity and bribe a police officer...and all for a cousin who was nothing but a burden on his shoulders.

The moment he entered the house, the terrified Indranath threw himself before him and pleaded,

'Chhorda, do something, I beg of you, they'll kill me!'

'I will kill you first, you rascal!' Samudranarayan pushed the young man away from him. Caught unawares, Indranath lost his balance and fell from the low terrace onto the cemented floor below. Surprisingly,...never to rise again! Perhaps, just to teach Samudra a lesson, he got killed! Otherwise, how could a small knock like that kill a sturdy young man? Or had the night's events weakened a blood vessel somewhere, which ruptured at the first blow?

The vivid memory of that night still haunted Hymanti...their Bagdi subjects silently crowding around Indranath's corpse...the eerie glow of the torch playing hide and seek in the wind, with the changing expressions on her husband's drawn face. The moon had set.

How the Bagdis helped him dispose of the body...how he escaped from the village that very night at their insistence...Hymanti's confused recollections had grown dim over the years. Only the last words of her husband remained with her,

'I don't have the courage to give myself up to the police, Hyma...I cannot make you a widow...I cannot die without you!'

And so, Hymanti had remained suspended like Trishanku between wifehood and widowhood these many, many years. Only two months to go before a missing person could officially be declared dead and then

Hymanti would have to rub off her *sindoor* and don her widow's weeds! From the age of eighteen to the age of thirty, how had Hymanti clung on to the fringes of a shameful existence through these long, weary years as the wife of a murderer, an escaped convict? Why did she not have the courage to kill herself? In the hope that if Samudra called out to her some day, she should be there to answer his call? Why, like Sabari, did she wait with endless patience? And how had a girl like Hymanti survived in that mansion with none but Shyama and Nutan Ginni for company, when at every step, her culture, her talent, her education must have risen in revolt? Poverty could be borne with ease, but this shameless vulgarity? It was intolerable.

Removing the withered flowers of the previous day, it was Hymanti's daily ritual to place a fresh garland around her husband's portrait and immerse the old one in the pond. Nutan Ginni was not unaware of this. Yet, as the edge of her saree was seen disappearing over the threshold, the old woman's voice could be heard from the other end of the courtyard, accosting Shyama,

'And where is the *memsaheb* gallivanting off to, Shyama?'

'The lake, perhaps, I'm not sure…'

'What do you mean, you're not sure? They say picked pockets are witness to a thief and a drunkard to a publican! A bride of the family slipping out of the house at every hour! For what? Such wanton tricks she knows…garlanding portraits, immersing flowers! Look at me! Widowed at sixteen, but can anyone point a finger at me?'

No one was alive to bear witness to what Nutan Ginni had done at sixteen. Poor Shyama could only try flattery,

'As if anyone can compare with you, Didima…' she began, but the old woman irritably cut her short.

'Don't you try to flatter me Shyami, can't stand it!'

These sudden assaults on the unsuspecting were her habit, but poor Shyama sat there in embarrassment, not having the guts to walk away either. Desperate for a new gambit, she volunteered a bit of news,

'You know Didima, I saw a strange young man at the bathing ghat near our pond this morning. He was hanging about around the *bakul* tree! Dressed in coat and pantaloons! Tall and strong he looked, too. I was petrified. I took to my heels at once. Must be a newcomer to the village.'

'As if there is anybody in the village you don't know! And what made you run away? Couldn't you have asked him what he wanted?'

'What should I ask him? As it is, I'm dead scared of a coat and a pair of pants.'

'Oh, my innocent babe-in-arms! What was a stranger doing at the women's bathing ghat, may I ask? Who knows, he may be a regular visitor. All that drama of immersing dry flowers every evening! God knows what that shameless hussy is up to? Husband missing these twelve long years…and what business does she have to doll herself up every evening for her jaunt to the pond?'

Shyama could not bring herself to be a party to this assault on Hymanti, even at the cost of infuriating Nutan Ginni. Her volleys began again,

'Old and bent that I am, I can scarcely keep an eye on the goings-on around here! Else, I'd have shown them what is what…' she gasped.

On her way back from the bathing ghat, Hymanti softly asked Shyama whether the day's newspaper had been delivered. Nutan Ginni had been busy blowing into the wood fire. Her shrill voice instantly rasped out at her,

'The memsahib can't do without her daily newspaper! If I were in your place I would have long ended my shameful life with a rope and a pitcher round my neck! And pray, where do you find the guts to hobnob with strangers at the lake? From those books and papers you stick your nose in all day, of course!'

Hymanti stood staring at Shyama in surprise for a moment, then slowly went up to her own room. Hobnobbing with strange men? She…who had almost wrapped herself up in a cocoon of shame and agony? Her only link with the world outside was that newspaper. Who could tell why she scanned its every corner with such despair? Why she devoured every bit of news like a starving man?

But was there no truth in those wild accusations of Nutan Ginni's? Why then did Hymanti stand trembling in the evening shadows, in that corner of the first floor balcony? And who was that stranger in western dress before her…their frightened glances riveted upon each other? Was it the same man that Shyama had described?

Who was it that held her so boldly in his passionate embrace? Was it Samudranarayan? Was he still alive?

After what seemed ages, Hymanti freed herself and asked in a trembling voice,

'Elope with you? But what will people say?'

'Let them say what they will, Hyma! How does it bother us?' He countered. 'But I will carry you off with me to my new kingdom in the forest where trees have been cut down to build a new township. There, we will rebuild our little nest together. There, I am not known as Samudranarayan. I am now Mr Mukherjee.'

'You have changed your name?'

'Of course! What else could I have done? Hunted like a dog, I wandered from one corner of the world to another. And while you slept peacefully in the moonlight, I slaved like a coolie in the scorching sun.'

Slowly, his life unravelled before her. He had spent long years in Japan and America. Braving the ebbs and tides of fortune, he had established himself as a forest officer and amassed a fortune. He had built his home in the jungles of the foothills, done it up with every item of luxury and comfort for Hymanti. All his toil and aspirations of these many years were centred round her.

'But you never enquired after me? Suppose I was dead?'

'Impossible! I had full faith, Hyma, that we would meet again! That all my efforts would not be in vain.'

Hymanti could only bury her head in his breast and weep silently. She had no words to express herself as he did. The night drew on with whispered fragments and tears for the wasted years. Samudra planned to escape with his wife in the wee hours of the morning. He could hardly contain his excitement at this romantic escapade,

'People elope with other men's wives, there's no novelty in that!...I will elope with my own,' he laughed, 'What a sensation that'll cause! But why these tears, my love? I criss-crossed through forests and mountains and across the vast ocean to be at your side and all you do is cry all night!' He looked around him, 'But, I hope no one will come up here...I have no wish to be caught after these many years!'

'Who will come? Grandmother can't climb stairs and Shyama is too scared of ghosts to venture out of her room after dark.'

'Then can I take shelter in your room for the night without fear?'

As Hymanti bolted the door and cautiously put on the light, Samudra looked around in wonder.

'Everything is still the same...the mirror, the cupboards, the pictures on the wall, even the moonlight bathing your face. You are as beautiful as ever, as if nothing has changed in your life. As if I have just been away on a brief foreign tour. And all the while this terrible storm wrecking havoc with my destiny!

Short bursts of laughter…whispered phrases…

'Whose portrait is that…mine or some godman you have adopted? Do you still put garlands round the portrait of this miserable wretch? If it's mine, then I'll have the garland. 'That garland does not match this awful khaki. What do you say…a dhoti? Where will I get one? You'll get it? Why, have you preserved my clothes through these many, many years, Hyma?'

'Aren't you going to identify yourself to anyone else? Grandmother…Shyama…or Khiroda? No one?'

'Have you lost your mind? The news will spread like wildfire and a fresh police circular for my arrest will be put up at every station. Far better that the prince should escape with his star-crossed princess on his flying steed in the dead of night like a fairy tale. I have not aged all that much, have I Hyma? Will fortune really be so kind to me?'

There was no end to their words, but the night drew on, the pallor of moonlight surreptitiously yielding to the new light of day. Perhaps they had dozed off for a while…

At the crack of dawn, Samudra awoke with a start. He shook her awake,

'Come, hurry up and get dressed, Mrs Mukherjee. We have to catch the train at 4.40. Why are you looking at me in surprise? Remember, I am Mr Mukherjee now, not Samudranarayan the zamindar, so obviously you are Mrs Mukherjee! Take off that awful dhoti-like saree of yours and wear something pretty. I hate it! But do be quick!'

Hymanti smiled wanly at her husband,

'I hardly have anything better than these.' In fearful anticipation of the public announcement of her missing husband's death, she had taken to wearing these narrow-bordered white sarees.

'Alright, it does not matter. I shall adorn you to my heart's content in our new home. Only do hurry up, my pet, my queen! It's almost morning and just think of the consequences of that!'

Hymanti looked around her, her eyes devoid of emotion. This was her familiar world, her austere universe…and this portrait, the husband of her dreams! Would she have to abandon it all? Could she not devote the rest of her life to this portrait and the daily offering and immersion of flowers? Somehow the presence of this strong, virile man in his coarse dress in her lonely, chaste chamber seemed distasteful to her. Had not this flesh-and-blood husband become redundant to her? This aggressive presence that made impatient demands on her chastity?

Surely, she could continue to devote herself to his portrait?

When the new day dawned and Shyama and Khiroda ran from house to house bearing the news of her escape, what would people say?

'Forgive me…!' Whose voice was that? Hymanti's? Hymanti, who clung to her husband's feet, her breast heaving with grief.

Samudra stared at her, aghast. 'You mean you won't come with me?'

'Please forgive me!'

Bengali original: 'Amay Kshama Karo'
Translated by Saumitra Chakravarty

The Red Saree

Ashapurna Devi

*A*S IT TURNED OUT, WE WERE THE ONES WHO HAD TO SHOULDER THE responsibility of carrying Anadi Babu's wife to the burning ghat. In any case there was little else to do. It had all happened so abruptly.

We did call a doctor however, but only for the death certificate. Dhrubesh Babu went off to fetch the bamboo bier and the funeral wreaths. Subodh wobbled off on his bike to round up the pall-bearers. And I was left in the silence of the night and its endless darkness to guard the corpse, after having switched on the electric light.

Yet, how was it that we had allowed ourselves to get so deeply involved in the matter? After all, we were not so close to Anadi Babu. Had he been here he would surely not have summoned any of us! I dimly remembered hearing that Anadi Babu was out on official tour, a bit of information that had promptly slipped my mind. Whether the lady next door was alone with her two children, or some well-wisher had been invited to act as guardian, I did not feel the necessity of trying to find out.

The chaste, cave-like interior of Anadi Babu' s 'andar-mahal' shunned the prying eyes of neighbours. I had heard about that. Perhaps, that was the reason why the neighbourly duty of making enquiries about the welfare of the woman who was alone next door had not been performed! And now her sudden death had thrown us, the gentlemen of the locality, into confusion. Who could have anticipated such a turn?

It was around midnight. I had just retired to bed and was pleasantly drifting into the bewitching interregnum between wakefulness and sleep, when the noise from the next door house made me sit bolt upright in bed. All the lights of Anadi Babu's house had been switched on. The two small children were wailing in unison and the maid was calling out loudly to us.

Putting on my slippers, I went outside, where my mother and my aunt had already taken up position.

'The master of the house has gone out of town. Taru, what if something has happened to the lady?' they asked anxiously.

'Well, what can be done? You can hardly expect the harbingers of death to await his return!'

There was scant comfort in this bravado, however.

Apparently, the lady had woken up in the middle of the night, feeling unbearably hot and had asked her little daughter to fan her. Before the stupefied child could locate the hand fan, the mother had fallen face down on the floor. This was the rather brief account of her death.

The account of what followed was hardly less dramatic. We did not know of any relative of theirs who could be summoned to observe the elaborate rites of mourning. Neither the children nor the maid could provide the necessary information. And so here was I sitting alone with the corpse, having sent off Dhrubesh Babu for the bier and the flowers and Subodh for the pall-bearers...all out of sheer neighbourliness and the fear of allowing a corpse to rot!

Outside, my aunt sat in the dim light, casting long shadows on the courtyard, trying to pat the little boy to sleep, but his monotonous, rather demanding wails did not cease. His sister who was just a little older, sat dumb as a doll, frozen stiff after that first scream.

My mother's curiosity had not been quenched. Again and again, she had the maid narrate the strange account of the sudden death in detail, trying to see whether she could arrive at any conclusion. It wasn't as if the same thought had not occurred to me, but when the doctor had himself wisely declared it a case of heart failure, I thought it best not to entertain any further suspicion. That could only aggravate the problem.

I was not aware that this was Anadi Babu's second wife. I got this from the maid who suggested that it would be better to inform his daughter by his first marriage, who lived somewhere near Rishra or 'Chirampore'. Undoubtedly a very valuable suggestion, but who in his right senses would do this noble deed and go hunting for 'a nameless daughter from a first marriage' down the streets of Rishra or Srirampore at this midnight hour?

I took another look at the dead woman. Certainly, she looked too young to be Anadi Babu's wife! I should have known that she was his second.

Even though we were neighbours, I had never had the good fortune of looking at her face before. The door of the balcony facing our house was always shut. Perhaps, the terrace was out of bounds for her as well. And to step out onto the street...that was certainly beyond her wildest dreams. A window occasionally left open might have provided the outline of a veiled female form. But if the truth be told, I had little curiosity about the wife of an elderly person like Anadi Babu. If anything, the elaborate veil provoked a derisive smile!

The news that Anadi Babu regarded all members of the male species with suspicion had reached me via the local grapevine. There was nothing new in that! Plenty of people did the same.

What was sensational was the posture in which the dead woman's body was found. A powerful electric light was burning in the room. The dead woman, having cast off the fear, shame, hesitation which had ever clouded that veiled face, now lay with her wide-open eyes fixed shamelessly on that bright light overhead.

I pulled a sheet across the sparsely-clad body, but it was not needed. For, she lay with an air of supreme unconcern for the male species of this world. The slack, dishevelled posture of the body was testimony to her utter disregard.

I sat staring at her in amazement! How strange it was that living so close to this matchless beauty, I had never had the good fortune of casting eyes upon her! What a beauty she must have been! How enchanting must the play of emotions have been across that face! Who knows...? Perhaps this was best, this triumphant smile lurking at the corner of those pallid lips. Could her living image have produced that smile, veiled and imprisoned as she had been all her life?

The task of summoning pall-bearers at that dead hour of night was not an easy one. Subodh was taking unexpectedly long. However, Dhrubesh Babu, a grey-haired veteran of many funerals, had accomplished his task to perfection...garlands, a couple of wreaths, a bottle of scent, even a packet of *sindoor*...he had scrupulously attended to every detail. It was he who reminded us about getting her a new saree! Exhaling a mouthful of smoke, he laughed,

'There is a custom of draping a corpse in a new saree! Well, forget that! When the living can hardly think of new clothes, getting one for a corpse seems such a waste. What do you say, Tarak?'

With all due respect to Dhrubesh Babu, at this moment his meaningless laughter and mouthful of smoke seemed sacrilegious to me, like wearing shoes inside a temple! I was irritated. I asked him whether it was possible to take her away in her present attire?

'What's the option? Alright, you can check whether there is a bit of red silk in the house. Some people do use those as shrouds for their wives. And this one's absconding from his wife's funeral! It's almost like that old saying, 'Who knows whose funeral falls to whom, when the Brahmin dies outside his shell.'

I realized it was futile to vent my anger on Dhrubesh Babu. The veteran of many funerals had lost his sensitivity towards them. I told my mother to get the maid to open the box and pull out a better saree for the lady. The maid was reluctant at first, saying that her master would skin her alive, but finally agreed after being pulled up by me.

As I unbound the bunch from the knot at the dead woman's shoulder, there was not a whisper of protest from its owner. She continued to stare unblinkingly at the powerful light overhead. Oh God! Didn't her eyes burn out in the glare?

At last, everything was done to perfection...the red saree was taken out, the red benarasi saree with silver motifs! It was the same red saree in which she had crossed the threshold of this house to seek shelter as a bride. Today, she would leave the confines of this bastion, re-cross the threshold on her way to the distant horizon of liberation with the same red saree draped across her body.

But why was I getting so sentimental? Anadi Babu's wife was in no way connected to me. Or, was I falling in love with a corpse?

Subodh was back at last. *Alta, sindoor*, flowers, scent...nothing was lacking. And so like a victorious queen liberated from her iron cell, where an ever-jealous husband had long held her captive, Anadi Babu's wife went proudly down the streets of Calcutta, her beautiful face unveiled.

Three days later Anadi Babu came back. Naran Babu had sent a telegram to his office. The man would be shattered, I assumed. Apart from grief, there would certainly be a sense of remorse for ill-treatment meted out to his victim. The doctor's certificate might have let him off the hook as far as the police were concerned, but the suspicion that she had poisoned herself had spread like wildfire through the locality. And there was sure to be a 'well-wisher' or two who would dutifully convey the news immediately on his arrival.

I had not thought fit to disturb him in the morning; the evening would be as good a time as any. The two motherless children had been in our custody for the last two days. I left word with my mother not to send them back till he asked for them, lest it be construed as reluctance on our part to keep them with us for a longer period...

But the report I received after my return in the evening was not only shocking, but enough to make my blood boil in anger. The moment I had left in the morning, Anadi Babu had stormed into our house, scarcely waiting to shake off the dust of the journey, cursed us in the foulest language and carried off the children.

I dispensed with the idea of a courtesy call.

Anadi Babu descended on us the moment I was back. My first thought was that he had come to repay the expenses incurred by us for the funeral that night, as any self-respecting person would. I was just framing a polite refusal, when the first grim salvo caught me unawares,

'How long have you known my wife?'

'What do you mean by that?' I shot back irritated as much by the question as by the uncultured tone.

'Do you think I am an innocent babe that I cannot understand the obvious! If you had not known her before, what made you get so involved?'

'If making funeral arrangements for the dead means getting involved, don't worry. I'll get involved with you in the same way, some day.'

The countenance that had resembled a wasp's hive, now assumed a tigerish expression:

'Oh, so now you are waiting for me to die! But what's the use? The bird has flown from the nest. Funeral arrangements, indeed! Trespassing into my house...laying flower garlands and bouquets on her...breaking open my suitcase to adorn her in red silk...what about all that? Who asked you to take these liberties, may I ask?'

'My conscience!' I retorted, 'You were away gallivanting in the west. And this is all the thanks I get for my pains! Being taken to task by you! Well, strange indeed are the ways of the world.'

'Thanks? For what? What business is it of yours whether my wife dies or rots within my house? Aren't you ashamed of laying your hands on another man's wife? How dare you spray scent and powder on her body? And you with your tall talk about your education! Ever tried to find out what law authorizes you to trespass into another man's house in his absence and take matters into your hands?'

Taken aback, I still managed to find an answer,

'You should thank your lucky stars for that so-called trespass. It saved you from the law. Do you realize that you could have been behind bars by now, had it not been for the doctor? And that too because he was a friend of Naran Babu's. That's what saved your life this time.'

'Oh, it's not so easy to put people behind bars!' he scoffed. 'The previous one hanged herself and what…! Anyway, that's beside the point. Now you tell me how you had the guts to waste that two hundred-rupee saree? Didn't the maid warn you? To think of the cost of those sarees in today's market!'

'Whatever its price, you couldn't have used that red benarasi, could you? It belonged to her after all and she….'

'How dare you? How dare you take the name of my wife? And what do you mean it was "hers"? What right has a woman to anything? During the *kanyadaan*, her clothes and jewellery are handed over to her husband along with her. I know I have no personal use for that saree. But at least, I could have used it for the next one's trousseau! After all, it was almost untouched.'

I still have vivid recollections of that night. Hardly two months have gone by.

But today the sight of a red benarasi saree brought it all back. A few minutes ago, I saw a figure draped in a red saree step into Anadi Babu's house, the edge of the saree knotted firmly to his dhoti. His third wife had just crossed the threshold!

Surely, this red saree will never be wasted. After all, you cannot expect him to be away from the scene every time, can you?

Bengali original: 'Lal Saree'
Translated by Saumitra Chakravarty

Padmalata's Dream

Ashapurna Devi

I T IS BUT NATURAL FOR A MARRIED GIRL TO WANT TO COME TO HER FATHER'S place every once in a while. Stifled by monotony, she may want to breathe easy at her father's, or have a change of scene. If a girl has no father, she could go to her brother's. But if a girl has neither kith nor kin like Padmalata, does she not have the right to return to the village of Sonapalasi?

After all, much of her childhood had been spent here and if the memories were neither pleasant nor glorious, even sorrowful and humiliating ones had their own attraction! And thus it was that for seven years, Padmalata had been possessed by a growing desire to establish herself there. It was a wild desire to savour the stir she would create among the inhabitants of Sonapalasi when she returned as Padmalata, the transformed version of 'Podi', daughter of the Brahmin cook at the Jodu Lahiri's. For ten years, Padmalata had built up this dream in a pleasant, whimsical fashion, adding spice and colour to the picture in her mind of the few days she would spend there. It was as if she had no other scope for fulfilment in her life. And so with great effort and persuasion, she begged a few days off from her husband to visit Sonapalasi.

Looking back, it had been worth the effort. She had literally astounded them, not by her arrival, but by her mannerisms. Overwhelmed them, in fact!

Rags to riches stories were not uncommon in these war-time years. Nothing was impossible in a market that had blown away the last shred of scruple from many a fortune-seeker. There really was nothing incredible about Podi, daughter of Jodu Lahiri's Brahmin cook, suddenly acquiring the Midas touch.

A suitable response was the important thing! A display of overwhelming affection.

For, if that simpleton of a schoolmaster husband of Padmalata's could have mounted the golden steps of success as a military contractor, surely he could find a job or two for the unemployed youth of the village. Could Padmalata herself not find grooms for the orphaned spinsters of the village? The same girl who had literally been scattering coins along her path? She had been here just a couple of days but already her paeans rang out among the villagers—from Ratan the carter to Bhattacharya the priest of the Kali temple. Such refinement, such generosity! Rare traits indeed, in today's world.

Padmalata's smile was charming, her words sweet, matchless, her behaviour! And it had been so since her childhood, they all knew that, didn't they? No wonder the villagers had doted on this beautiful, talented girl! So, it was hardly surprising that she should be so much in demand today.

Padmalata was in a quandary. Only four days in hand and so many invitations? After a long, long time the Lahiri household had come alive with her presence. The pomp and grandeur had departed from this house with the death of Jodu Lahiri. It came back with the return of Padmalata. Endless streams of visitors were literally pouring in. Padmalata welcomed them all with a gracious smile and a golden touch as if she were indeed the mistress of this household!

Even at this moment, people could be seen going down the stairs, tucking away the five-rupee note offered as a token of respect. Like Sotyobala, who, in a voice oozing with honey, told Padmalata,

'Tomorrow you must have a morsel of fish and rice at my place, Padmarani! I'll not listen to any excuses.'

'But Roy Jethima has staked a prior claim, Sotu Pishi,' Padmalata's voice was the epitome of modesty, 'she'll be so disappointed if I don't go.'

'Oh, and who is she to do that? Roy Jethi, indeed! Must be that sister-in-law of Mukunda Roy's! We all know what lies behind such invitations. Pure flattery, that's all. Well, I'm not one to mince words.'

'What flattery, Sotu Pishima? Am I a person worth flattering? Just because she insisted that I visit her...'

'And we can't "insist", can we, child? And why should we have to? Are you a stranger to us? I can stake the first claim on you. You may not remember, but your mother had a lot of respect for me...' Sotu Thakurjhi meant the world to her. Those intimate bonds can hardly be analysed, my dear.'

Was there really any necessity of doing so?

Had not Padmalata survived on the morsels of this village for the first sixteen years of her life? Morsels of misery and humiliation?

How could she forget the 'respect' that her mother had for Sotyobala's venomous tongue? Was her memory indeed, so weak?

Padmalata did not quite feel sorry for her mother's plight, but those memories were enough to cause a turmoil within her. Memories of this very courtyard of the Lahiris'...of bitterly cold nights, the icy wind piercing her to the bone, the cough that racked her mother's body throughout the year...that frail, emaciated widow trying to draw the edges of her thin, short widow's weeds around her body to shut out the cold...laying out the *naivedya,* making preparations for the next day's puja and coughing all the while. The echoes of that racking cough seemed to be lurking in the cornices even today, to come alive perhaps, on a winter's night. A little girl would be at her heels, clad in nothing much warmer than her mother's apparel...a tattered and patched long skirt of coarse material, discarded by one of the Lahiri grandchildren.

She would huddle against her mother's breast for a little warmth, but the icy wind stabbed her shoulders like a knife...and after a while it all became numb. She would not feel the chill any more, only a thousand pinpricks. The problem was with her hands, her frozen little hands. She would try to assist her mother, but in a trice, her fingers would stiffen and bend in the cold water. And that meant double work for her mother. Warming the edge of her saree over the hurricane lantern to foment her little one's fingers, she would draw her into her lap and chide her gently for exposing herself to the cold. Her own chores in the Lahiri household were endless. Being their cook didn't mean that her duties ended with cooking! Shouldn't she take on part of the servant's job as well? That useless little girl of hers, wasn't that an extra mouth to feed? Was that for nothing?

And so, her mother would gently prod her to bed. But the frightened child shuddered at the thought of the dark room, the bare bedding and the oil-stained pillow, cold as if water had been poured on to it. How could she survive there without the warmth of her mother's breast?

Besides, who knew what ghosts and demons lurked behind those dark, unplastered walls?

Jodu Lahiri's wife was bedridden, but it was funny how nothing ever escaped her notice. If on a cold night, Padmalata's mother coaxed her child to bed in the light of the oil lamp, the cracked voice could be heard cursing irritably from upstairs,

'Do you think you are a nawab's daughter? Stop pampering that brat of yours! Oil for that lamp costs us a pretty penny. If you had a grain of sense, I wouldn't have to take the trouble of reminding you again and again. Bad enough having two extra mouths to feed, mother and daughter dragging on their few chores till midnight. On top of that, such a waste of kerosene! Have you ever thought of the money that's getting wasted, Brahmin woman, because you want to get your work done at your convenience? But why should you, it's not your money, after all! You know that old saying, "Fattened on the Brahmin's alms, what do I care for the price of rice?" And infirm as I am, I have to depend on ungrateful wretches like you!'

Once it started, it went on and on.

The lamp would have breathed its last by then. And what ghost or demon could compare with that woman's venom? On the other hand, the memories of the monsoon nights had a bitter-sweet tinge about them. It was real fun trudging to the pond with her mother in knee-deep slush. But even there her mother's racking cough was an agony. Instead, it was better to lie huddled together on that tattered bedroll and forget about meals for a couple of days. But that was easier said than done! Hunger made its presence felt, even in her tiny belly.

This memory gave way to another one...the same house, the same courtyard, only the two people were different. The thin, bronzed child in the tattered dress had given way to a young girl, bursting with youthful vitality and health, struggling as much to keep the cold out as to cover her blossoming body with the short saree. Gently chiding the frail widow, she insisted on taking over all the chores. She would prod her mother to bed early,

'Why don't you want to go to bed by yourself? What are you afraid of? Ghosts?' She would say with a laugh.

How could the mother make her daughter understand that the dangers of youth were far worse than those of ghosts? And then for a poor Brahmin widow's daughter to be cursed with such beauty! As her daughter went about her chores, the mother watched wide-eyed with wonder. She had really lived up to her name...Padma! Her feet were like a pair of lotuses. This young body, blooming with health and vitality, where did it get its nourishment? From that handful of rice carelessly flung at her? No wonder, Mrs Lahiri cursed! Her own two grandchildren, black as bats, got thinner and paler with each successive attack of malaria, while this girl, hardly fourteen years of age, grew more beautiful by the day! The advice she gave was harsh, but perhaps sound,

'Here, Podi, eat a little less, will you? Just because it's free, doesn't mean you can hog as much as you want. Getting to look like an elephant day by day...and that hag your mother, her blood gets more and more watery just looking at you!'

Having swallowed the insult, 'Podi' smiled with an effort,

'Does my mother have any blood left in her body, Didima? It's all water anyway.' Upon which one could hardly blame the mistress of the Lahiri household for cursing that cheeky girl for her audacity.

But of course, it was not Mrs Lahiri alone, the whole neighbourhood had had its fill at her expense. Podi's youth, her beauty, her talents were an eyesore to all. Her ways were suspicious, her behaviour was...

But no more of that. 'Podi' was dead and no one would be foolish enough to grudge Padmalata her dues now, would they?

Mrs Lahiri peered through her hazy, cataract-coated eyes and waxed eloquent,

'Such a beauty she has turned out to be, like the goddess Lakshmi, no end to her talents either, even as a child! A thousand pities your mother isn't alive to see you! But we aren't gone yet, my child. You must come home to us every year. After all, you and my Kamli-Bimli, you are just the same to me!'

But perhaps, not quite the same! Kamli-Bimli never referred to their grandmother except as 'old, burnt-out hag' and Padmalata had just handed over three crisp hundred-rupee notes towards her 'grandmother's' pilgrimage expenses.

At the Roy Jethima's, banquets were always a memorable experience. Not only today, but in times past, in what was now history. Like that time...it was the ritualistic observation of Mukunda Roy's mother's vow, or some such occasion. The entire Lahiri family had been invited and with them had come Podi's mother, as the workhorse there too. Meanwhile one of the servers had seated Podi along with the other invitees, possibly because she was a Brahmin girl. The server was none other than Murari Sanyal. The neighbours had made a terrible fuss over the incident, with their sly glances, their insinuations and innuendoes. The sharp-tongued Sotyobala had not minced words, literally reducing Podi's mother to tears on another occasion. If a young pair laughed and talked so freely on their way to the village pond, nothing was left to the imagination, she said. It was lucky for her that it was Sotyobala who saw it, or Podi's hopes of marriage would be ruined forever. Anyone could vouch for that!

Fortunately for her, Podi's mother never had to encounter that disgrace. For that very month, with some help from well-wishers, Podi was married off to a boy from a distant, obscure village. He was a matriculate, teaching in a village school for a monthly salary of Rs 30 and was said to have a bright future. But that is immaterial in this chronicle. What was foremost in her mind was the memory of that banquet at the Roys'. She had not been allowed to sit with the other invitees. She had been forcibly removed from the scene. While the storm of glances and innuendoes waged on, Nibhanani, Mukunda Roy's eldest daughter, abruptly stood up. Her logic was sound enough. If a cook's daughter could be accorded the status of a Brahmin girl, what was wrong in glorifying a cockroach as a bird?

The ten-year-old memory came back to her as she was going down the stairs. Abruptly, the cheerful greeting of Mukunda Roy's daughter-in-law broke into her thoughts:

'Come, come Thakurjhi. At least you could spare some time for your sister-in-law. You haven't visited us even once ever since you've come here.'

'What to do, Bowdi? I've been here three days now. Seemed to have met everybody, but haven't had a chance to really sit down and talk. And I'm here only on a four-day leave.'

'Oh, come off it! How can you stay for just four days, you're here after such a long time? You write and tell that husband of yours, he's monopolized you for a long time, it's our turn now! Besides he's a business man, busy with a hundred things, how can he be tied to his wife's apron strings?'

'That's just the problem. That's why I can't come here more often. He's such an eccentric person!'

A faint patronizing smile lurked in the corner of Padmalata's lips, the symbol of her affluence and status.

After a moment's hesitation, the real question popped out,

'How come you don't have much jewellery on you, Thakurjhi? Don't you like jewellery?'

It was indeed a complex issue. The absence of gold on her body contrasted oddly with her status. The surprising thing was, it had taken all of three days for the question to surface! Perhaps, the silver she had been scattering on her path had helped screen the absence of gold on her person.

The answer followed quickly with a smug smile of contentment:

'As you can see Bowdi, your brother-in-law has thrown me out of the house after snatching away my jewellery!'

'God forbid! Is that your idea of a joke?'

'No seriously, Bowdi, my husband thinks every village is a den of robbers and rascals just waiting to kidnap his wife for her gold. You take as much cash as you want, he said, but no jewellery. So, I could just keep on these few tokens of marriage. By the way, is that weaver-woman Giri still around?'

'Of course, she is! Bloating up like a bull-frog with her ill-gotten gains.'

'Oh, let her charge as much as she likes, but can she get me around fifteen or twenty sarees with pretty borders?'

Her hostess's eyes grew wide with amazement,

'Fif…teen or twe..nty? Whatever will you do with so many?'

'No, I did not mean for myself. I've come home after such a long time. I want to give each one of you a saree as a token of my respect.'

'To each and every woman in the village?'

'Yes, with your blessings, Bowdi.'

With this, the last trace of suspicion about the absence of jewellery abruptly vanished. Padmalata was served her meal by Mukunda Roy's elder sister-in-law herself, with many a sigh about the short duration of her stay at her ancestral village.

Well, Padmalata had no regrets. She had driven home the last nail in the coffin of 'Podi', daughter of Jodu Lahiri's cook, and Padmalata could now reign supreme in the village of Sonapalasi. Only one small task remained to be dealt with…and that pricked like a burr. Murari! The same Murari who had once taunted her with a laugh,

'Do you think I will marry you? Some hope you've got! My mother will not welcome you with the lamps on her *kulo*, she will thrash both of us with one!'

Padmalata no longer had any qualms about looking him up, just in passing. Very casually, she asked about him just as she had about other people in the neighbourhood.

'And how is Murari-da, Roy Jethima? Isn't he in town?'

'Oh my dear, don't talk of that wretch!' said Roy Jethi with regret. 'Chronic illness has wasted away his body, doesn't have the strength to earn a pie,…even his house has been mortgaged…his wife and children are in a pitiable condition. Only thing left is his tall talk!'

Oh, that was still there, was it? Perhaps, Padmalata had the means to silence it!

Murari was just putting down his cup of barley water with an expression of distaste and getting ready to demand a clove of his wife, when Padmalata pushed open the wicker gate and entered. Before he could summon a smile to his contorted face, Padmalata asked him in surprise,

'What's that you are having? Sago?'

Murari waved his hand dismissively,

'Sago? Oh God, that's a dream of the past! This is barley, pure, undiluted Mondal's barley water!'

'What's the ailment?'

'Ailment? Not one, but many! Poverty, fear of the usurer, marital feuds, gall bladder, liver, dyspepsia, fever…'

'Enough, enough,' scolded Padmalata, 'where's your wife?'

'Should be around somewhere!'

'And your Boro Dada and Bowdi?'

'Pushed off as soon as my mother died.'

'And since when have *you* been reduced to this state?'

Murari cast a quick look over his own emaciated body,

'Why, what's wrong with my state?' he sneered. 'Not everyone has the luck to bloat like you. You know the old proverb, the finger bloating into a banana plant!'

'Well, banana plant or not, at least that's better than a cane.' Padmalata retorted sharply.

'Pity, the cane can't bite into the thick hide of the rich!' And Murari laughed again.

Padmalata ignored the insult and seated herself,

'Well, may as well sit down, since you won't ask me to. Big man, after all! And where's my hostess? Why no sign of her?'

Meanwhile, the hostess was busy trying to make herself presentable. Poverty had reduced them to such a state that she could hardly present herself before a guest without notice. The two children truly looked like Father Adam's offspring. Some sprucing up was certainly necessary. Padmalata quickly sensed the situation and did not press the matter further. She took on Murari instead.

'Your talk is as tall as ever, but look what you've done to the house! The very sight of it is...!'

'House? Why bother about something that belongs to someone else?'

'Belongs to someone else? What do you mean by that?' Padmalata feigned ignorance.

'Oh, you mean that piece of juicy gossip hasn't reached you, yet?...Neck-deep in debt...house mortgaged...etc., etc...'

'Mortgaged your ancestral property? Why, that amounts to ruining your family honour!' exclaimed Padmalata, the very picture of sympathy and concern.

Murari smiled thinly, 'Aren't you going to thank your stars that this piece of misfortune will give you a chance to patronize us further? Really, Podi, that smug superiority of yours makes me want to laugh. What did Mukunda Roy's daughter say, wasn't it something about a cockroach sprouting wings to fly like a bird? Very appropriate, don't you think?'

Padmalata realized this was a deliberate insult, perhaps in retaliation for her own. When close relationships turn bitter, the bitterness swallows up the sweetness. The two faced each other, ready to draw blood. But on second thoughts, she could not afford to lose her cool. She laughed,

'Your memory is quite sharp, Murari-da! Thank God, there is still someone left in this village to call me Podi. Ever since I've come here, it's been Padma and Padma everywhere! Well, let's have the latest?'

'Oh Madhusadan, what could be the latest with a bygone like me? That's your monopoly... I believe you're so rich, you're literally scattering money in your path! Well, well, good for you!'

'How did you get to know that? You hadn't even met me before this!'

'Oh dear, for the last three days, my ears have been worn thin with your praises! Puja fund, school fund, funds for the village tubewell, funds to repair the courtyard of the Kali temple...you seem to be inundating the village with funds! I feel so sorry for your foolishness. But maybe, the good name's worth it all!'

Padmalata laughed dismissively,

'Oh, it's just a trifle, hardly worth a name! I wanted to do so much, but in a hurry I could only carry a few thousands with me, apart from the eight hundred my husband gave me before I left. And maybe, a couple of hundreds here and there. What name can you earn with that? I wish I could have given Bhuti Pishima a little something to get her granddaughter married. Well, I suppose, I'll just have to send her something after I return.'

Murari's pinched nostrils quivered in disdain. The faint sneer at the corner of his mouth grew more pronounced,

'How many lakhs has Abinash stashed away? What contract has he taken up? Rice?...Wheat?...Cattle? Or is it women?'

Padmalata refused to lose her cool. She had come here to taste victory, not to cower in humiliation. So she feigned innocence,

'Who cares what he trades in? As long as I get as much money as I want! But about you...I can't even die in peace, worrying about your plight! What made you mortgage the house...suppose you can't redeem it later? Then what? How much did you mortgage it for?'

'Five hundred. Why, are you planning to give it to me?'

'Of course. You think I'll allow you to lose your ancestral property for that paltry sum?' Padmalata began to untie the knot of her saree.

'Do you carry thousands in your pocket these days, Podi?'

'What's the alternative? Mrs Lahiri refuses to take charge of even this trivial amount, so whatever I've brought, I carry with me. Well, what's money for, anyway? So long as I have enough for my return fare.'

As she took out five hundred-rupee notes and laid them down beside him, Murari abruptly gave up his banter.

'Look Podi, a cockroach sprouting wings is fine, but don't overdo it, don't try to be a *garuda*!'

'You have to accept this from me, I don't care how much you insult me after. I'll not let you be thrown out of your ancestral house for this paltry sum.'

'But why should I take your money? Oh, I know you're rich, go buy off the Bhuti Pishimas of this village with your money, don't flaunt your wealth before me.' With that, Murari thrust aside the money and vented his anger upon his absent wife, 'I've been shouting for a clove this one hour... Can't you hear me? Are you dead, or what?'

Murari's wife had probably been making herself presentable all this while. The talk of money had brought her to stand behind the door. In response to her husband's summons she made her appearance on the stage,

'I wish I *was* dead! I would have been well rid of you,' she said irritably, 'Thakurjhi, have you seen how this man talks?'

'Of course, I have! He's lost his mind, that man! Bowdi, just put away this money, will you? The house must be redeemed.'

Murari's wife had, of course, been eavesdropping all along. Casting a surreptitious glance at the notes, she said in a dull voice,

'Who would be foolish enough to lend this man money? Do you think he will ever be able to repay you?'

'Are you crazy? Who's asking for repayment? I never did give you anything for your wedding. Take this as a wedding gift. Now, where are those little ones of yours? I didn't even get to see them. Hidden them in a treasure chest or something?'

Murari's wife needed no second bidding. Snatching the money from the table, she called out excitedly to her children,

'Pushpo, Khoka... Come and touch your Pishima's feet.'

Murari glared at his wife, but it was useless. Gesturing furiously at her, he said roughly,

'Give that money back to her, Choto Bou! Do you think I will take alms from her?'

But the lady was not such a fool as to return what she had already put away. Tucking the money securely away, she cooed,

'Huh, return the money and take shelter under the tree with my children? Is that what you'd have me do? And pray, why should I return a gift from her? Is she a stranger to this family? Ain't I right, Thakurjhi?'

Meanwhile, Thakurjhi was busy tucking a note apiece into each of Pushpo's palms and trying to hunt for little Khoka's.

Well, Padmalata had no regrets, no complaints any more, nothing left to wish for in life. She had savoured the ultimate joy of fulfilment.

Just at that moment, in a damp, squalid room, tiny as a pigeon coop, her husband Abinash was lying on his stomach on a wobbly wooden cot, composing a letter to his wife. What was the purpose of this long letter? Expression of the sweet sorrow of separation? But how could he express his heart broken anguish except through a long letter? Even though he knew she would be home the next day?

'Padma,' he wrote, 'we are ruined. That job I'd applied for in Patna, that's now out of my reach for ever. That would have assured us of relative peace and security for the rest of our lives. But Fate willed otherwise. I had sold all my land and property and put together four thousand rupees for the security deposit. That money's gone. You know, I had put the little pouch of money in the quilt cover instead of the trunk, for fear of theft. Well, it is strange how it has not escaped the thief's eye even there...

I strongly suspect this to be the handiwork of someone known to us, some relative hostile to us... Whatever it is, today I have become destitute. I see no ray of hope for the future. Perhaps, that's the retribution I must suffer for selling off our ancestral property. And to think that just at this time the Lakshmi of my house should be away! Had you been here, my dear, things might never have come to such a pass. You must come home immediately... I have no strength left to go and fetch you, indeed, scarcely any, even to face you...!'

Bengali original: 'Padmalatar Swapna'
Translated by Saumitra Chakravarty

Shirish

Bani Basu

ONCE THERE WAS A LAND, A LAND LIKE ANY OTHER THAT YOU AND I HAVE known, a land of cities and hamlets, fairs, festivals and marketplaces. Only there was no beauty, no harmony anywhere. Its songs were like the cawing of the crow, its dances no better than the cavorting of ghosts, out of tune, out of rhythm and tempo. Its grain tasted like chalk, its vegetables like chaff. Its fish floated lifeless in the stream. The air hung heavy with smoke and soot, din and darkness.

No one knew from where Shirish had appeared in this land of growling ghosts. Not even Nabinmadhob, its oldest resident! No one knew that name anymore, they called him Sandel Khuro. He could neither see nor hear. In hot weather or cold, you could see him, a monkey-cap upon his head, locked in useless query about who went where. Not even he could fathom the secret of her arrival. If one asked him how Shirish Thakurun came to be here, he would cup his hands behind his ears till the question was repeated a dozen times. And then with a frown upon his brow, would come the answer, in a voice shrill as a cracked reed. He did not know how it all came to pass.

For, there at the bend of the road, lay an enclosed meadow and in the north-eastern corner of that meadow, stood a giant tree. The tree was full of birds' nests. Birds chirped in the evening, their chirping grew loud as the gushing of a mountain stream, as it cascades down the boulders one by one. Sometimes the tree was full of leaves, sometimes it shed them. Birds built their nests in it, laid their eggs, the fledglings emerged and flew off. Who kept track of all that? Yet, the tree grew stronger and stronger, its giant arms offering shade and refuge. No one knew its history either.

No one knew when Shirish's ancestors had bought the pink house at the corner of the meadow. No one knew where Shirish was born or where she grew up or got married or why this youthful widow (?) came here. No one knew her day of sorrow, or when her Sankhya Yoga ended and her Karma Yoga began. Who cared to remember? Even Nabinmadhob, who harboured many secrets like a buxom matron in a household, would say, 'Don't ask me all that! I have enough on my shoulders.'

Shirish's household consisted of a *durwan*, a coachman and a gardener in the outer quarters and in the inner, a servant, a maid and Shirish's only daughter. These were the people who moved about freely across the outer and inner quarters of the huge mansion and its sprawling gardens. They were the ones who looked after the household and tended to the plants in the garden. The pretty little girl rarely stepped out of the ancient phaeton that drove her in and out. The neighbours occasionally caught a glimpse of the Thakurun's daughter, lovely as a *champaka* in summer, or a gardenia that had drained the essence of sunlight into itself. She played and danced and sang all by herself in the inner gardens, or with her mother for company. But her mother Shirish was gradually emerging out of the inner quarters into the outer, onto the porch, the verandah and into the garden. From the garden, her presence permeated into the road, the shops, the market, the bank, the school, the college, the club, into sports, yoga and exercises, swimming...

It all began when the neighbourhood children came to ask for donations for their Saraswati Puja. Ramkhelwan, the durwan, drove them away. His logic was simple. Had any of them consulted his mistress before installing their Saraswati idols all over the locality? If not, then let them get lost! He knew these neighbourhood brats, sharp as rats they were, not child-like at all. Some quite feline, too, formidable in a group! But right in the middle of Ramkhelwan's remonstrations, one such rodent slipped past him into the house, screeching at the top of his shrill voice,

'Mashima, he's not letting me in!'

Shirish was at that very moment, suspended motionless in the centre of her cheerless existence like a bee embedded in its own honey. The shrill, sweet voice of the child pierced her to the core. She felt as if she herself was denying someone entry...and that someone was a supplicant at her door whose shrill, sweet voice was pleading desperately with her...! She fled her marble chamber and ran down the stairs, the tide suddenly rising in her sluggish bloodstream. The stunned and stupefied child stood in the centre of the courtyard, on one side the tall, sturdy, be-whiskered Ramkhelwan, on the other, an unnaturally pale, emaciated woman, indifferent to worldly concerns.

It was Shirish who said,

'What will you do with the money, my child?'

The boy burst into tears,

'Eat!'

'What do you want to eat?' asked Shirish, a faint smile lurking at the corners of her mouth.

'*Luchi* and *aloo dum*...' The child whimpered.

By then the other members of the juvenile train had filtered into the *andar mahal*, one by one. Slowly they voiced their complaint, which was, that in the local Saraswati Puja celebrated by their elders, the children got their share of the afternoon's *khichuri-labra* all right, but that was their limit. They were not given even a single morsel of the evening's royal banquet of *luchi, aloo dum*, cauliflower curry and *payesh*. The children had therefore decided to have their own Puja that year. The wooden Saraswati idol in Tulu's house would be set up in Mintu's drawing room and with a little help from Ganesh's father, a part-time priest, the rituals completed. And the money raised could then be spent on their own feast of *luchi* and *aloo dum*. They were dead set on that.

'How many of you?' asked Shirish tenderly.

'Seventeen.'

'I celebrate Saraswati Puja at my place. You are all invited for dinner in the evening. You will get *prasad,*' said Shirish.

Ramkhelwan's jaw dropped. Mouth agape, he wondered whether he had ever seen any puja being celebrated in this mansion.

But the children came, at first hesitantly in ones and twos. And then the trickle grew to a flood as child after child summoned up the courage. And in the great hall of the ancient mansion, Shirish spread out mats on the floor and fed them all a children's banquet...puffed, white *luchi,* red-gold cauliflower curry, pale-green and white peas and potatoes, scarlet chutney, creamy *payesh* and orange *rasogollas*...whatever each one could eat.

Oh, dear! Where was the idol of Saraswati? What about the rituals of the Puja? Where were the gongs, the cymbals? As the children played happily in the hall, Shirish's beautiful daughter, Proserpita entered, clad in a milky white saree edged with blue lotuses. With her *tanpura* in hand, she was the epitome of a child-Saraswati. She would dance for them and sing for them the songs of Saraswati, of Lakshmi and Durga and the entire range of the *Yasho Dehi, Dwisho Johi* for the divine pantheon.

The days flew past. Proserpita's song awakened the buds in the garden, joyfully lighting up the trees. If Proserpita smiled, the birds vied with each other, chirping and twittering. In storm and in rain, the seasons of Baisakh and Ashwin, of Aasarh and Falgun danced to her rhythm, and the fluffy, white clouds were like swirling ballerinas. And Shirish joined the gatherings of the children and then that of the young people, the maids and the matrons. Unnoticed by all, she changed the spirit of these gatherings. Strange as it seemed, it was true. The graffiti disappeared from the walls in her area, the processions stopped. People went to work on time and came home to rest. Children played happily and returned to their homes by dusk. The loudspeakers that had blared out the aazan, the Granth Sahib, the Geeta, fell silent, for their preachers were otherwise pre-occupied. The *maulvi* combed his beard, touched his eyes with kohl and sat down to teach Arabic. Sardar Balwant Singh's business of solar heaters was flourishing too well for him to spare a thought to any other matter. And Neelmoni Pundit, learned in the *Bhagvad Gita*, had people flocking to him in his grammar school at home, for lessons in spoken Sanskrit. It all started when the children heard Neelmoni Pundit chanting a verse in Sanskrit, when the rains came down at the close of Saptami Puja. This is how it went, in effect,

> Raindrops are falling, drip, drip, drip
> The mind is restless, flip flop, flip
> Hold the umbrella quick, quick, quick
> Young Montu, don't say, 'no'.

The children insisted that they should be taught the easy version of Sanskrit. Shirish accommodated them all in her courtyard. Her presence permeated everything, everywhere. She was no longer a chalk-like, clay doll. The shell-white woman with a face like a ghoul had been transformed into a golden princess whose auspicious footprints like those of the goddess Lakshmi, left behind a trail of peace and prosperity in their wake, as she went about her chores. The neighbourhood overflowed with happiness and fulfilment and pride. Every season now brought its own celebration, the drums and gongs of the *chhat* festival, the rangoli, the *bihu* dances, the joy of the *Baisakhi*, the ritual chanting of the paeans to Lakshmi, the soft, sweet songs of the monsoon reverberated again and again through the air, like the tones of a monochord.

Thus pre-occupied, the throbbing little centre of pain, thick as honey, in Shirish's life grew smaller and smaller as the days passed. When the moon was high up in the sky and the stars twinkled in darkness amidst the waving coconut-palm fronds, Shirish would wake up from slumber, go up to the roof and raise her radiant face to the night sky, and speak to the dark, secret past,

'Wherever you may be, my deceiver, whatever heavenly peacock throne maybe your seat, I am free of your bondage at last. You dwell in a jewel-studded, treacherous heaven, but I will fill this harsh world with abundance and plenty. The green fields will turn greener and then be tipped with gold, the air, heavy with the scent of ripeness. And your Midas-hoard will pale into insignificance beside this living world of green and gold that will unravel in the wake of my endeavour.' A smile would slowly spread over her face, not in overt challenge, nor in loud, scornful laughter. It was a smile suffused with serenity, like the glow of the aurora in the northern skies.

As she descended from the terrace to her bedroom, after her midnight chant like the Samveda, her daughter, the moonstone of her heart, laughed in her sleep. Shirish touched her delicate forehead lightly,

'Are you dreaming, my love? Will you take on the mantle from me, the task of making the lotus bloom in its bed of slime? I will impart to you the secret mantra. I will bequeath to you the secret of the unceasing flute that has the power to tame the wild birds and beasts and insects. It is a power I have acquired at great cost.'

Proserpita turned in her sleep. Her eyeballs quivered within their lids and she whimpered. Shirish gently uncrossed her hands over her budding, lotus-like breasts. It was said that the stone-demons would crush you if you slept with your hands crossed over your chest.

'Sleep, my child,' Shirish murmured. 'In the light of the lamp, I'll watch over you silently, the cool touch of my hand will be on your brow. Sleep in peace, my child.'

Her daughter was the joy of her life, the peace of her mind, the object of her wonder, her delight. She saw the world through her. If Proserpita asked her why she was an only child, her mother would say,

'Just once, my child, the upper and the nether regions, earth and sky came together in harmony. The act cannot be repeated.'

And if Proserpita asked,

'Who is my father?'

'Your father is Man, who plays no role other than the sowing of the seed.'

And if the girl should ask whether her mother was all she had in this world, Shirish would hold her daughter close in her arms and say,

'I know not whether I am everything to you, my child, but you are my all.'

She heard the echo of her daughter's laughter in the chirping of child voices that gathered around her and struck answering chords in her breast. In the music of her child's voice, she heard the whistling of the magpie-robin in her garden and beyond, on the high walls of the neighbours, the rocking of the fork-tailed passerine, the glint of laughter as that of a woman walking by. And when her own youth brimmed over to the clarion call of the cuckoo on a spring night, she clasped her daughter to her breast and desperately stilled the urgent demands of her body, just past its prime.

It is people like Shirish, who, unnoticed by all, impose order on the chaos of the hamlets and cities. Others may mould the shapeless clay into form, but it is people like Shirish who whisper the magic word of creation. No matter who the king might be, rising out of the need of the hour, he who brings harmony into chaos, is the real ruler. With the rhythm of joy rising out of the depths of sorrow, spreading across her own life, Shirish's dream of fertility had touched the barren yellow land with its wand of green and gold. No one knew that at the centre of her new-found happiness, was the apple of her eye, the flesh and blood image of her daughter who was like the beating pulse of her heart. Perhaps, Shirish herself was not sure what had resurrected her from the abyss of deceit and treachery in her past and brought the spark of beauty to her eyes. Today, she fluttered around like a diaphanous butterfly, spreading her pollen from tree to tree so that even the highest branch of the barren mango tree burst into bloom. Where lay the source of this strength? Who gave it to her? Did she know all that, did she care to know? And because no one cared to know, word spread from mouth to mouth across the land, and the forces of darkness waited, breathing hot and heavy.

It was a Spring evening. The last rays of the dying sun trailed their luminous fingers over the world like the dying strains of *madhu-madhavi sarang*. The evening mist leapt lightly from bush to bush, shutting the eye of the day. Ramkhelwan, the porter, watched as a cavalcade of motorcycles roared up to the gates of the mansion. One by one, he counted six...six huge ogres who strode up to him. They had steel bangles on their wrists and silver rings on their ear lobes. Gold chains gleaming on hairy chests made one shudder, said Shantimoni, the maid. Ramkhelwan, who had long forgotten the duties of a *durwan*, could drive away little more than the urchins and beggars of the neighbourhood. His hands stopped grinding their tobacco. The huge iron gates noisily creaked open and six pairs of boots marched down the drive towards the inner quarters.

'Is Shirsha Devi at home?' they demanded.

'Who are you? There is no Shirsha Devi here.'

'Oh, Shishir Devi, or Shishirkana or Shishirbala, or——mala or whatever.' Shirish stood before them in silence.

'Have you heard of ChottoRaj-da? Mohitbaran ChottoRaj?'

Who had not heard that name? Shirish did not answer.

'Mohit-da wants you to contest the next election as our leader. You have to topple his rival, Abhaybindu Daw.'

'What do I know of all that?' she asked gravely.

'Oh, you'll be tutored. By Mohit-da himself.'

'I'm not interested in party politics.'

'Mohit-da will take care of all that. You'll just stand for the elections.'

'I detest all that.'

'But he thrives on it.' They roared with laughter, these denizens of the underworld. 'Elections are our bread and butter and we will not hesitate to pull the trigger of the stengun to the temple of anyone who dares defy us.'

With that, the motorcycles roared off. The neighbourhood quaked in fear. The people, including Nabinmadhob, gradually descended in torrents upon her in her inner courtyard with piteous appeals. She was their daughter, their mother, their sister.

'Don't say no to them, Mother. Mohitbaran and Abhaybindu are man-eating ogres. You cannot escape their talons, one of them will certainly get you. There is no escape.'

The older ones shook their heads and said that there was more in this than met the eye.

When they had gone, Shirish continued to sit upon the step, the blue vein in her temple throbbing. Her hair was dusty and wild and there was a curious set to her jaw.

The days passed one by one, dragging their feet, like the lull before a storm. A week passed. Slowly, Shirish got back to her work and Ramkhelwan to his post, opening and shutting the iron gates.

On the seventh day, Shirish came home to find Ramkhelwan beating his head in despair. Shantimoni was senseless with grief. Mohitbaran's huge LandRover had carried Proserpita away from her gate. Shirish ran to his house, but the huge gates were firmly padlocked, one behind the other. The neighbours said Chattoraj-da was away on a honeymoon, no one knew where. She ran to the police station. The officer-in-charge said her eighteen-year-old daughter had gone with him of her own volition, there was her signature to prove it.

'It's forged!' she shrieked in anger.

The officer had her forcibly removed for breaking the peace. She ran to the *zilla pradhan*. He congratulated her on her daughter's great good fortune. After a long, long vigil at the district magistrate's, he finally turned her away saying it was impossible for him to keep track of all the girls who went astray in the huge area under his jurisdiction.

The large pink house at the corner of the meadow has long since fallen into decay. Its plaster has flaked off, its huge iron gates have come off their hinges. Ramkhelwan no longer sings Ram-bhajans at the gate. And Shirish has vanished. No child comes to play ball in the garden overgrown with weeds. But grown men do.

Every night as darkness falls, the muffled hisses and stifled laughter tell their own tale. So do the withered tube-rose garlands, the broken bottles, the paper bags and pellets—the ugly debris of the night which the gardener sweeps away every morning with a smile, as he pockets a hefty tip. The ogres of the night tear around in their monstrous motor-cycles, brandishing their vicious cycle chains on any unhappy victim that falls into their clutches. Entire families fall prey to the demoniac fury of their choppers. No one knows these killers, but rivers of blood flow and people shudder. Bombs explode in crowded marketplaces, on crowds of shoppers, smashing everything to smithereens. Nabinmadhob lies paralysed. The women in his family avidly devour the neighbourhood gossip.

That year there was no rain. The Earth sizzled in the heat, scorching the paddy to hay. The red earth was cracked, dry and barren to the edges of the horizon. Ramzan *miya* and Surinder Singh, Dulal Hazra and Gobinda Majhi, clapped their hands to their heads in despair. The well water dried up, the spade yielded nothing from the furrows. In the dry bed of the stream, there lay a few handfuls of wet mud. The huge tree in the northeast corner of the meadow, crashed to the ground, its trunk eaten by termites.

And then the rains fell. It poured and poured without end and the people looked up and watched in amazement as the torrent reared its head like the frothing fangs of the serpent, sweeping away cattle and cowherd and the thatched roofs and walls of huts, shaking the houses to their foundations. From pole to pole stretched this vast sheet of water. The deluge devoured everything in its wake, from Kailash to Ararat. No ark promised refuge.

Translated by Saumitra Chakravarty

The Call of the Sea

Bani Basu

O
UR CHILDHOOD WAS SPENT IN POVERTY. BUT CHILDREN DO NOT DEFINE
affluence as their parents do. So my siblings, particularly my
brother Binu and I, did not realize that we were poor. My
father had a rip-roaring, hearty laugh. My mother was like the flame of
the evening lamp. And we lived in a corner of a mansion that included a
portion of a courtyard as large as a field.

Our share of the mansion also included three big rooms with high
ceilings and a huge, enclosed balcony in which one could play a game of
badminton. Which of my friends could boast of a house like that? By
way of furniture, we had a large almirah, a heavy chest of drawers, a
table with a brass top and five or six peculiarly shaped chairs—all of
polished, reddish-brown mahogany. To my child's eye, the legs of those
chairs were like molten jaggery. And of course, what intrigued us most
was the angel of white marble. It was taller than I was and seemed to be
descending upon us with folded wings and bent head, in the courtyard.
One foot had already touched down, the other, half-broken, was still
raised in flight. That broken leg somehow made her all the more human
to us. She was someone we could sympathize with.

These were all antique pieces. Who knew how old they were? They
had never been polished, nor had I ever seen the rooms acquiring a coat
of paint. But everything was kept spic and span. My parents and my
elder sister always saw to that. Whenever I pointed out our house to my
friends, they would stare awe-struck and wonder whether my father
was a king that we should live in a house this size.

If I ever happened to mention this to my parents, the smile on my
father's lips would abruptly vanish and the familiar glow of the evening
lamp would go out of my mother's face. And my elder sister would be

sure to find some opportunity to chide me absent-mindedly even in the midst of all her household chores.

'Can't you find anything better to talk about, Tuni? What's all this talk of kings and queens, huh? You longing to be a princess, or what?'

God knows I had no such desire. The world of princesses was a forbidding one in which they got turned to stone by demons. Demons put them to sleep in garrets and when they did awake at the touch of gold and silver wands, it was only to stare fearfully at the monster-faces of those ogres. No, it was not a world I wanted to be in. So I would secretly ask my younger brother Binu why I had been scolded. What was so annoying about my father being called a king?

Binu was younger but certainly more wise.

'Don't you know Tuni, that our great, great-grandfather was given the title of "king"? You know, the one who built this mansion, these sprawling courtyards for their Pujas, these grounds and all?'

'So? What's wrong with that?'

'You stupid girl, don't you know they drank away their wealth? None of our ancestors ever did a day's hard work other than racing their pet pigeons and celebrating their cats' weddings and licking the white man's boots. That's half the reason we are in such dire straits now!'

That was a phase of our life when Binu worked hard at his linguistic skills using such grandiloquent phrases in Bengali that even his teachers stared at him in amazement. Well, simple as I was, all I could gather from his lecture was that it was bad to be called a king and that kings were evil folk, perhaps worse than Tetul-da, that one-armed rogue down our lane.

There were just two occasions in the year when we children became conscious of our poverty. One was during the Durga Puja, and the other, during the annual school vacations, when it was time to go for a holiday.

During the Durga Puja, our courtyard would come alive with festivity. People from all over Calcutta would flock to see our deity dressed in the traditional *daker shaaj*, of pith and gold. But we children never got more than a couple of new dresses to wear. My mother's sewing machine whirred away all through the months of Bhadra and Aswin, right up to the day of Panchami. Mountains of petticoats and *kurtas*, blouses and frocks, vests and underwear, shirts and pants had to be stitched...not only for her own, but for all the members of that extended Roy family!

And from that heap my mother would perhaps pull out a stiff, golden dress with frills and ask me whether I liked it. I would come running to her in joy. How could I not like such a dress?

'Ma, shall I wear this for Astami Puja? And these others, are they for Shashti, Saptami and Nabami?'

But all that my mother's hand could pull out a second time from the heap was a plain printed frock,

'Here, this is for you to wear on Shasti.'

'And?'

'What more? Can't you see me slogging day and night stitching other people's clothes? How can I find time to stitch more dresses for you? As such, I'm aching all over.'

Though I loved my mother dearly, at that particular moment I could not sympathize with her plight. I would begin to cry in right earnest. For right in front of my eyes was the image of my cousins Putul and Bithi, their ten new dresses, two for each of the five days. Some would have frills, others have collars like a dog's ears or a mickey mouse appliqué on silk...each one unique in its own way! And I, in my one golden organdie each and every day of that week!

'Why do you have to stitch clothes for all those people? Why can't you make them only for me and Binu and Didi and Baba and yourself? Why? Why?' I wailed.

My mother would sit gravely at the sewing machine, with her cheek resting on her hands as I whined on and on. My elder sister would try her best to drag me away from the scene, and right in the middle of all that, my father would enter,

'What's the matter? Why is Tuni crying? And Bula, why are you tugging at her leg like that?'

'Just look at her, Baba! She's not allowing Ma to work. Just fifteen days to go for the Puja and so much stitching left to do!'

My sister was always at my mother's side, fixing buttons, making button holes, hemming the edges, stretching out the yards of silk for her to cut, helping out in every possible way.

My father would listen gravely to her remonstrations. But the very next afternoon, he would come home sweating profusely, calling out to me,

'Tuneee...Tun...Tuneeeee!'

And as I leapt over to his side, he would hand me a packet,
'Just see whether you like this, Tuni?'
And out would pop a heavenly white frock of Swiss silk, with tiny
embroidered rosettes. I would hold the dress close to my face, breathing
in its scent, a doll-like picture of ecstasy, floating in an ocean of happiness.
And just at that moment, my mother would make an appearance,
'What's this? Where did you get that dress from? It must have cost
the earth!'
'From the New Market.'
'Oh God! How much did it cost you?'
'Do you like it or not? Why do you go on harping on the price?'
'Of course, it's pretty. But the price must be equally so.'
'Forty-five rupees.'
'Wha...a...t? We could have got her three dresses for that amount.
How will we...'
'Ugh! Shut up, will you?'
'And that's not all. She will demand shoes and socks and ribbons to go
with it. And she will whine for all the goodies during that week of the
Pujas...' My mother departed, leaving the sentence hanging in mid-air.
At night, while stroking my forehead to put me to sleep, my sister
would say,
'Tuni, Baba had something that he urgently required to buy. Instead,
he got you that expensive dress with the money. Tomorrow, you'll ask
him to return it to the shop, won't you? Tell him you don't like the dress.'
'But I *do* like the dress so much, Didi! I adore it. Why should I tell
him a lie? Can't Baba buy his stuff with some other money?'
Didi did not give up, however,
'Tell Baba you don't like the white colour, that you don't want any
more dresses!'
At that I would burst out tearfully,
'Ugh, you horrible creature, I hate you! I adore that dress and now
you want me to say I don't. All my cousins, Putul, Bithi, Jhari, Dipu,
Manju...every one of them has a new dress for every single day of the
Puja week. Everyone!...And I...?' My sobs would drown my words and
that would bring my mother to my side,
'Bula, why is Tuni crying? Have you scolded her?'

And before my whines could rise to a crescendo to attract more attention, my sister's hand would come down heavily on my mouth.

'Look at her, Mother!'

'Let her be, Bula, she's only a child.'

Ma would stand beside me for a while.

And then came those five heavenly days of the Durga Puja...days filled with endless sticks of candyfloss, sweets and ice lollies and the screeching, squealing sounds of gas balloons! In the huge courtyard assigned for the annual Durga Puja, the chandelier would come alive, the gold and pith robes of the idols would gleam and glisten. And just then, one of my many aunts would call me aside to ask who had given me that silk dress.

'My father, of course. Who else?' And I would be off to join my friends, my heart bursting with pride at my father who got me gold and white dresses, not unlike the pith and gold robes of the goddess. Milky-white it was, with fine gold lace and multi-coloured rosettes, and it smelled so good too...like lozenges!

'Tuni!' That was my cousin Bithi, 'What pretty shoes!'

'These shoes are called Irene, the latest from Bata,' I would add breathlessly. 'Baba...my Baba, got them for me.' I was beaming with pride.

Leather shoes were forbidden near the altar, so I would hastily jump off. In the sea of faces floating in front of me, another pair of eyes would focus on me and then on my dress, perhaps another voice would pick up the cue,

'That's a lovely dress Tuni's wearing. Can't you get one like that for our Minu?'

I could see my mother coming down the steps in a new cotton saree with a scarlet border, her head covered, her feet rimmed with red *alta*. She would be carrying an enormous brass platter of mysterious Puja accessories to where my father sat near the priest on the altar, the edge of his unbleached *dhoti* drawn across his bare shoulders. Who...ooo...oosh! That was the blue gas balloon slipping through Binu's fingers. And there was my Didi in a striped yellow *Dhaniakhali* saree taking up her place alongside our cousins near the altar. So many Didis, all daughters of my father's relatives or of neighbours...some in silk, some in organdy, some even in Benaras silk sarees.

The Sandhi Puja began amidst pomp and splendour. In the unearthly glow of the earthen lamps, in the fragrant haze of incense and joss sticks, the reverence on my mother's half-covered face was ethereal. I glanced at her again and again, as the incense-laden air played hide and seek with her. And all of a sudden, that voice carping in my ears,

'Look at that coarse saree Bula's wearing! Do you suppose it's because she doesn't want to spoil her good ones while helping out with the Puja work?'

'Nonsense!' came the pat reply, 'she can't afford a better one!'

I was too young to comprehend the real impact of such comments, but I was conscious of a growing sense of discomfort. My ears would grow hot with anger and sorrow. My head would feel strangely light. My sister Bula's saree was coarse and cheap? But she looked so beautiful blowing the conch-shell, her puffed-out cheeks, her forehead, her nose and chin, pink like that of the goddess! I ran away to hide my tears, the voices trailing behind me. 'Where are you off to, Tuni?' In that tumult of sound and festivity…beating drums and clanging gongs…a voice would be hammering in my chest…I was poor…we were the poor folk in the family…my sister's saree was cheap, my brother's half-pants baggy, my father's bare shoulders were covered only with the corner of his coarse dhoti! All this fun and festivity…all that the Durga Puja meant …it was not for poor folks like us…only for the likes of the Putuls and Bithis, the Manjus and Dipus, the Madhu Didis, Nil Mashis, Nutan Kakimas and Gitali Didis. And I, in my white silk dress, was off to the utter solitude of our lonely garret to hide my tears, the cruel words about the dress, swirling around me.

With the festive week drawing to a close, the hurt would also fade away. It was back to school and the world of school bags and the textbooks, covered ever so carefully by my sister, the tiffin box full of *ghugni* and the Maths and English lessons with my father. And *Monimala* in the evenings. The days simply flew past and I bustled along with them. The nights were spent in the warmth and security of my mother's or my sister's arms, nodding off, in the limpid pool of memory, after a hectic day at school.

The scorpion of poverty would rear its venomous tail again in vacation time. Come summer, Puja, or Christmas, the little scorpion would sting repeatedly. All right, during the Puja season, you could say it was impossible for us, the famous Mullicks of Mullick Palace, to abandon our century-old Durga Puja. My father never got leave from his boss during the summer, so that was okay? But Christmas, what about Christmas? Those fun-filled days under an azure sky with baskets of golden oranges in every shop, when all of Calcutta broke loose for endless picnics? Besides, all my friends were going on holiday...Mitali would say, 'Tanima, aren't you going anywhere this winter? We're off to Giridih, with the famous Usri Falls...such a beautiful place!' Keya said she was going to Hazaribagh where they'd see the forests, play hide and seek in the garden and have chicken every single day...Shipra, of course, claimed the upper hand. Hazaribagh and Giridih were a hop, skip and jump away by train and no fun at all. She was off on a two-day journey by train to Delhi to see the Qutb Minar and the Red Fort and then to see the Taj by moonlight at Agra. Her father had assured her of all this.

I stared at them, speechless with wonder. Shipra would actually see the Qutb, the same Shipra, who sat beside me on the bench and shared my *ghugni* and I her *gulab jamuns*? The Qutb, built by Qutb-ud-din Ibek and completed by Iltutmis? And the Red Fort with its peacock throne, its Dewan-i-khas and Dewan-i-am? And the Taj, glorious and pristine through aeons of time, as the poet had said? Could one actually visit them, see them? To me, they were just names locked away within the pages of an old history book.

'Baba, where are we going for Christmas, this time?'

And my father would turn to my sister in mock surprise,

'Bula, what is this tiny Tuntuni bird chirping about?'

'No Baba, seriously. You have to tell me where we're going! See all my friends are off on their tours...Mitali, Shipra...*all* of them!'

'Everyone's off?' My father would smile, 'then the whole city of Calcutta will be as free as the Maidan. Just the few of us here? We'll go out every single day.'

'Baba, you're joking again. You must tell me where we're going.'

At that point, my sister would get up from the *masalas* she was grinding, wipe her turmeric-stained hands on a little red towel and make her entry,

'Tuni, why are you interrupting Baba's work? Can't you see he's checking his accounts?'

I had never been scared of my parents, but my sister's was certainly a daunting presence.

'Didi, you tell Baba to take us to Delhi this winter. I want to see the Red Fort and the Taj. Please, Didi!'

Didi's brow clouded, 'Which of your friends is going?'

'Shipra…Shipra's going.'

'So, you have to go, too? Why do you always have to imitate others? Do you know what such people are called?'

I was sure it was something dreadful, but I had lost the guts to protest. Fighting back my tears, I wondered whether going to Delhi was some sort of crime. It wasn't, was it? Then why did my sister scold me so? And late in the night, as I was drifting off to sleep, I could hear my mother's voice pleading,

'Can't we take her for a day or two to some nearby place?'

And then my sister's voice, snapping at my mother,

'You be quiet, Ma. As it is, Baba finds it so difficult to cope with the expenses. Children will always be unreasonable.'

With that, I would fall asleep, the little scorpion at work again within me. The scorpion would sting and crawl back into the hole as in the rhyme. And a voice would be humming in my mind as I dozed…you don't have money…you are poor…your father does not earn enough to take you on a vacation. Like the monotonous grinding of train wheels, the same voice would be chanting within my hurt mind, that the only train I would ever be on would never take me to Hazaribagh or Usri or Delhi. Its destination was the land of the have-nots where fathers had no money, sisters wore cheap sarees, mothers showed their red-rimmed feet under the sarees they wore high up above their ankles as they went about their endless chores.

Then, all of a sudden something happened to lift the clouds off my horizon. One morning, my father came running down the courtyard to the kitchen door in a state of excitement. He was waving one of those blue envelopes with foreign stamps that we had been getting off and on for years.

'Phutkun is coming, do you hear, my dear?'

My mother was stirring the boiling milk on the mud oven. She stood up, her face even more radiant than his,

'What? Really? Phutkun Thakurpo is coming?'

'Yes, with his whole family…Phutkun, his wife Stella and their two children.'

'They'll stay with us?' The alarm bells began to ring in my mother's mind. 'His foreign wife and their white-skinned children? Oh, where shall we put them up? What shall we feed them?'

My father smiled, 'Will you listen to what Phutkun has written...'

My dear Mejda, I am coming down with my family to see our ancestral Durga Puja. But I will stay with you. I know I'll not be welcome in any other part of that house and in any case none of the others keeps a house quite as neat as Mejo Bowdi. Please don't put yourself out in any way on account of our visit. I'd love the typical Bengali dishes...like that *lau shaker charchchari* with *daler bara, lau chingri,* and *patal bhaja* and *mourala macher bati charchari*. And as for my family, they'll be happy with boiled potato and cabbage, half-boiled beans and raw tomatoes and carrots. Only the water should be boiled. We'll spend the Pujas with you and then make a short trip to some nearby place before getting back to England. I'll be on a three-week vacation. Please convey my *pronāms* to Mejo Bowdi. Bula must be a grown up girl now and as for your smaller fry, I haven't even seen them yet!

Yours
Phutkun

My sister was at my father's side by then,

'Don't you worry about anything, Baba, I'll make all the arrangements. Sahib Kaka and Stella Kakima can be accommodated in our room, Leela and Subhas in yours. You and Binu can occupy the wooden cot in the drawing room and Ma, Tuni and myself will spread our bedding out on the floor.'

My father smiled affectionately at my sister,

'See, everything has been worked out already. What would we do without Bula?'

Phutkun's, or Sahib Kaka's, was a name familiar to us since birth. Apparently, a cousin of my father's had gone abroad to get his barrister's degree and had settled down there with a foreign wife. Obviously, his children were considered 'foreign' too, and my uncle's father had promptly disinherited them all in anger. As a result, ties had been severed with his next of kin, and the only part of the family of which Sahib Kaka was especially fond, was that of his Mejda and Mejo Bowdi. They had maintained regular contact for the last seventeen or eighteen years with us. The same Sahib Kaka and Mem Kaki were coming.

Binu and I watched in some trepidation as my father marshalled his scant resources to put up western-style fittings, a commode and a wash basin in our bathroom. We giggled privately at the new chair-like structure. Apparently, foreigners could not squat. We could hardly stop sniggering. But along with this funny side of the situation, our main problem was the thought of communicating with our 'foreign' cousins with our limited English vocabulary. We started memorizing phrases of the type, 'What's your name?'…'My name is Miss Tanima Mullick'…'My name is Master Binayak Mullick'…'Where do you live?' Then, realizing that this last would be unnecessary, we'd begin giggling again…'Which class do you read in?'…'I read in Class IV'…'I read in Class III'… But Binu eventually lost patience, flung his hands up in the air, bared his teeth and went off to play ball, yelling words like 'hat, mat, cat, that, rat…fie, high, nigh'…in fun. Baba overheard us practising one day and burst out laughing. He told us we did not have to struggle so hard with our English. Better to speak slowly in Bengali and they would surely catch on, because for all that Phutkun was nicknamed a 'sahib', he never had been one and never would be.

And so, my Aunty Stella arrived in a shiny silk saree, her hair knotted at the nape of her neck and looked around her with delight at the high ceiling, the ancient architecture, the beautiful, antique statues. In her broken Bengali, she exclaimed excitedly,

'All this is fit for a king's castle! Why don't you open it up for public display? In my country, the dukes and barons are opening up their manor-houses for the public, it helps raise funds for maintenance, too.'

Sipping his tea, my uncle Phutkun reminded his wife that she should not try her business acumen in this place,

'Here in India, darling, history comes alive, it is not relegated to museums.'

'What's that you said in Bengali about business sense? Not some abusive word, I hope?'

'Oh, I haven't been able to teach you the nitty-gritties of Bengali grammar yet.'

Happy to change the topic, with a wink at my father, Phutkun Kaka continued,

'Remember I told you about our own private Durga Puja. Well, even though it started off as a family affair of the Mullicks', it has now been thrown open to the public.' He turned to my father, 'How many share holders to this property are there, Mejda?'

'Thirty-seven,' counted my father.

My cousin, Leela had affectionately nicknamed me little Red Riding Hood. She and Subhas-da had defied all their father's predictions and refused their boiled vegetables. They vowed to taste everything, only there was a request for less chillies from Stella Kakima.

As the days passed, they wandered around our huge mansion, its labyrinthine corridors, its winding staircases used by the sweeper for entry, its roof big as three or four football fields, its friezes, its angels with a look of wonder frozen on their cherubic faces, its wall lamps, old paintings and family photographs, above all, its Durga Puja. We picked up a close relationship with our cousins, my sister Bula with Leela-di, Subhas-da with Binu. The boys spent their time flying kites on the roof and discovering the narrow, ancient North Calcutta alleys, which fascinated Subhas-da. And I became Stella Kakima's pet,

'Meddi (Mejdi),' she would say, in her broken lingo, 'I'm taking this Tuni-doll home to England with me.'

'Go ahead,' laughed my mother, 'she's such a prattler!'

'Seriously though, you won't back out later, will you?'

I listened in growing excitement. What fun to be in England, in Phutkun Kaka's house with its sloping roof like a hut, and sprawling gardens, its chimneys and fireplaces, the pet dog, the spotlessly clean roads. I would get to see the Buckingham Palace and the Thames and the tube train. I would even acquire a fair skin like my cousin Leela's, like a foreigner's, and wear pretty dresses and see lots of interesting places. What fun that would all be!

Phutkun Kaka told us he was planning a trip to Gopalpur-on-Sea after the Pujas and that he expected us all to join them. My father immediately protested saying he would have to get back to the office the very next day after Vijaya Dashami. So, naturally, my mother had to stay back to take care of him. She suggested that Bula and Binu should accompany them.

Leela-di said, 'Bula, you must take a holiday.'

'Next time, Leela, next time, please don't mind.'

I knew my Didi would not go, she was such a homebird, this sister of mine.

Eventually, after a lot of discussions, it was decided that Binu and I would go. We started packing our clothes in great excitement, the white silk dress of last year, still as good as new, the golden organdie and all those amazing clothes my Aunty Stella had got us, which were called 'dresses'. Binu looked smart in his new clothes. And when my sister Bula saw me in my new pair of slacks with the printed top, my little pigtail bobbing up and down, she held me close,

'Pretty as a picture in a story book,' she said.

Binu and I bounded into the waiting taxi, hands tucked into our pockets. We were impatient to be off. Mitali came running up, asking where I was off to.

'We're off to the sea. Gopalpur-on-sea!' I said, my face lit up with happiness.

The train chugged off, its air-conditioned interior cutting off all outside noises. I sank happily into its cushioned comfort, my cold hands clasped tightly over my chest. Leela-di instantly wrapped a triangular pink shawl around my shoulders, so snug and yet so light. You could not see the world beyond the window, only our own reflections. Within its lighted interior, my Aunt Stella's ruddy face, Leela-di's red blouse and black skirt, the glint of Subhas-da's gold-rimmed glasses and Binu's endless chatter. I was hemmed in on all sides by wave after wave of English conversation, not a word of which was comprehensible to me. From the food basket came the tantalizing smell of unknown delicacies. The label on the box spoke of Spencers, a Calcutta hotel. And after dinner it was off to sleep on my very own berth, rocking endlessly and leaving the past behind. I slept and woke and rocked by turns, each in its own way a new experience, as if I had never done it before. The sun was like a vermilion ball. Fields and lakes, ponds and rivers and canals rushed by. White herons, cormorants and black, fork-tailed passerine birds, the fields drawing close and receding, the sun playing hide and seek behind the leaves. In my child's mind, the monotonous grinding of train wheels was an endless chant...Tuni, Binu,...Binu, Tuni... Leela-di, a book on her lap, Binu clutching his toffees, Mem Kakima, Sahib Kaka, Subhas Dada reading the news, jumping up, jumping down, and far, far away the ageing city of Calcutta, an old house, its winding alleys, dirty lanes, Id-dul Joha, Id-dul-Fitr...chugh...chugh...Tuni-Binu's first tour...and on and on to Berhampore!

The hotel van was waiting at the station, its tyres getting embedded in the sand in much the same way as Binu and Tuni had, into their cushioned berths. The thought made them both giggle.

'And what makes you laugh, Tun-tuni?' asked Phutkun Kaka.

'Little ones don't need a reason to,' said Kakima.

And then that wondrous scene, those amazing sounds! Tuni–Binu fell silent in sheer wonder. Subhas-da jumped out of the car and raced down the beach with his camera. Stella Kakima jumped up,

'Oh, it's wonderful!' she gasped.

'Better than Brighton,' put in Leela-di.

'Of course,' purred Phutkun Kaka, with a wink at Tuni and Binu, 'you should see whose country this is!'

The hotel was a dream come true, with its amazing rooms, bathrooms, beds, its palm-fringed lounges, its exotic food. But best of all was the sea, its edges like Ganga waters laced with soapy froth, a luminous emerald beyond and far, far away, a deep, metallic blue like the gleam of a peacock's throat. And endless sandy beaches and sand dunes tipped with blue-green waves. Dingies floated by and far away, a trawler. They were forbidden to bathe in the sea for fear of rocks but Binu would not listen, he sat laughing on the black rock with Subhas-da, his legs dangling in the water. Tuni however was more timid, she clung to the edge of her uncle's shorts and paddled in the water. Waves broke over her head again and again, before she could recover from the one before. She watched the endless crash of breakers against the rocks. She watched the play of mortals on the shore of the vast sea, all day and all night. Her aunt and cousin, their fair skins exposed in their bathing costumes sun bathed, rose from the waves wrapped in towels, furry as bears, their hair tucked away under their bathing caps.

As they came close to each other, playing in the water, Binu giggled. They pretended that they were in England... So many white-skinned people, reclining like Leela-di and Stella Kakima on the beach with their sunglasses on, or bobbing up and down amidst the waves in their colourful swimsuits. Back at the hotel, it was a lesson in how to use cutlery for Tuni and Binu. Napkins folded like stiff white flowers to be unfolded and spread on their laps and food to be swallowed noiselessly without puffing out their cheeks as Leela-di had showed them. Bearers saluted them, their caps like coxcombs. When the atmosphere became too alien for Tuni, she stared hard at the bronzed faces of her uncle and her brother. And the strange roaring of the waves at night, as she lay beside her cousin Leela, wasn't that exotic and foreign, too? Had Tuni really left her own city, her own country behind and come to England?

She woke to the soft swishing of the waves outside their window, the breakers pouring out their white froth upon the sands. Breakfast was on the balcony with her cousins, drowned in their foreign lingo, some of which was gradually becoming intelligible to her.

Phutkun Kaka—'Stella, are you enjoying yourself? Leela, my girl, what about you?'

Stella Kakima—'Wonderful! Feeling at home here.'

Kaka—'Oh, so you didn't enjoy your stay at our Jorabagan house?'

Kakima—'Jorabagan is alright. But here I am not forced to wear a saree and I can heave a sigh of relief, away from all that curiosity.'

Leela-di—'Actually, Dad, I enjoyed it as much as I would an adventure in a foreign land.'

'Well, how do you think I feel in your land, for your sake... And how I have felt amongst the Mullicks in Calcutta over the past one week?' laughed Phutkun Kaka.

Kakima—'I am really sorry for you.'

Subhas-da—'I've decided on a tour of India, not Europe, after my graduation. All those narrow alleys and vast terraces are fascinating. And the people, too. I've never met anyone quite like my Uncle and Aunt before. The ordinary people on the street however, are so peculiar. Some treat you like a god, some behave like absolute lackeys, others are no better than animals or inanimate objects.'

Phutkun Kaka—'You should include Tuni and Binu in your conversation, or they'll feel left out.'

Leela-di—'Right. So, Tuni, do you like it here?'

Tuni—'Very much!'

Leela-di—'And how about you, Binu?'

Binu —'I'll go to England when I grow up. Is England like this place?'

Subhas-da—'Not all of it. Here and there, yes.'

Phutkun Kaka (with a smile)—'That's settled then. Subhas comes to India and Binu goes to England...a youth-exchange programme! And Tuni, Leela, do you have any such plans, too? Oh, of course, Leela...I forgot...!' And all of them started laughing for some unknown reason, leaving Binu smiling foolishly without any comprehension of the joke and running off to the edge of the balcony. Tuni with a glass of milk shake in her hand and Leela-di wiping the froth from the milk shake from Tuni's lips with a napkin.

Soon, it was time to say good-bye to what was their 'England', this Gopalpur with its cashew groves, its sand dunes and its luxurious hotel room. Good-bye to the blue sea dotted with dozens of dark fishing boats like scythes, to the beam of the lighthouse which scanned the midnight waters of the sea, to the lights of the trawlers twinkling in the darkness and the specks of phosphorus dancing on the crests of the waves. One by one, they fell back into the past...Gopalpur-on-Sea, Berhampore, the emerald and turquoise waves. Tears welled up unnoticed, in Tuni's eyes. They were going back, as they must. It was all over...these last few days of building castles in the air, playing a game of make-believe, playing at being this little empress in the comfort of the hotel room, this tiny mermaid riding the crest of the waves. Closer and closer they came to the old city of Calcutta, the old house, the mundane life with its torn text books, its cracked, ink-stained school benches. It was back to the old alley with its screeching tubewells, its teeming crowds of bald pates, bristly moustaches, ear-splitting sneezes and sly guffaws. Back to the screams and the fights in the nearby slum and the youths who loitered in the narrow alleys.

Clutching a child in each hand, Phutkun Kaka went up the broad staircase of the old mansion. He bid good-bye to my father, in a broken voice, hoarse with emotion,

'Well, Mejda, I don't know when we'll see each other again...'

And Leela-di, 'Thanks for a wonderful experience, Jethima! Bula, I'll miss you.'

Kakima said, 'Meddi, you must visit us.'

Subhas-da, 'Binu–Tuni, we must meet again, soon.'

And then, down the stairs and into the waiting taxi, to the airport hotel and off by plane.

Back home, there was a nip in the air in the early winter morning on the latticed verandah. And there under the century-old beams and rafters, was a new Binu and a new Tuni... Binu with his bag of sea shells and Tuni in her straw hat. And the same old Ma and Baba and Didi. Baba still had the corner of his coarse, white dhoti wrapped around his bare shoulders, Ma and Didi, the same radiant, welcoming smiles lighting up their faces. Baba called out, 'Binu...Binu', but Binu was busy rattling the shells in his bag. Baba held out his arms,

'Tuneee...Tun-Tuneee...!'

Tuni flew into her father's outstretched arms, her head resting securely against his bare chest. The familiar beating of his heart was music to her ears, the music she had heard in the depths of the emerald and turquoise waves. Wave after wave of this wonderful feeling broke upon her, unending, bright and beautiful like the silvery glow of the full-moon night. The soft curve of the child's cheek was like the bend of the shore, frothy with tears.

Bengali original: 'Samudra'
Translated by Saumitra Chakravarty

Her Own Seat

Bani Basu

AT LAST, IT WAS ALL OVER. THE NEGOTIATIONS WERE COMPLETE, THE SALE deed executed, the income tax clearance too, had come. Having concluded the business, Sunanda came home, hot and sweating, at 3.30 p.m. She soaked herself in a hot steaming bath in the ancient bath-tub, dating back to her grandfather's day. Ahhh!...It was like shaking a huge burden off her shoulders. The bath was an ablution in more ways than one.

What a relief it was! Nothing to hold her back and no one to care for, except herself. Like an ascetic with nothing in the world, except his loin cloth! Sunanda glanced at the photograph of her gurudev, perhaps for the seventh time in these few days and folded her hands in silent prayer. Property was such a burden. For one who wanted to shake free and spread her wings like a bird, this brick and mortar was like a dead weight stifling her. It could only be her gurudev's blessing! In the end, it was Sharad Desai who had agreed to buy Sunanda's share of the huge ancestral mansion, which accounted for approximately one-third of the whole house.

Thanks to her father, who had done up his portion of the house to his taste, Sunanda's was the only section of the house that was habitable. He had cleared out a rectangular area in the courtyard for a bit of lung space. He had retained the neem and mango trees, they kept the air fresh and healthy. The curling tendrils on the mango boughs turned copper with Spring. The rest of the space was planted with decorative plants, mainly foliage, so dear to her father. And when you crossed this open space, neither wholly garden nor fully courtyard, your eye would fall on the sloping red-tile roof, where the bougainvillea, with its burst of magenta and cream blossoms, flowered right through the months of March and April and well into May.

The verandah was spacious as a mother's lap, its confines serene and secure as Sunanda's memories of her own mother's embrace. It had been her refuge for a long while as she well remembered. Until of course, her mother abruptly departed without so much as a backward glance. Perhaps, the burden was too much for her? Perhaps, she had forgotten that this child Sunanda could not sit down to her daily music sessions, without a plate of hot, white puffy little *luchi,* round as ping-pong balls, and potato fritters, fried as only her mother knew how.

Her father had shouldered all the responsibilities for a long while. The transition from mother's lap to father's shoulders is not an easy one. And God knows it was not easy for a happy-go-lucky, child-like man like him to shoulder a mother's responsibilities. It never is easy!. If only to remind us of the void left by the mother which no one else can fill! It is essential to understand that, if only to experience the enormity of the loss. He could not take her mother's place, but the effort he made, made him a better father than most. Hordes of well-wishers immediately appeared on the scene, as they normally do in such cases, urging him to re-marry. His eye would be fixed on the photograph of the plump, matronly woman on the wall, with her head demurely covered, her smile laden with the pain of what she had left behind her. And then he would glance at the sleeping child with plump cheeks and full lips, her eyeballs quivering behind the veiled lids. How helpless she was and yet Sunanda was the tiny seed of a tall family tree! Her mother's family had been exponents of Classical instrumental music, her father's, that of vocalists. The slim, little fingers were full of calluses formed as they expertly skimmed over the strings with all the adroitness of a Roshanara Begum humming a tune.

Her father warded off the hopeful parents of unmarried girls with the stunning reply that one could not have more than one set of parents in a lifetime.

As the child progressed into adolescence and the adolescent into youth and maturity, her father was there, shouldering all her responsibilities, never relaxing his vigil, even for an instant. Whether it was the reminder, 'Suni, there's a nip in the air, time to unpack the quilt,' or the admonition, 'Suni, your voice sounds hoarse, better have a shot of ghee seasoned with bay leaves, ginger and pepper', or the affectionate advice, 'Suni, that was three hours' practice at a stretch, don't get into the kitchen today, leave the servant to cook whatever she can!' He was always at her side.

However, he failed to find a match for this motherless daughter of his, somewhat spoilt, sensitive and so exceptionally talented. If there was a groom to his taste, the family was not quite suitable. If he approved of the family, the groom was not quite up to expectation, not good enough as a partner for the talented sitarist daughter of a father versatile in *dhrupad*. He may not match the girl in talent, but should he not be a connoisseur at least? And if the father approved of a boy, the daughter felt there was nothing behind that solid, handsome exterior. If on the other hand, the girl found a singer for herself, the father feared that a clash of egos would ruin his daughter's life. That was, in short, the history of their attempts at match-making.

The years passed and Sunanda's sitar poured out the exquisite syllables of *Raga Bageshree* or *Darbari*, netting its own catch of suitors, overwhelmed by her music. But no one could meet the expectations of father and daughter. For, the father's real dhrupad was his beloved daughter and the daughter had tuned the vicissitudes of her life to those of her father, just as she had done the octaves of her music.

Time passed, for, time and tide wait for none. The twilight shadows gathered under his eyes, his hair thinned out and the first streaks of grey lightly touched her temples. On a gloomy winter evening, her father set aside his *pakhwaj* and his betel leaf case,

'Have I ruined your life my child, by being too selective?'

His daughter laughed and brushed aside his fears,

'Of course, you have! And rightly so! Come on, give me a couple of betel leaves with a generous sprinkling of *zarda* from your case. Don't be miserly, mind you.'

But the shadows did not lift from her father's face.

At length, Sunanda held out her ridged and callused fingers to him,

'Baba, don't you realize that this *sitar*, this *surbahar*, this *Saraswati veena* of mine will not tolerate a rival?' She pleaded with sadness in her voice, 'These calluses and ridges on my fingers, these are my only wedding symbols, my vermilion, my shell bangles!'

'But who will look after you when I'm gone?' Her father's face was overcast.

'Why, this beautiful, secure refuge of mine, this house where nothing can hurt me, my bedroom where I reign supreme, my Puja room with its thirty-three crore gods and goddesses, my hanging balcony where I can relax and Baba, above all my music room downstairs, my seat of meditation... Why do you worry?'

But the fear and insecurity never really lifted from her father's eyes. As the liver cancer ravaged his body, his eyes, sad and full of guilt, fluttered helplessly over his daughter till they finally closed forever.

That was more than ten years ago. Time had flown since, she scarcely knew how. Since then Sunanda had surged ahead in her career as a musician. Ten years of radio and television programmes, of national and international conferences and concerts. When the realization of loss finally dawned on her, it was another gloomy winter evening. She had been unjustly denied the prestige she deserved at a conference. A brazen youth, dizzy with instant success, who knew nothing of music, had invited her to sing popular Hindi film songs. A middle-aged singer had edged closer and closer to her on stage till his expensive after-shave could no longer cloak the stench of stale sweat trapped in his teri-wool *sherwani*, literally assaulting her nostrils.

In the courtyard outside her house, winter had taken its annual toll of the neem leaves. The crows cawed in the hollow of the ancient mango tree. The loud and foul-mouthed marital squabbles next door shattered the magic of *Raga Bhopali*. A pair of inquisitive eyes peered at her from the neighbouring verandah on the left. It was her cousin, a *raktabeeja* sprung from the same bloodline, but what he wanted from her she could never guess. Music she knew and understood, but worldly wisdom, scarcely! And how he, a scion of the same music-loving family, could be so grossly materialistic, was beyond her comprehension. If he met her outside the house, either he would threaten to report her to the Corporation authorities for failure to separate the common sewerage pipe, or make a caustic comment about her greying hair and advancing age. She could not understand his choice of words nor his inability to pronounce his words correctly. To her, he seemed like a vengeful death angel at her door, waiting to grab her share of the property.

Staring at the wall of darkness in front of her, she gave up. She was disgusted with the world. She got up from the arm-chair on the verandah and wandered into the bedroom on the ground floor. Her eyes swept over the polished wood of her solitary bed, her wardrobe and at her own plump face in the mirror. And again she felt weary of the world. She went into the small, adjoining puja room and glanced at the golden image of Gopala and the stone one of Radha and Krishna which were her household deities, which she had inherited. But the marble Shiva, the Buddha of papermache and the brass Nataraja on the shelf, were offerings from her students and hosts of admirers. There was a huge crack running diagonally down the side of one wall from the ceiling to the lintel. The white walls were bare, too bare, except for the framed portrait of an ascetic. Sunanda gazed at it for long moments. At last, she seemed to make up her mind,

'You are the ultimate truth of my life. My last refuge!' she murmured.

She took out the large envelope with the word MADHURASHRAM stamped upon it, from her drawer. It was for the third time that day. It was a letter written in an almost illegible scrawl on rough hand-made paper. Her Guru had written to her from his sickbed. She could well imagine the calm smile on his face, his body stretched out taut as an arrow, a small, sloping desk pulled close to his chest, his head at a slight elevation. It was a letter she had received from Thakur Siddhadas almost six months ago. Today the time had come to make the crucial decision.

Sunanda, my child,

You have achieved the ultimate, divine grace through your music. I have been giving much thought to the dilemma that you seem to be in. Who am I to make up your mind for you? Perhaps, it is His wish that the ocean of your melody should be at low tide today. If you have heard the call within your heart, then who am I to try and stop you? Cast off your conflict and hesitation my child, and come to us. Dispose of your property as you deem fit. You are aware that a nominal amount has to be paid to the ashram for boarding and lodging. If you choose to become a permanent resident, it is customary to wear white sarees with red borders, you have to make the necessary arrangements, but please see to it that your clothes do not surpass those of the others. Be sure to bring all your musical instruments along with you. If you choose to convert this house of God into a celestial abode of music, then I shall not prevent you. Your music is your path to salvation, wherever you may choose to live. I will ask Dhananjay to arrange your room for you. Let us know the time of your arrival, the ashram car will meet you at the station.

May God bless you always,

Siddhadas

For a long time Sunanda sat cross-legged on the prayer mat on the
floor, the letter upon her lap. Slowly she roused herself, lit the lamp
and the incense and made the floral offerings at the altar. She crossed
the threshold of her solitary chamber and went down the black granite
stairs to her music room and flicked on the switch. The beauty of the
room instantly came alive. And what ethereal beauty! The glass cases
that lined the walls contained an assortment of musical instruments.
Her *tanpura* tuned to its highest pitch, was laid out on the top. In the
next rack lay the *tarafdar sitar* prepared by the late Nibaran Chandra
Goswami himself, a gift for her sixteenth year from her.father. Lying
close by, was her polished mahogany *surbahar* with its intricate ivory
inlay. And in the lowest rack of all, like a magnificent pair of celestial
breasts, the double-domed Saraswati veena, with its deep and guttural
twanging sound, named after Tansen's illustrious daughter. To the right,
her father's percussion instruments, the *khol*, the *mridanga*, the *pakhawaj*
lay on the low platform. And in the corner stood an image of Saraswati
delicately carved out of bamboo strips and paper by a reputed craftsman.
But most awesome of all was the white marble statue of the goddess
her guru, her music teacher had got her from Jubbalpur. He called it
the 'colourless Mother', the pristine white which is the absence of all
colour and yet its source and fusion. Across the carpet, blue as the sea,
with its pattern of pearly shells, was a low glass case containing the sitar
and the *tabla*s with their double-layered leather tops, which she used
for her students. There were low sofas, wicker stools and tables strewn
across the room. The anti-macassars and cushion covers on the sofas,
embroidered by Sunanda's mother, still retained their gloss.

Sunanda usually lit a lamp and incense every evening before she sat
down for her practice. As she unlocked the door, the captive scent of
years filled her nostrils. The smell of the *Agaru* scent wafted through the
room. She lit the tall, multi-layered brass lamp before the marble image
of the Muse. She switched off the electric light. In the faint, flickering
glow of the brass lamps, the room was transformed into the ethereal
abode of the Gandharvas. Sunanda sat cross-legged on the floor before
her Saraswati, Nibaran Goswami's sitar in her hands. Were those the
faint echoes of her father's *pakhawaj*? Or just his blessings? Was that the
flawless *barhat*, the spell-binding *tarparan* of her guru? Sunanda sat cross-
legged before the Muse in the lamplight, Nibaran Goswami's sitar in

her hand, amidst the shadows of the dimly lit room. Her fingers armed with the *mejrap,* skimmed over the silvery strings of her sitar. She chose *Raga Desh*, her guruji's chosen one, as expressive on the sitar as he was on the *surbahar*. His fingers would move swiftly tracing the course of the Raga from *alaap* to *jor*, like a swimmer darting across the torrents and eddies of the swirling waves and rising triumphantly to the surface. Such was the maestro's skill that it was like a fairy tale, a dream come true. It was his practice to sit before the portrait of his own guru, with his veena in his hand. He avoided playing at conferences. Sitting before a select group of students and music lovers, he would say,

'Today, my veena's strains will bring tears to your eyes, my children. My music will make you sob your hearts out.'

Lost in the past, Sunanda's fingers moved absently from Raga to Raga, from the soul stirring strains of Desh and Tilak-kamod to the haunting, rural cries of Brindavani Sarang. She played on, losing all count of time, unaware of what she was doing. This had been happening over the last few months, or was it years? At last, she laid down her sitar and folded her hands in mute appeal before her instruments, before her Saraswati, her marble image of unblemished purity,

'I can no longer continue in this way,' she thought, 'I must renounce the world! Forgive me if you can.'

Perhaps, her lost essence of music would come back to her in the beautiful environment of Madhurashram, with its haunting smell of the *sandhya malati* blooms and the stars raining down from the skies into her eyes. Perhaps, she had lost it forever. If so, so be it. Perhaps, she would achieve divine grace through a path other than her music? She was desperate to find the path that lay ahead.

Sunanda pushed open the wicker gate and stepped into the Madhurashram hermitage. A climbing vine of twinkling blue flowers trailed like a welcome arch over the gate. The atmosphere of the ashram lived up to its name. In the sprawling gardens within, were orchards and flower beds and kitchen gardens. No sound other than the ceaseless chirping of birds disturbed its tranquillity, no sound either of man or machine. Sunanda came here at least once every year to rejuvenate herself.

Her student, Mamataben, had introduced her to this place ten or eleven years ago, at a time when Sunanda's parched soul longed for the nectar of peace. It was immediately after her father's death. Mamata, seeing her plight, took on the role of mentor. Mamata's family members were all disciples of Thakur Siddhadas. And his blessings had given her the first taste of peace after a long, long time.

Mamataben was also responsible for introducing her to Desai. As Sunanda grew firm in her resolve to retreat to Madhurashram permanently, her share of the house hung like a millstone round her neck. The house was situated on a small plot, hardly 800 cubits square. No promoter could think of putting up a concrete colossus of flats on a plot this size. No one wanted to buy it for personal use either, wedged uncomfortably as it was between those of the other two share holders. With real estate prices soaring sky high, who would be interested in investing crores on a disputed plot like this one? At such a time of distress, Mamata had come to her rescue. Desai was a millionaire industrialist, committed to social service. This small house would be ideal for his plans of a social service centre with a primary health care clinic, a family planning and child welfare unit. The drawing room could be partitioned for the purpose. He liked the house, clinched the deal and paid her a handsome price.

All subsequent arrangements were made by Mamata and her husband. The deal included the furniture—her mother's bedroom set, the sofa set, the chest of drawers, the show case full of dolls and curios, the mirror with its ornamental frame, the chandelier, the wall lamps— just about everything that was part of Sunanda's house. The marble Saraswati would be a gift to Mamata, the cane and paper one, Desai had chosen for his own drawing room. Even after the deal was struck, Desai generously allowed the house to remain as it was during the last days of Sunanda's stay in Calcutta. None of the neighbours knew anything about the sale.

Staring at the crack in the wall in the puja room and the stain on the left side wall of her bedroom, where water had seeped through, Sunanda heaved a sigh of relief. That roof had been converted into a half-terrace and later fitted with tiles, but there had been no let-up in the leakage of water. She realized it was all beyond the powers of a lone woman to handle. It made Sunanda cry out in despair in the middle of the night. Well, she was free from all that. A white saree with a red border and a sitar in her hand. What a perfect picture of bliss!

Madhurashram seemed more tranquil than ever before. Her *gurubhai,* Dhananjay, had arranged the same room she always occupied on her annual visits. It was a long and narrow room, around 6 feet by 12 feet, with a low door, painted green. Opposite that was a window with four shutters, which overlooked the garden, which was known as the honey-garden because bee-keeping was done here. There was a low bed with hard bedding in the room. The only other furniture was a wooden stool on which she could keep her trunks and suitcases. There was an earthen pitcher of water on four bricks, containing the water from the deep tube well of the ashram. Her suitcases would have to double up as a writing desk and her sitar would share the cot with her. Sunanda washed her hands and feet at the tube well outside her room and wiped her feet on the doormat. She poured herself a glass of water from the earthen pitcher. It was like the nectar of the gods! Dhananjay reminded her that if she wished to meet the Thakur, it should be done now.

She changed into a white Begumpuri saree with a red border and went off with Dhananjay to see Thakur Siddhadas. High overhead, the intense blue sky, its vastness, its profundity was like an anodyne to the empty cage of her heart. She touched her guru's feet and they smiled at each other.

'Are you happy, my child?' He asked of her. The radiance on her face was his answer.

Thakur Siddhadas hardly stirred out of his room on the eastern side of the ashram, except at dawn and dusk when he took a walk through the hermitage garden. The rest of the day he would be deep in meditation, sitting cross-legged on his prayer mat. Sunanda usually met him at dawn in the garden, when she went for her morning walk. But he would be absorbed in his thoughts and scarcely spoke to anyone at that hour, walking briskly through the garden. Looking at him one could hardly discern any trace of his recent illness, which had confined him to his bed.

Life at the ashram was stern, austere and pure, almost reminiscent of the Vedic age. Sunanda always got the feeling that if you strained your senses, mythology could come to life here, so pure and serene was the environment. You would almost hear the faint echoes of Vedic chanting or detect the lingering fragrance of ancient Yajnas, even catch a glimpse of the sages, Jamadagni, Swetaketu, Nachiketa or Upamanyu meditating in some remote corner of the forest.

Strangely, the nights in the ashram seemed to transport her into the mysterious world of the Arabian Nights. Under the clear, star-studded sky, Sunanda seemed to hear the rustle of silk trousers of the dancing girls, embroidered with sequins, their veils draped across the night sky, the wild jingle of their dancing bells, abruptly silenced by the sharp, staccato order, 'Khamosh!' The suppressed sound of trapped musical instruments reached out to her from the surrounding air and the sky like the twanging of a loom.

Sunanda grew increasingly restless. She gave up her early morning walks. Her bedding remained rolled up on the cot. She placed a freshly plucked rose on the silver plate, and offered obeisance to her invisible Muse. Yet, as her mejrap trailed across the sitar strings to the *alaap* in Raga Lalit, starting from the middle octave, the strings did not respond to her touch. They were out of tune. She screwed up the knobs to tune the sitar and listened to the familiar hum from within the heart of the gourd. She began the *alaap* again, but the notes failed to obey, the instrument fell out of tune. Finally, the tautened strings snapped of their own accord and coiled like hissing serpents around her helpless fingers.

During the evening meditation session in her Guru's chamber, Sunanda rose noiselessly from the prayer mat and returned, unnoticed by the other disciples sitting in rows, deep in silent prayer. But she felt as if a pair of raised eyebrows followed her out of the chamber. The torn strings of her sitar had pierced her heart.

A letter from a colleague told her how her decision to renounce the world of music was regretted and if that colleague had been around, she could have prevented it, though why she said so was unclear. Was Sunanda so infirm that she could not make her own choices? Sunanda could not sleep at night. She allowed her uneasy mind to merge into the vastness of the azure sky—a sense of space such as she had never experienced in her house in the narrow lane of the congested old city. But try as she might, she could not focus her attention as her fingers travelled over the strings.

Three months later the Thakur sent for her in the privacy of his chamber,

'Are your religious rituals taking up too much of your time, my child?'

Sunanda remained silent.

'I don't hear the sound of your sitar?'

'I have stopped playing the sitar,' she confessed.

He was stunned,

'Do you no longer experience the need? A day may come when music will no longer be needed as your intermediate path to salvation. Your soul will instinctively reverberate with the music of the Universe.'

'I have not experienced such a call,' said Sunanda in a dull voice. And then blurted out, 'My fingers seem paralysed. They no longer move of their own accord on the strings. I am forgetting everything. My heart is parched. Everything seems so bitter.' Tears poured down uncontrollably. 'Forgive me, my Master, nothing appeals to me any more, everything seems turned to poison.'

Siddhadas said to her,

'Forgive you? It is I who should beg your forgiveness. I have failed to guide you on to the correct path. My people tell me you have stopped eating and have given up your morning walks. You do not join us for the sessions of meditation. Your mind is not at peace. Be patient, my child, Your hour of deliverance will come. This ashram will never confine you against your will. You must go wherever you find peace. That is God's will.'

That night, Sunanda tossed and turned on her cot and finally drifted off into an uneasy sleep. She dreamt that she was sitting on the seashore, playing her veena. The huge instrument, with its twin domes was slipping down the silken pleats of her saree. She changed into a starched cotton saree. She tried a complex set of notes spanning several scales, but try as she might, she could not control it. The stubborn veena merely wailed its angry protest like a frog in frenzy. Her fingers slipped off the strings. She awoke with a start, her body bathed in cold sweat. She looked around. Where was her veena, her *surbahar*? She had not brought them with her to the ashram. With the edge of her saree, she wiped the dust from the *sitar* and clenched her teeth in despair.

In the wee hours of the morning, she drifted off again into an uneasy sleep. Again, she dreamt the same dream. She was bobbing up and down on a turbulent ocean, her veena slipping from her hand. She screamed and cried out in her sleep. Someone was knocking frantically on the door and rattling the knob. Sunanda opened the door. It was Mamatha.

'How it poured all night! But when I came here, I found that the water had receded from the sand and it was all so beautiful.' Mamatha chattered on, and then, 'What's the matter? Have you been crying Sunanda-di?' Mamatha asked in surprise.

Sunanda brushed away her tears,

'What a surprise, Mamatha? Have you brought my veena?'

'Oh, that's a long story,' said Mamatha, 'why only the veena, I should probably have carried your whole house with me on my shoulders.'

She sat down. 'I hope you won't be upset, Sunanda-di, but Desai is unwilling to have your house. He claims it is haunted. Before starting work on the re-modelling, Desai and Joshi wanted to stay for a few days in that beautiful bedroom of yours. They claim they kept hearing strains of music all night.'

'How absurd,' said the bewildered Sunanda, 'and what instrument did they hear?'

'What do they know of music, to be able to differentiate between one instrument and another? They kept hearing all sorts of music every time they drifted off to sleep. It faded away as they woke up.'

'And why was that?' Sunanda grabbed Mamatha's hands.

'For no particular reason, other than the sheer beauty of the room. Even a tough businessman like Desai didn't have the heart to dismantle the furniture. He kept putting it off.'

'So, my room is even now as it used to be. Is that what you are saying?' queried Sunanda.

'Not only your room. The whole house is exactly as it used to be...every last article of furniture in every room.'

Sunanda dashed out of the room calling out to Dhananjay. He asked what she wanted.

'I'm leaving for Calcutta by train today. Please see that my musical instruments are carefully packed and loaded onto the train.'

Siddhadas Thakur was walking towards his room over the wet grass when Sunanda dashed across to him like a meteor over a dark sky,

'Thakur, I'm going home!'

Smiling benignly at her, the Thakur raised his right hand in benediction,

'May you find peace at last, my child,' he said.

The house was empty, totally empty. No, that was not quite true. There was her Muse, colourless, yet the confluence of all colour. At her feet, the rivers of the many branches of knowledge and music merged into the vast ocean and a thousand others sprang. She laid down her sitar and picked up her veena. Her Guruji's final lessons to her had been on this instrument. My daughter, he would say, just as the turbulent rivers find their home in the sea, the notes of the veena are like the ocean, like the profound stream. The veena is an instrument which one should struggle to arrive at. Sunanda had arrived. Sunanda played on as if in a trance, notes she had dreamt of. Her fingers plunged into its depths, the music was an ecstasy mingled with pain.

But yet her fingers could not attain the complex threads of the notes. Sunanda struggled on, she wove webs of melody, they remained incomplete, while the shadows gathered in the courtyard outside the open door. Still the climax eluded her. The trapped music wailed for the release of expression. She began to sweat, the trapped music like an iron fist around her chest. Sweat like tears, like the blood of her body in its lifelong struggle for expression, poured thick and heavy, down her body.

She heard those familiar footsteps. And then saw her Guruji, gently chiding her for the notes that had slipped her fingers. He captured the elusive notes and brought them back and they slipped into her fingers from the abyss of memory. Sunanda was swept along on a tide of ecstasy, the veena with its twin domes thrilled to her touch. The floodgates of memory had released the trapped music. Her guruji had departed as silently as he had come,

'Your seat of music, my daughter, this is your seat of meditation, your prayer mat. It will never abandon you even if you turn aside.'

And he was gone, his footsteps retreating. She had not even offered him the betel leaves.

The grandfather clock on the wall chimed the hour. It was 2 a.m. Sunanda awoke from her trance. She carefully laid down her veena and stood up. Was it indeed her Guruji who had come at this late hour? And she had sent him away without even his favourite *paan*? Where was he? She came to the open doorway. No sign of anyone in the courtyard outside, the neem tree flooded with the light of the full moon. Her Guruji had passed away in Kashi, three years after her father's death.

Sunanda quickly shut the door and picked up her veena again. This time her fingers found the perfect note, the disobedient chords fell in to tune. Her distant dreams were coming to life. She spiralled higher and higher into the world of sound, effortlessly picking up more and more expansive, more and more complex notes, striking deeper and deeper into the essential core of human existence, where man-made boundaries fade away. Was her Guruji's appearance a mere hallucination? Sunanda was too engrossed to wonder.

Sunanda was on her seat, her own dearly won seat. There were the pearly white shells on a deep blue sea, this the seat of the seven-year-old child, whose tiny fingers plucked music from the veena like a three-stringed harp, reproducing the precise notes of a Roshanara Bai or a Kesar Bai, exactly as she had heard on a gramophone record. Seated before her pristine, white Muse, Sunanda played on all night with her head bent, moving closer and closer to the distant call of the sea of the Infinite. The strings of the sitar lying beside her, reverberated in tune. The doors of the glass cases were open, the *surbahar*, the *tanpura* emitted a variety of notes.

Who awaited her on the other side of this ocean of sound? Her fingers on the string raised the query again and again. The answer was, music. Wave after wave of music, torrent after torrent, vast as the ocean, infinite as the sky. Who could surmount it? May the pollen of my music, sacrosanct as the dust of Brindavan be smeared on my body, she said. I float upon the sea of melody. I meditate upon its seat. My heart is the eternal lamp of its harmony.

Bengali original: 'Aashon'
Translated by Saumitra Chakravarty

The Indir Thakuruns

Suchitra Bhattacharya

THE SCREAM JOLTED SUPREETI FROM HER SLEEP JUST BEFORE DAWN. JUST that one scream from Indumati. There was nothing unusual about that. These intermittent screams had become a part of Indumati's recent illness. You could not even call it a scream, it was more of a piercing cry. Supreeti woke up with a start and sat bolt upright in bed, the last traces of her dream rudely shattered. It took her a while to comprehend what had happened. She could still feel her heart beating wildly. She shut her eyes and sat still for a while, trying hard to control herself. After some time the pounding in her chest subsided. Fear gave way to wonder and then to irritation. By then her heartbeats were back to normal.

This was a new symptom Indumati had developed after her last stay in hospital. She lingered on against all odds, in the terminal stages of liver cancer. Though the blood seeped relentlessly out of her body day after day and the strong medication kept her drowsy and speechless, the intermittent screaming continued. God alone knew where she found the strength for those ear-piercing wails,

'Oh, my dears, take me home just this once! Oh Subbo, just once...!'

She seemed to be addressing her nephews and her niece each time, individually by name. Then she would subside into her near-comatose state. Day and night these heart-rending cries could be heard. The inmates of this home listened. Oh! The poor, frail, helpless thing, she'd been here from the very beginning, practically one of the first inmates! How could they have the heart to be angry with her? She had lost her vision and hearing long ago, now even her mental faculties were fast fading. She could hardly recognize anybody any more. Her whole body had knotted itself up into a small, pathetic bundle, the brown skin hanging loosely in folds around the protruding bones and the corded veins. Being toothless, her cheeks had retreated inwards, leaving two enormous craters on either side. Spikes of white hair stood out on her head like fields of '*kash*' flowers. Her eyes, yellow as an old nanny goat's, were rimmed with pus. Who would not have pity on such a creature? Naturally, all the old women were volunteering their services, taking turns to change her sheets and rubbercloth. The office had hired a day *ayah* to take care of Indumati, but she hardly did anything for her. The woman was irresponsible and stayed away every now and then. So, it was the old women in the room who had to take care to feed her and give her her medicines on time.

A thin, shrivelled hand would reach out to grasp another frail and emaciated one.

'Come hold my hand, hold it tight. That's right, come now, slowly...! That's it.'

And the old woman would be propped up, though her weak body trembled violently and her yellow eyes were fixed and vacant.

Anurupa heaved a deep sigh,

'Poor thing. What a state she has been reduced to! Even Death seems to have forsaken her.'

'Death will come at its own time, Didi,' said Charulata pensively. 'Meanwhile, she has to suffer. It's all her *karma,* who can prevent it?'

'I believe her nephews are bearing the cost of her treatment.'

'Yes. There ends their responsibility.'

'What bad luck! Couldn't they have taken her home for these last few days at least? Isn't this the Pishi who had brought them all up?'

'What are you saying? Didn't you hear what the doctor said, Didi? The old woman may linger on in this condition for anything between 7 days and 7 months. Which nephew would want to take on this burden after having cast her off once?'

A shiver ran down Supreeti's spine at her own words. Anurupa had lapsed into silence. Charulata's ancient cheeks trembled, the loose skin flapping over toothless gums in agitation. A chill descended over the room.

A sound made Supreeti prick up her ears. Had anyone else been awakened? Anurupa, Pratima or Charulata? Perhaps. Hardly anyone was capable of enjoying a good night's sleep at this age.

Supreeti realized that her body was drenched in sweat. She wiped her neck and shoulders with the edge of her saree. The only fan in the room was a good distance away from her bed, nearer Anurupa and Pratima. Hardly any air percolated through the rows of mosquito nets. She looked absent-mindedly at the window on her left, a south-facing one. The one directly behind her faced the east. Time, on this Bhadra night, seemed to stand still, it was so hot and sultry. Supreeti switched on the tiny torch she kept under the pillow. Her throat and tongue were parched, she needed a drink of water. She was suffering from bouts of acidity these days. Was that what made her throat so dry? Or, was it Indumati's cry? Or, that dream of hers?

It was, indeed, a strange dream! She had not quite been able to identify the golden cottage with the lush green garden, or was it blue? The grass was blue with tiny flowers. Rows of marigolds and roses, and *champaka* trees bordered the compound wall. On one side there was a dense undergrowth of the *kalachita* and the *rangabaran* that bloomed so profusely. Was it Chotku's house, or Bablu's? But that was impossible. The *kalachita* and the *rangabaran* were memories from a distant past when Supreeti wore her hair in thick braids coiled around her head.

'Tha..amm..aaa!'

Was that her little grandson, hiding amidst the *kalachita* creepers? Or, was it behind the rose bush and the marigold plants, or the golden cottage? Panting and gasping, Supreeti groped in search of the child playing hide and seek with her,

'Bumba, where are you?'

'Here I am.'

Her grandson ran to her and hid his face in her lap...a child with soft, silky hair, plump cheeks and bright, glistening eyes.

'Thamma, I've come to take you home!'

As she watched, the child's face grew older and older till it was transformed in a jiffy, into that of a young man. Supreeti shivered. Whom did this face remind her of? Bablu, her son, or Bablu's father? In her dream, her husband was asking her whether she was happy in the new house. She stretched out her hand towards him. Immediately, the face transformed itself into that of Bablu,

'I don't think Bombay suits you, Ma. It might be a good idea to go and spend some time with Chotku.'

'But it was Chotku who sent me to you. He is a senior officer and has to socialize a lot. My presence in the house is very awkward for them.'

Supreeti pushed aside her mosquito net with a jerk. At which point of her dream did Indumati utter her cry? When she was talking to Bablu, or later, when she was running on the blue grass in the blue light holding her grandson's hand? She stood near the window and clenched her right fist. The feel of her grandson's touch was even now with her. It was years since she had seen him. She rested her forehead against the window. The darkness outside and inside was almost impenetrable, but there is always a kind of light within the darkness. Or maybe, that's because your eyes slowly get accustomed to it. She could discern the outline of the neem tree in the compound. The shaggy head of the tree had a ghostly presence in the darkness, like one's ancestors. The moon had set, and perhaps that was why the darkness was so profound, the sky black and shadowy. As she continued to sit there, she felt a gentle breeze stirring outside. The earth was cooling down at last. The sultriness was beginning to subside, bringing some relief to her exhausted body. What scents did the breeze carry along with it? Did it bring with it the touch of her Bablu or her Bumba from the Arabian Sea shore of Bombay? Or, had it trailed its soothing fingers on Chotku's infant daughter in the officer's quarters at Burnpur? Supreeti closed her eyes. The salt air of the faraway Arabian Sea was filling her eyes with salt tears. Her mind was becoming moist and sentimental. Oh, God, she thought, let Indumati not utter her piercing cry now! Not at this moment when the darkness was slowly lifting over the eastern horizon.

'Indu-di, just raise your head a bit...let me bathe it for you. Indu-di, can you hear me?'

There was no response. Indumati was lying fast asleep in her foetus-like position.

Anurupa pulled up a stool and sat down beside the sick woman. She herself was gasping with the effort of having carried half a bucket of water from the bathroom. She became tired so easily these days. Just at this moment, the task of lifting the old woman and bathing her head for her, was proving too much for Anurupa. But she was left with no choice. It was already 8.30 in the morning and the ayah had not turned up, as usual. Anurupa turned around and glanced at Pratima. She was busy folding her clothes and putting them away in the trunk. Anurupa decided to do without that arrogant woman's help. She would be sure to deliver a lengthy lecture on the irresponsibility of hospitals which should, in fact, be taking care of her, or express her irritation about the screams that rent the room all day. Anurupa turned her head away.

The long dormitory was now home to five old women. Each was allotted a high iron cot, a small wooden cupboard, a tiny store cupboard, a stool and a small space bordering it all. Within these confines, each woman had built up her own household in her own individual manner. Some had set up rows of gods and goddesses on a wooden plank below their beds. Photographs of gurus had been established on top of the cupboard. Imaginary walls sprang up to demarcate the boundaries of each little household, complete with pictures of Kali and Krishna, Mahadev or Balgopal, and of distant but cherished relatives. Charulata was next to Supreeti with Pratima beside her. Pratima's neighbour was Anurupa and Indumati was closest to the wall at the end of the room.

Anurupa left the room and came out onto the balcony. She leaned over to see whether she could catch sight of a familiar face, whom she could summon to help with the bathing. Not a soul was in sight. Not a sound from the first floor rooms. Yet, just a few minutes ago the building was abuzz with early morning activity. The prayer room bells were summoning the trembling voices to the chanting, punctuated by coughs and wheezes and bursts of conversation. The women, including Supreeti and Charulata, had completed their morning's rituals and had perhaps assembled in the kitchen to cut and peel vegetables, clean the rice and the lentils, trying to play at housekeeping to keep themselves busy. They talked and argued and squabbled among themselves. After that it would be lunchtime followed by a short nap. At dusk, they went down to the office room, to search for the day's mail. Sometimes there was a visitor for one of them. After that, again the endless rounds of talk and gossip, a session of choric chanting from the Upanishads or the *Bhagavad Gita*. Some of them listened to music or watched a dance or drama programme on television. Once in a blue moon, a Sadhu Maharaj would visit them and chant the names of gods.

Anurupa sat down on the balcony, on the arm-chair next to the wall. Her hips were aching. The ayah had absented herself as usual. Someone should inform the office. She had no energy left to go downstairs. And

Three Sides of Life

no one would come up before 10 or 10.30 at the very least. If there was nothing better to do, some of them would take a stroll in the garden. Those who found the steps difficult to manage, would come up only after lunch. That still left the problem of bathing Indu-di's head unsolved. Even if you left the arrogant Pratima out, what about Supreeti or Charulata? No concern at all for Indu-di?

Why blame these inmates when their own kith and kin had forsaken them all a long while ago? Anurupa drew a long deep breath. Her own son Manik had told her that his two-roomed shack was hardly enough for his own family, with the three children needing space to study. There was no place for a visitor. He had requested her to bear with them for a while. Her son had paid the money for Anurupa's old age home from his father's fixed deposit. He had promised to take her home the moment he was able to construct a third room with a loan from the office.

That was five years ago. Would the loan ever come? It was so long since she had slept on her own bed at home. She remembered the guava sapling she had bought at the annual *Rath Yatra* fair. She had planted it in the courtyard of her house, it was just beginning to bear fruit when she left home. She remembered the crack in the courtyard that had appeared after her husband's death. Had Manik found the money to repair it? Would she ever see her son again?

A gentle hand on her shoulder brought involuntary tears rolling down her cheeks.

'What's wrong Anu-di? Why are you sitting here all by yourself and shedding tears?'

Anurupa sat up straight. She wiped her eyes with the edge of her saree. She hesitated to confide in her, for it was none other than the haughty Pratima, who had come out to stand beside her.

'No, I'm not crying,' she said, 'just sitting here for a while. Is Indu-di still asleep?'

'She's in her usual state.'

'It would be better if her head could be bathed, it seems to bring down the screams.'

'I have done the job,' said Pratima, her hand on Anurupa's shoulder, perhaps for the first time in the many years they had been together. 'Come, get up. There is no point in sitting here and making yourself miserable, is there?'

Anurupa gulped, 'Not miserable, just wondering what we should do, the ayah's absent again.'

'You should have asked for my help.' said Pratima, 'Why stand on your pride? And what were those tears for?'

They went into the room together.

'For no one, my dear, except my cursed destiny,' Anurupa's voice cracked again, the words choking in her throat.

'You are too sentimental, that is why these tears flow so readily.' Pratima was her normal self again. 'How many times have I told you that when your time is up in the scheme of things, you have to vacate your station in life. Your son must have his own life with his own family, his wife and children. You have no place in that little circle.'

How many times had Anurupa listened to these words? How many times had this same habit of offering unsolicited advice caused a serious rift between the two? Today, however, these words of wisdom did not sound so officious. Neither did they provoke the usual retort.

'You're different,' said Anurupa listlessly, 'you're much stronger. You've relinquished your position in the household of your own accord.'

Pratima let that pass. No doubt, she had had the strength of mind to take the bold step on her own. As soon as her husband died, she herself put forth the proposal, before she could be discarded. She had asked her sons to make the necessary arrangements to send her to a home with the money she had in the bank. Her sons had turned a deaf ear at first. Where was the question of a home, when they were there to look after her? Pratima persisted, she even threatened a hunger strike. Her daughters-in-law had been apprehensive. What childishness! What would people say? Pratima smiled,

'You should not heed what others say. Everyone is born to occupy a particular niche in the scheme of things. When your time is up, you must learn to surrender that place to others. For example, when I was a little girl, my place was with my parents. From there, to my in-laws...another station in life...and then onwards to my own household to rear my children. My children grew up, they got married, all of them had their own independent households. When his time was up, your father-in-law also departed, giving up his place in life. Now, it is my time to give up mine.'

Her daughters had broken down, 'As long as we are there, you can't go anywhere, Ma, and that's final,' they sobbed.

The smile vanished from Pratima's face. Every human being was essentially alone in this world, caught up in an island of her own, within her own heart. The stark reality of this dawned upon every mother, a little late perhaps, but as her children grew up and age overcame her, it came to her with great intensity. Her daughters were too young to understand. She tried a different approach,

'God only knows how many more years I may have to linger on in this world. Before I grow too incapacitated and a burden to all of you, let me go. That way I will have time to get accustomed to my new environment.'

When she returned to the dormitory, she found Anurupa folding her clothes in silence. The white sarees with narrow borders, the white blouses, part of the widow's weeds she wore, all of which she hung up on the plastic rope.

Pratima went back to her own place. At sixty-five, her frame was yet tall and straight. Her dentures gave her face a youthful look. The greying hair she wore coiled at the nape of her neck was thick and long. Her complexion was the colour of ripening wheat. She was particularly neat about her attire. Strong as she was, it was difficult to explain the sense of weariness overcoming her today.

Outside it was growing hot and sultry, with no hint of rain, though the sky was overcast. Beads of sweat gathered on her brow, even under the fan. Exhausted, Pratima gave in, and sank down upon her bed.

Suddenly, a crow cawed harshly from the branches of the neem tree outside. It shattered Indumati's stupor,

'Oh, take me home...just once...Oh Choto Khuki..!' It was not a cry, only a pathetic plea. The bent and broken body shuddered violently and was still. Pratima covered her eyes with her left hand. As the darkness descended, she began to see that river...the vast, silvery river. The little boat sped across the mighty river, causing ripples on either side, ripples that spread in waves to the shore. The boat left marks of its passage on the surface. Just for a few moments and then all was calm again, all traces of its voyage erased. Was it a dream, or a reality...this boat? If it was a reality, surely, surely someone would have come to persuade her, indeed to force her, to return home? A flush suffused Pratima's fair face. It was an illusion. Only the vast river was real, not the boat.

Anupama was looking down at her in astonishment. Pratima was not one to be found lounging in bed at midday. What was wrong? She ventured a little closer,

'Is anything amiss, Pratima? Are you not feeling well?'

'No, nothing.' Pratima sat up.

'Is everything alright with your family? I don't recall having seen your children coming for a visit for quite some time now.'

After a long, uneasy pause, Pratima laughed, 'People in exile should not expect visitors, Anu-di!'

The doctor laid a finger on Indumati's pulse.

'How long has she been like this?'

He was standing at Indumati's bedside, surrounded by all the women of the home. From all the floors. Each forehead was a maze of a thousand creases, so anxiety could hardly put its fresh stamp there anymore. Or at least, none that could be made out.

The doctor was addressing the girl from the office, but it was Pratima who answered,

'Even this morning we heard her screaming a few times...you know the way she keeps calling out. We bathed her forehead. Then in the afternoon...'

The doctor put his stethoscope on the bony chest and listened to the beats of Indumati's heart.

'Where is Mrs Dasgupta?'

Mrs Dasgupta was the manager of this home, the official guardian of forty-seven old women. She had not accompanied the doctor upstairs. The young secretary offered to fetch her. The doctor shook his head. With a sigh, he put his stethoscope back into his bag. He went down the stairs accompanied by the secretary, followed in silence by Supreeti and Pratima and all the ladies. At the head of the stairs, Supreeti stopped him,

'What is it, Doctor Babu? Is she...?'

The doctor looked around. What could he say? There was an Indumati reflected in every face, Indumati's heartbeats fluttering in every chest. He cleared his throat awkwardly. Turning to the young secretary, he murmured,

'It may be a matter of minutes now. Or, even hours. Does she have any children?'

'No, only nephews and nieces.'

'Well, let me talk it over with Mrs Dasgupta. It's better if she can send for them. Also, we need an oxygen cylinder immediately.'

The doctor went down the stairs. Even after he crossed the stairs and entered the office room, the women continued their silent meeting on the balcony. Unconsciously each was searching the other's face. Madhobilata and Suroma, both ground floor residents sank into the chairs next to the balustrade. The effort of climbing the stairs had been too much for their arthritic, old limbs.

Charulata invited them to their own dormitory to rest and stretch out for a while on her bed.

'No my dear, I think we'd better get back to ours. We've been so worried about Indu-di all day.'

'Yes, she really did give us a fright,' said Charulata, nodding her head, 'the way her eyes rolled over and her chest began to heave. I thought she was gone.'

'Charu-di, perhaps you had better come down with us and stretch out a bit. These days you don't even get proper sleep at night.'

Charulata heaved a deep sigh, 'No...o, I think I'd better get back to my own room,' she said pensively.

Sleep had indeed become a long forgotten luxury. The night would be spent in a daze, wisps of memories trailing through the long drawn-out hours of darkness. So many memories tucked away in that bosom. Memories came and went. Increasingly, Charulata was getting confused about the past, unable to fix dates. For instance, last night she just could not ascertain the year of her husband's death, try as she might. Was it the year of the war with Pakistan? Or, the one with China? What she did remember, however, was that her daughter Rini was a child at the time, a mere schoolgirl. How old would Rini be today? Thirty-five? Or, thirty? She could not remember. She only remembered the hardship, the struggle to bring up the child. She had taken up orders for stitching and preparing pickles and *boris*. Her brothers had helped her. Her husband's younger brother had given them shelter. Rini was a late arrival and consequently a pampered child, a fatherless child, brought up with great difficulty. Charulata had been lucky to get a good match for her. At last, she did not have to worry about finances any more.

The money came in regularly. They came to visit her, her only daughter and her son-in-law and pressed a little something into her hand each time. Still, the ache refused to go away from the frail, old bosom. She would have dearly loved to fondle her grandson and hold him in her arms, give him an oil bath and pat him to sleep on the mustard-seed pillow with a lullaby. Well, that dream would never be realized now. She could never bring herself to request her daughter to take her home with them. There was no point in blaming Indumati's nephews and nieces if one's own daughter, brought up with such hardship and struggle, did not care to understand a mother's secret pain and desire, was there?

The crowd had thinned out on the balcony. One by one the old ladies had gone back to their rooms. Only the last rays of the setting sun lit up the now-empty space. Charulata plodded back to the room to join the others, each lost in her own thoughts. In spite of the daylight outside the window, the room was gloomy and still. In the darkest, gloomiest corner lay Indumati's inert body, her toothless gums wide open, exposing the abyss within. The swollen eyelids quivered. Her limbs had bloated heavily in the last few hours. At a glance she appeared to be dead. Only the laboured rise and fall of the bony chest gave evidence that Indir Thakurun was still there.

That was the day before yesterday. She was there yesterday, certainly there last evening as well. But in the stillness of the night she had quietly slipped away. None of her roommates knew when. Neither Supreeti, nor Charulata, nor Pratima or Anurupa.

And now, they were all lined up on the balcony, gazing dry-eyed at the scene below. At last, her nephews and niece had arrived to take her back. Indumati had been dressed up in a new saree...her first, in a long, long time. She now lay bedecked with flowers. The ladies on the balcony stood up straight. Dressed in her floral ornaments Indumati was entering her bridal chamber, covered with flowers, her glass bridal chamber atop the shiny black hearse. Her nephew sprinkled a bottle of scent on her body. Her niece lit a bunch of joss sticks and wiped away a tear with her handkerchief.

There was a pounding in Supreeti's chest. Anurupa leaned over for a last glimpse of Indumati's face. But the hearse was carrying her away beyond their faded line of vision, through the gates of the old age home. Like a queen, Indumati was going home at last. As the hearse rounded the corner, Charulata lifted her hands to her forehead in prayer, 'Durga, Durga!' she said. Instinctively, the others followed suit,

'May she go home in peace at last.'

'Home?' muttered Pratima, trembling. Her voice shook. No one ventured a reply. With misted eyes the four old women stared vacantly at each other, unblinking, silent.

Bengali original: 'Indir Thakurunera'
Translated by Saumitra Chakravarty

Bonds

Suchitra Bhattacharya

C OMING HOME FROM THE MARKETPLACE, SUKHOMOY STOPPED SHORT
on the threshold. Two children were jumping up and down in
an uncontrollable manner in his beautiful drawing room on the
ground floor. Having left their mark on the intricately woven carpet,
they were now in the process of climbing onto the expensive sofa set
with their shoes on. The mosaic floor, once spotless, was now littered
with two or three kitbags, cheap water bottles and plastic carry bags.

Sukhomoy frowned.

'When did you turn up?'

Amal flashed a toothy smile, offering no direct response to the
question.

'Just dropped in. Let's suppose, just to look up you old folks. You're
all alone!'

Sukhomoy was not pleased. He had heard the tell-tale signs of the
confusion within from outside the door. A veritable frenzy! He could
hear the shrill cries of the two children shattering the serenity of his
hermitage-like mansion. But even then he had not realized that it was
Amal, that useless, vagabond of a nephew of his, come all the way from
Seuri, bag and baggage!

Sukhomoy took his shopping bag to the kitchen. The two naughty
little ones were taken aback for a moment and stopped to stare open-
mouthed at him. The elder was around five years old, the younger could
be three at the most. Measuring them up with a glance, Sukhomoy
settled himself under the fan. Turning to his nephew, he asked,

'And what news of you people? How's Mejdi? And Jamaibabu?'

'Oh, my parents? They are as people of their age should be…arthritis,
piles, palpitation, blood sugar, blood pressure….!' Amal put his feet up

and sat cross-legged on the sofa. 'For that matter, Mamima is not looking too good either.'

'Yes.' Sukhomoy's voice was grim. 'She's been having her breathing problem again for some time now. Last night it took quite a serious turn.'

In fact, the previous night had been terrible. Anurupa's proneness to coughs and colds had for the last eight years or so been accompanied by asthmatic wheezing. At first, her asthma had been seasonal, occurring during changes of seasons, now it was becoming chronic, no matter what the season. Last night, the regular heaviness in the chest had got progressively worse as the evening wore on till it erupted into a full blown attack after dinner. When her regular medicine failed to provide even symptomatic relief, Sukhomoy was forced to contact their house physician on the phone at midnight. But despite the fact that he regularly checked in on Anurupa, the man refused to oblige at such a late hour. Instead, he simply discharged his duties by rattling off the names of some medicines over the phone. Sukhomoy rushed to the day and night drug store at the nearby C.A. Market in the middle of the night. But even after the capsule was administered, Anurupa sat up all night. She heaved and gasped painfully, like the bellows of a furnace, with a pillow clutched to her chest, terrible sounds emerging from her throat. Each one was like a final death rattle. Sukhomoy hovered anxiously around, alternately propping his wife up on pillows and spraying medicines into her mouth at regular intervals. He hardly knew how the night dragged on.

'I'm very worried about your Mamima, Amal,' he confessed.

'Has our arrival inconvenienced you?' Amal asked bluntly, rocking his chair.

About to admit that it had, Sukhomoy checked himself with a bitter smile,

'No, this is your uncle's house. You have every right to be here.'

'Co—rrect! That's exactly what I was telling Manju. She's rather petrified after seeing Mamima's condition.'

'Manju? Oh, you mean your wife? Where is she?'

'With Mamima, in her room. She's been clinging on to her ever since we've landed up here.' With that, Amal bellowed for his wife, 'Ma—n—ju! Come down here and touch your Mama's feet.' And then, abruptly lowering his voice, he confessed, 'Actually, she's more intimidated by this mansion of yours, than by Mamima's illness. I told her that she shouldn't judge all our relatives by her own in-laws. She used to think all our relatives were paupers like them. I told her my uncle is a lord. Lives in a regular palace at Salt Lake. Let her see for herself now. Such a classy house, such first class furniture! Has she ever seen anything like this in her whole life? She? A naked, destitute schoolmaster's daughter? Ha!'

The two children had literally been devouring their father's chatter. Suddenly, the elder one clapped his hands,

'Wait till I tell Ma!'

Amal giggled,

'What'll you tell her?'

'That you've called my grandfather naked!'

'Yeah, go and tell her. Tell her with relish. And get lost from here. Five years old and ripe as a pear! Interrupting grown-ups' talk! Three kicks you'll get for that.'

Somewhat chastened by the shout, the child shrugged.

Sukhomoy could hardly contain his irritation. Amal had always been so uncultured…so uncivilized. That raucous laughter, that coarse, vulgar language, that unfettered tongue! No education, that was what was wrong with him. He'd barely scraped through school, and then it was curtains for Goddess Saraswati! His mother had had enough problems with this one. He had found himself a job in a cold storage company, but in what capacity, God only knew! From his sister's letters, Sukhomoy gathered that he did not earn much. And with that frugal income he had had the temerity to plunge into a love marriage and produce three offspring in quick succession! It was the proverbial last straw on the camel's back! One was literally a babe in arms, born during the Pujas. His sister had kept them informed about these developments.

Amal's wife was awkwardly descending the wooden staircase winding down to the drawing room. Coming closer, she pulled the corner of her saree over her head and bent down to touch Sukhomoy's feet.

He had never seen the girl before. Amal did make occasional visits, but he always came alone for not more than half a day or so. And Sukhomoy himself did not believe in visiting relatives. In fact he did not like to visit, not even for weddings or rice ceremonies. He hardly kept up his contact with them, beyond the occasional letter. Anything beyond that, he knew could only complicate matters. It could only lead to never ending requests for loans for daughters' weddings and sons to be fixed up in jobs…and all for what? Was it his fault that he was literally a giant among Lilliputs? Moreover, familial bonds meant the inevitable rounds of gossip and scandal. He hated all that.

But he was not entirely displeased with what he saw at first glance. The girl looked sober and humble enough. Dark and comely she was, but far too emaciated and frail. The child in her arms looked equally frail, possibly a victim of malnutrition.

Her head bent, Manju informed him that Mamima was asking for him. Sukhomoy cleared his throat, 'Is your Mamima able to lie down now or is she still sitting up?'

Manju shook her head, her reply inaudible to him. Half-way to the stairs, Sukhomoy turned to her,

'Have your children had their breakfast?' he asked.

'You don't worry yourself about all that, Mama,' Amal volunteered, 'they will fend for themselves.'

'Well, you people have also come a long way. You too must be hungry. Just go and see whether Pushpa is through with the breakfast preparations.'

At that Amal roared with laughter, 'Oh, our stomachs are like the proverbial Ravana's pyre...constantly on fire! If you're going to try to quench this flame, your pantry will be empty in a day. You just go ahead and see what Mamima wants of you.'

Sukhomoy glanced surreptitiously at the girl. She had covered her mouth with her saree and was giggling at her husband's wit.

By nine-thirty, it was already warming up on this morning of the month of Chaitra, the hot air swirling in gusts outside. Spring was on its way out, its last whisper rustling in the fronds of the stunted coconut palm outside the window. Fourteen years old to the day! Anurupa had planted it on the day of their house warming. Did the breeze whisper a message from the past? Maybe. Maybe not. Maybe, they swayed by themselves, leaving their echoes in Sukhomoy's heart.

Twenty-five years ago, Sukhomoy had purchased this plot of approximately 1,280 cubits. There was no greenery here then, only wide open space. The huge fish spawning ponds were just being filled up for the giant metropolis to expand and move itself slowly in this direction. The sand grains still glistened in the soil. Very few people lived here at that time. Only two buses plied between this place and the main township of Calcutta. It was so sparsely populated at the time, that people were hesitant to construct their houses here. But it had been a godsend to him. He had got it dirt-cheap if you considered today's land prices. And six years before he retired as General Manager of the South Eastern Railway, he began construction with the proceeds from the sale of his share of the ancestral property at Rampurhat. By then this satellite township was already bustling with activity. Houses were springing up, pretty as a picture, spacious roads, green boulevards. Though the traffic was getting denser by the day, the place still had its own serenity and charm. And he had built his own house in keeping with the elegance of the surroundings...the spacious drawing room, the huge dining area, the small family library-cum-study, kitchen, store room and servant's quarters on the ground floor. The first floor had three self-contained, one-roomed units for themselves and their two sons, Babin and Chottu, with a pleasant south and east-facing balcony. They had called it *Swapnateet!*

Anurupa was ecstatic when she saw the house. So were her two sons, Babin, already into Engineering at I.I.T. and Chottu, a student of Class 9. The two boys set about gardening with great enthusiasm, filling the flower-beds with seasonal flowers, their mother supervising the laying of the lawn all day. Babin and Chottu plastered the walls of their rooms with posters. Babin was a film buff, everywhere there was Amitabh in all moods and poses, Chottu, a sports enthusiast. His walls were a veritable sports gallery of Gavaskar, Vishwanath, Imran, Kapil Dev, MacEnroe, Bjorg, even the shaggy-headed Mario Kempes! With that the dream gallery of the parents was picture-perfect too—a kaleidoscope of hope and happiness and idyllic bliss of retired life.

It should be midnight now in Babin's USA and dawn would scarcely have broken over Chottu in London. Calcutta was already simmering in the sun.

'A penny for your thoughts?'

Sukhomoy turned with a start at the window and came to lay a hand on his wife's forehead.

'Nothing.'

'Why didn't you call me earlier?'

'I thought I should allow you to sleep a while.'

'Sleep? I only wish I could.' Anurupa closed her eyes wearily.

'Have you taken your capsule?'

'Yes.'

'Why did you send for me?'

'What did you get from the market today, the usual *rahu* fish?'

'No, I got *bata* fish today. But why do you ask?'

'What do you mean, why? Your nephew and his family are here, the girl for the first time, and should we serve them just *bata* fish curry and rice?' Anurupa was still wheezing a little, 'Shouldn't you have got some mutton for the children?'

'Oh, those kids will hardly get to have their share before that rhinoceros Amal devours it all?' laughed Sukhomoy. 'You leave all that to me. Just you be a good girl and try to get some rest. You're not getting out of bed today.'

Anurupa raised herself to a reclining position on the bed, 'Amal's wife seems to be a nice girl. A bit of a simpleton perhaps, but quite efficient, nevertheless. I could make out from her words that she takes good care of your Mejdi and Jamaibabu.'

'Well, who else but a simpleton would fall in love with that boy?'

'Not only in love, she seems to be quite in awe of him, too.'

'You seem to have garnered a lot from your half hour of conversation.' Sukhomoy smiled wrily. 'Perhaps, they told you why they have descended on us, lock, stock and barrel?'

'How can I ask them that if they don't choose to tell?'

Without another word, her husband picked up some important papers from the cupboard, electricity bills, prescriptions and the like, and some cash.

'In a way,' joked Anurupa, 'it's a good thing they have come. It'll give you a chance to play with these grandchildren of yours, it's an opportunity you don't often get.'

Babin had come down last year. Jumbo had got quite attached to his grandfather, clinging to him like a burr... 'Dadun, come and play with me...Dadun, I want to sleep with you...Dadun I want to lunch with you...from your plate...Dadun, come, let's go for a walk.'

Sukhomoy abruptly turned his face away, 'Have you seen the look of those children? Absolutely shabby, like peasants!'

'You shouldn't say such things about little children,' scolded Anurupa, 'after all, they are your grandchildren, too.'

The maid, Pushpa entered the room. She put down the breakfast tray on the bedside table—tea and toast for Sukhomoy and for Anurupa, a glass of Horlicks and some biscuits.

'Ma, would you like some *luchi*? Shall I fry a couple of them for you?'

'Have you served them?'

'They didn't wait to be served. They devoured the lot.'

Pushpa was the family's live-in maid. She had been with them for quite some time and had literally turned herself into a sort of blind man's cane for the elderly couple. The unexpected arrival of Amal's regiment had ruffled her feathers quite a bit. Still, her attitude appeared quite unseemly to Sukhomoy.

He turned to her with a sombre expression on his face, 'You just run down to the market, and get a couple of large chicken, some sweets and sweet curd. Have you given milk to the two children?'

Pushpa's face turned even more sulky, 'That woman helped herself to two large tumblers of milk with liberal helpings of sugar for the children. All that after a full breakfast of platefuls of *luchi* and curry!'

Anurupa smiled. 'What if she did? What are you getting so worked up about? They are our relatives after all. And you must refer to her as Bowdi, not "that woman".'

'I know that,' Pushpa snapped, 'just go down and see for yourself how they are splashing water and messing up the bathroom.' She took the money and went off.

Anurupa slowly sipped her Horlicks, 'You should have gone yourself. Maids cannot be trusted with these things.'

'Where do I have the time? Your mouth spray is exhausted, I'll have to check it out in B.D. Market, can't get it in Shanker Medicals. Today is the last date for payment of the electricity bill,' Sukhomoy bit into his toast. 'Must get aerogrammes from the post office, too.'

'Haven't you answered Chottu's letter yet? So many days since his letter arrived?'

'Hardly a day since the letter came and that too, two and a half months after I wrote to him.'

'They have just set up house in a new country! He has a new job…and what a responsible job it is…researching into diseases! Naturally, he finds it difficult to correspond.'

'Hardly new! Eight months have passed since he joined.'

'Eight months, after all is not such a long time. And what about your Babin? He's been there for eight years now. How many letters does he write in a year? Four or five at the most? That too, postscripts to his wife's letters.'

Sukhomoy was instantly sobered,

'For them everything tastes new. Always. Except their old parents.'

'Don't take it like that.' Anurupa finished her Horlicks and lay back on her pillows. 'Finish your tea. It is getting cold.'

He glanced at the door. Amal's elder son was peering at them from behind the curtain.

'Come in, my child,' Anurupa beckoned gently.

The child shook his head.

'Are you crying? Why? Has your mother scolded you? Oh dear, tears are literally rolling down your cheeks.' Anurupa's voice softened further.

The child wiped his eyes with the back of his hand and spoke up, 'What a bi—ig roof you have! My brother and I have crept upstairs and taken a look at it.'

'Really?' laughed Anurupa, 'And what else did you see? The flower pots?'

'Ye-es. And my brother's plucked one. A red flower.' The child pushed aside the curtain and came in. 'Which room have you kept for us, Thamma? My mother wanted to know. My baby sister has gone off to sleep, you see.'

Anurupa turned to her husband in embarrassment,

'Haven't you given them a room yet? Where will they put their things? Have Babin's room opened up for them? His double bed is large enough for their family.'

Babin's and Chottu's rooms remained locked throughout the year. Once a week Pushpa dusted them as best as she could. Once, Anurupa had tended to this cleaning up with her own hands. With her increasing allergy to dust, she had given it all up.

'Even Babin's bed will not suffice for that lot!' said Sukhomoy with disgust. 'Chottu's room will also have to be opened up.'

'Open it up then. Let it be used. They have become ghost chambers now.'

Dissatisfied with her elaborate show of hospitality, Sukhomoy angrily opened the drawer and tossed the keys onto her bed. The charm would be dispelled. Amal would desecrate the sacred intimacy of those rooms with his uncivilized presence.

He stalked out of the room, pausing at the door to tell his wife that Pushpa should do the needful as he was going out.

It was noon by the time the real reason behind their arrival became clear. Amal himself let it out during lunch. Amal's elder son had an eye problem, his eyes watered all the time. Occasionally there was pain in the affected eye. He had consulted a few doctors in Seuri, each had voiced a different opinion. One suggested a problem with the glands, another, with the nerves, a third, that it was to do with the cornea. He had come to consult an ophthalmologist in Calcutta with a letter of recommendation from the local doctor. Dr Suren Sarkar of the Presidency General Hospital would conduct the investigations. The name rang a bell. Chottu had probably mentioned it to Sukhomoy.

Sukhomoy retreated into his study and lit a cigarette. He had this habit of relaxing after a meal with a cigarette. Once, it had been twenty or twenty-five a day. Now he had brought it down to one after each meal and perhaps a couple more during the day. He was planning to give up the habit altogether. Of late he had been experiencing a feeling of pain and uneasiness in his chest if he walked quickly. He was also tiring easily. He had not told his wife about it. No point in worrying her with his problems, the poor thing had enough of her own.

The afternoon had been sultry. A sudden gust of wind blew dust into the room. The wind chased a few dry leaves down the road. Sukhomoy got up and shut the window. How many times had he instructed Pushpa to keep the windows closed in the afternoon, the dust messed up the rooms, but she never bothered. Today, of course, it was excusable. She had her hands full enough with the dust that had blown in from Seuri.

Amal was really disgusting, as dirty as he was irresponsible! All the result of a lack of education, of course! His behaviour at lunch had been really atrocious. With the child suffering from his eye problem, here he was, busy tearing the city's doctors to pieces, while he sucked at a bone of mutton. 'That doctor in Seuri was useless.' He complained. 'Tried to act smart with me. I marched into his chamber and gave the blighter a piece of my mind.' What an indecent posture he adopted! One leg was tucked onto the dining chair, the other swinging below. The only garment he wore was a checked and garish *lungi*. You could see his hairy chest. Awful! And the way he slurped noisily as he rinsed his mouth!

Sukhomoy put out his cigarette and went up to his bedroom. Ah, his worst fears were confirmed. There was Amal firmly established on a wicker stool, prattling away endlessly to Anurupa. Had the fellow no sense at all? He knew his aunt had not slept all night! Should she not be allowed to sleep? Why on earth did Anurupa encourage him? It was sure to be pure family scandal…who was teetering on the brink of bankruptcy…whose daughter was planning to elope with whom…who had grabbed his brother's land in Rampurhat! What could Anurupa gain from all this? He himself had never encouraged Amal. If he came home, he was not prepared to extend anything more than elementary hospitality, beyond which he expected them to take the cue for departure. And this applied not only to Amal, but to all members of his family.

Instead of going into his own room, he wandered into the corridor that lay between his sons' rooms. The doors were wide open. Chottu's bed was littered untidily with Amal's belongings. Amal's wife Manju was lying on Babin's bed with the baby at her side. The elder son was sprawled out on the floor, the younger one curled into a tight ball on the edge of the bed.

Sukhomoy turned aside and walked on to the spacious, circular balcony, facing the east and the south, from where the sunlight usually withdrew by noon. He lowered himself into an arm-chair. This arm-chair and a couple of wicker stools usually lay scattered across this balcony. His sons' rooms were very dear to him, his sanctuaries in loneliness. Unknown to Anurupa, he would occasionally unlock them and wander around, picking up mementoes from the past. He would finger the furniture in the room. The posters were long gone, but the faded outlines on the walls were his own picture gallery…. Babin's birth…his first tottering steps…his earliest syllables…his first day at school…Anurupa being rushed to the Railway Hospital at night…Chottu's arrival…the two brothers growing up together…a frieze of memories on the walls, a complete picture. Babin came back from the States to get married and left with his wife. Chottu got an offer for research in London and married the girl of his choice before he left... Sukhomoy at the airport bidding them good-bye, embracing his sons and later his grandchildren...how many tender memories these rooms held captive! He would secretly open the door and gaze at them hungrily.

'Asleep?'

Sukhomoy opened his eyes but did not answer. Amal pulled up a wicker stool and sat down—and strangely enough seemed to respect the quiet of the afternoon's shadows which surrounded them.

'You are looking old these days, Mama,' he said suddenly.

His uncle sighed, 'Well, I am growing older!'

'Nonsense, you have hardly touched 70 yet. How old are you? 68 or 69?'

'That's no mean amount.'

'Not a great deal either. Look at my Jetha. 81 years old and still refereeing football matches for children! And my father? Prostrated at 76! Bedridden all his life!'

'Jamaibabu was always the sickly type,' said Sukhomoy absently.

'Nonsense! You know where the shoe pinches! When you are duped by your favourite one, your body caves in.'

'Who has duped your father? You and your wife are there to look after him.'

'Do you think he loves us? Not at all. He was always partial to his elder son...good in studies...got a couple of degrees tucked up his sleeve! May not be a patch on Babin and Chottu. But nevertheless, my father's hopes and aspirations were all pinned on him. Now, he has cut off all relations with the family. And I, the eyesore of my parents, kicked around and cursed all my life by my father...just think of him having to tolerate me day in and day out.'

'Has Nirmal really partitioned the house?' Sukhomoy had learnt of this from his sister's letters, but he still felt compelled to ask.

'A solid ten-inch boundary wall between the houses. Hen-pecked, totally hen-pecked, that brother of mine! My father had a mild heart attack, I met my brother on the street and informed him. He never even bothered to pay us a courtesy call! Probably afraid of having to shell out cash. He doesn't even get Mother a saree for Durga Puja.'

Sukhomoy tried to make light of the issue, 'Anyway, good for you! Taking care of your old parents and reaping a harvest of virtues for your after-life!'

'Virtue, vice?...I am not clever enough to understand these notions, Mama! All I know is that our parents looked after us in childhood and it is time the roles were reversed. No issue of charity involved anywhere! Just hard debit and credit! Grudgingly or otherwise, they did give me shelter, didn't they? The debt has to be repaid.'

In some remote corner of his heart Sukhomoy experienced a mild qualm, he couldn't quite pin it down.

'I believe Babin is planning to settle down abroad,' said Amal abruptly, 'Mamima was telling us he has got some green card or something?'

'That he has. But he has never said he is not coming back.' Somehow the father's voice lacked conviction. Mentally, he cursed his wife for confiding in Amal.

Amal's curiosity was endless, 'But rest assured, Chottu will never settle abroad. He was always so attached to Mamima.'

'Well, if it suits them to settle there, they should certainly do so.' Sukhomoy's voice was firmer now. 'What is there in this country to attract men of their calibre?'

'You are right. They shouldn't come back, they're so brilliant.' Amal said sagaciously. 'That is what I always tell Manju. You have only seen me and my brother, two perfectly ridiculous specimens. Me, a total washout and a failure and my brother, that fake scholar, absolutely hen-pecked, wagging his tail beside his wife! You should see my uncle's boys, so polite, so cultured and well brought up. Never stood second in their lives.'

Even if that were a trifle hyperbolic, there was some truth in it. Babin had stood third in his Higher Secondary exam, Chottu was second in his Joint Entrance exam for the Medical stream. Their father had spared no effort, either physical or financial. This was the culmination of all his efforts. He had been the ideal father, carefully steering them on the right path since childhood, and this was his reward, his success as a father! Their wives were equally well educated and well brought-up. Babin's wife taught in a school abroad and Chottu's wife was of course, a doctor like him. Success, prosperity, happiness, there was no dearth of all that in Sukhomoy's contented life. Why then the vague, stabbing pain and the loneliness of an afternoon?

'Don't you want to know what I wrote in my letter?'

Anurupa was finishing her light supper, a couple of *chapattis* and a bowl of chicken stew that Pushpa had specially prepared for her. Under normal circumstances, she would have enjoyed this light repast, but tonight a chill ran down her spine. What, if the attack recurred?

'Do you want to hear or not? Or, shall I seal the letter?' asked Sukhomoy impatiently.

Anurupa's breath whistled through her chest, 'What is there to hear? The same old tune? We are alright...how are you? Don't worry about us...your mother wasn't well, had an asthmatic attack, she's better now.'

Sukhomoy was a little offended, 'Is that all I write?'

'Isn't it?'

He glanced sharply at his wife, 'Well then, what should I write? Should I tell them how I sit beside you night after night, watching your eyes bulge with every gasping breath?'

'Have I asked you to?'

'Or maybe I should say, "Dear Chottu, the *gul mohur* you planted beside the gate is in full bloom. As also your brother's *palash*. The two trees form a red canopy over our gate?"'

Anurupa stopped eating and stared at her husband, 'Why don't you admit the truth? That there is nothing further to say. That this vain effort at correspondence is only a confirmation that we are still around?'

In silence, her husband sealed the flap of the air-mail...the bright electric light looked suddenly dim, even hazy.

'You are inhuman, Anu!' he said in a low voice.

'Not inhuman, simply honest! Can you really bring yourself to write what you'd like to? Or, allow me to do so?'

'Why should we?' His voice was hoarse.

'Don't then. Sit guarding your Kuvera's mansion like a *Yaksha*.'

Downstairs, Amal had switched on the television full blast. Strains of a song from an old Hindi movie floated up the stairs. Anurupa strained her ears to catch the words of the lyric. Rinsing her hands into her plate, she gently chided her husband, 'You have become too unreasonable these days. Did you have to be so harsh to that child?'

'Serves him right. Why should he be shouting while I'm trying to listen to the news? And that woman? Equally irresponsible. Mother of three and can't control even one of them! The baby wet the sofa, she simply brushed it off. The boy was opening and shutting the door of the showcase noisily. She didn't say a thing. They've reduced the house to shambles in a day.'

'Let them be. Don't be so squeamish. They've just come for a couple of days, after all. Are we going to take your sofas and show cases with us to heaven? That military friend of yours was just commenting the other day that after our generation is gone, there'll only be a row of ghost mansions here. He was right.'

Sukhomoy put his spectacles back into the case. He couldn't help smiling at the tone of Anurupa's voice, 'And I'll be the Yaksha guarding them! The Yaksha of Salt Lake!'

'That's exactly what you will be,' laughed his wife. 'Okay, now that's enough. Give me my capsule.' She washed down the medicine with a lot of water, 'It's nearly ten o' clock. Aren't you going to have your dinner?'

'We will. Let your Pushparani finish watching her serial. This morning she couldn't stand Amal's wife, now they are the best of friends.'

'Amal's wife is a nice girl. She is very unhappy. Even your sister exploits her cruelly,' said Anurupa after a moment's hesitation.

'Why?'

'What do you mean, why? She didn't bring any dowry, beyond the clothes she was in, that's why. Her mother-in-law abuses her day and night. Poor thing, she was in tears.'

'Amal is quite a tough fellow. Why doesn't he protest?'

'Does he have the means? With a meagre salary of just a thousand rupees, he has to depend on your brother-in-law's pension and the interest from the fixed deposits.'

Sukhomoy was stunned, 'Then why did he claim to be looking after his old parents repaying his debt of gratitude to them?'

'Nonsense, that girl wants to set up a separate household. But your nephew is helpless. If they move out, they will starve. They are hanging around out of dire necessity, Roy Mahashay, not out of reverence for their parents. Even for that child's treatment, your brother-in-law had to take money out of his bank account.'

Pushpa removed the dishes from Anurupa's bedside and announced that dinner had been served downstairs.

Sukhomoy finished his dinner, smoked a cigarette, took his after-dinner stroll on the circular balcony. Went to bed. The oppressive heat of the day had subsided, a soft breeze was blowing, caressing the furniture, its occupants. The tube light across the fronds of the coconut palms flickered. But Sukhomoy could not sleep. The terrifying memories of last night and his own helplessness were too fresh in his mind. He could not sleep even after the commotion had subsided in the next room.

Suddenly, he heard a sound. Then there was silence. Then again and again, rising and falling. After listening intently for a while, Sukhomoy realized its source. Amal was snoring. About to lose his temper, Sukhomoy controlled himself. His nerves relaxed. The sound spiralled through the dark house like a moth, a comforting presence.

Anurupa did not have an attack that night. Sukhomoy fell asleep.

She did not have an attack the next night either. Nor the next. For two whole days Amal and his brood trooped through the house, jumping up and down, messing things up. The children uprooted the plants on the terrace. The child was examined by a doctor. There was nothing much the matter, it was a glandular problem, the medicines would continue, there would be a check up after a month. Amal joyfully took his family on a whirlwind tour of Calcutta, the Metro, the second Hooghly Bridge…he left nothing out. Today, they were leaving, bag and baggage, by the afternoon bus from Dharamtolla. Anurupa prepared *luchi*, curry, *halwa* with her own hands, to pack for the journey. She had given Manju a new saree and a set of clothes each, for the children.

Manju shed a few tears. Amal laughed his raucous laugh. The children did neither.

They left in the scorching heat of noon.

Babin and Chottu's rooms had been swept clean by Pushpa. Back to their old spic and span appearance!

About to lock them up once again, Sukhomoy stopped, taken aback. For, standing silently in the shadowy corridor between the two open rooms was Anurupa, alone in the shade of the afternoon. How utterly lonely and destitute she looked! Babin and Chottu's proud mother, alone, absolutely alone, in the last quarter of her life.

A deep sigh tore through Sukhomoy's body. If only one of his sons had been uneducated, unemployed, worthless, like Amal!

Bengali original: 'Taan'
Translated by Saumitra Chakravarty

The Testament of
Madhobi

Suchitra Bhattacharya

I AM MADHOBI, THE DAUGHTER OF KING YAYATI, CELEBRATED FOR HIS PIETY and virtuousness. Who is my mother? Why should you ask? A mother is after all no more than a womb, her identity is immaterial. I am born of the loins of the invincible king Yayati. That is my identity: a maiden should have no other. And why talk of an identity? Do I even have an independent existence?

This story begins on a Spring day long ago when I had just stepped into my youth. I was in the royal gardens, gathering flowers with my closest handmaidens, when I received the summons to the royal court. I found my father on the throne, his grim countenance clouded with anxiety. Before him stood two men—one, a young rishi of celestial appearance, the other, a huge and powerful man. I was familiar with the second. He was my father's friend Garuda. I bent down and touched his feet and the rishi's, too.

My arrival seemed to have created quite a stir in the court. The clouds seemed to lift from my father's brow.

'Listen, Madhobi,' he said in a deep voice, 'My friend Garuda has brought Rishi Galab to me. The rishi has made a request to me, for something that he has not been able to find in spite of his search across many lands.'

I wondered why I had been summoned. My father did not grant me a second glance. Turning to the sage and without so much as a tremor in his voice, he said,

'*Munivar*, at this moment, I have no means of granting your request. However, it would be wrong on my part to turn away a *brahmarishi* like you, empty handed, or the Vishnusakha, for that matter. So, I suggest that you accept my daughter Madhobi in lieu of the 800 horses you desire. She is a beautiful and gentle girl. I can only pray that your objectives can be met through her.'

Me, in lieu of horses! I could not understand head or tail of my father's words. I could hardly ask him what he meant. Anyway, I had no right to question. Overwhelmed, I stared at my progenitor for a while and then glanced at the Rishi. Would I henceforth be under him? The idea was not without its appeal. What mattered if he was not a Kshatriya warrior? He was wise and perfectly beautiful. I was lucky. Young girls like me dream of such men, don't they?

A pall of gloom descended upon the inner chambers of the palace. My handmaidens, my companions, my mother, my stepmother, they all wept. I bade farewell to them all one by one. And then, taking nothing but the clothes I was in, I left the royal palace with Rishi Galab.

My father's friend Garuda went his way. Rishi Galab walked ahead in silence. Trembling, I followed him. I was mentally preparing myself. Renouncing the pleasures of the royal palace, I would have to spend the rest of my life in the forest hermitage. I would have to learn to make myself worthy of him. Would I be able to accomplish that? Of course, I would. I was in love with Galab. A woman can make any sacrifice for her chosen one.

We walked on and on. Leaving the confines of the capital and then that of human habitation, we walked through a small forest. Beyond that was a gurgling brook. The weary sage sat down to rest on the banks of the river, under the shade of a *shingshapa* tree. With some trepidation, I too seated myself a short distance away from him.

In the shade of the tree, the silence seemed unbearable. Yet, I did not have the courage to start a conversation on my own. After a while out of sheer despair, I blurted out,

'Rishivar, should I have the honour of waiting upon you?'

Galab smiled thinly and shook his head,

'There is no need. We will resume our journey in a while.'

What a pleasant voice he had! I was overwhelmed,

'Are we to cross the river?'

'Yes.'

'Is your *ashram* a long distance away?'

'Yes,' he replied without looking at me, his gaze fixed on the swiftly flowing stream.

I spoke in an amorous voice,

'Why are you so grave, Rishivar? Have I failed to please you?'

A look of irritation flitted across his face. Momentarily, he glanced at me and then back at the stream.

'Daughter of Yayati, listen to me,' he said gruffly, 'this is hardly the time for caprice or pleasure. Do you know why I have brought you here?'

I gave him a vivacious look,

'Yes,' I said, 'you have accepted me in lieu of 800 horses.'

'You are wrong. You have been brought for the purpose of securing those horses, not in lieu of them.'

'What do you mean?'

'So King Yayati has not told you the whole story?'

For an instant, Galab's mind seemed to wander. He went down to the stream and splashed water from his cupped hands on his face. He came back to stand before me,

'Daughter of Yayati, listen to me. Let me tell you the truth in the clearest terms,' he said. 'I have not brought you here to accept you. At least, not yet. You have to accomplish a task for me, a very difficult task.'

My heart pounded,

'What is your command?' I whispered almost inaudibly.

'My Guru, Vishwamitra, has asked for 800 horses of a very rare breed as his *gurudakshina*. These horses are of a milky white colour, each having one dark ear. I have heard that King Harshashwa of Ayodhya has such horses in his possession. But I am told he will not part with these for nothing. He will demand in exchange, such a woman as can bear him a son fit to be a sovereign. I am taking you to him. If he approves of you, I shall leave you with him so that I can claim the horses in exchange.'

I stared at him, speechless with shock. What was he saying? I was a woman, no doubt, but was I not a human being? He was treating me as an item of financial gain. It was shameful.

When I could recollect my senses, I asked him outright whether my father was aware of this.

'Of course,' said Galab, 'he was the one who gave me this suggestion.'

Tears welled up in my eyes, tears of anger and sorrow. That my own father, my lifegiver, could do this to me...!

'So, I have to spend the rest of my life in Ayodhya?' I blurted out.

'Yes. Or, at least till you are able to bear him a son.'

'And then?'

A strange smile hovered at the corner of his lips,

'And then I may bring you back,' he said in a softer voice, 'I have to. I have been entrusted with the responsibility.'

Strange indeed are the workings of a woman's mind. Hope instantly flickered within me like a lamp. A deceptive voice whispered into my ears that it was the duty of a woman to come to the rescue of her chosen one in distress. If only I could overcome my sense of revulsion and spend a while with the King of Ayodhya, Galab would be mine.

Blessed is the lure of hope! Blessed the power of male attraction over a woman's mind!

We resumed our journey, across rivers and mountains, dense forests and bustling highways to Ayodhya. When we reached our destination, I was duly presented at the court of Harshashwa. Galab put forth his proposal.

The king looked me up and down in much the same way as a trader measures animals at a fair. At last he smiled:

'I must confess this girl is auspicious. I have no doubt she will bear me the heir I covet. But Rishivar, I must warn you that I cannot offer you your toll in totality. I do have the horses you desire, but only 200 of them. Will that be enough for you?'

This was sheer bargaining. My heart churned in disgust. Teeth clenched, I waited. For Galab...only for Galab.

Galab had turned pale. Not at my impending fate, but at his own frustrating dilemma. Taking me aside, he muttered,

'Daughter of Yayati, what should I do now? If I cannot carry out my Guru's commandment, I shall be guilty of sin. I will be denied all happiness on earth and forfeit any hope of salvation in the hereafter. You have brought me no luck. My lifetime of penance and toil are of no avail.'

His words pierced me like an arrow. But only for a moment. My frozen heart slowly began to thaw in pity. For him, only for his predicament. A beautiful woman was at hand, yet he was worried about salvation after death. Deliberately suppressing my anguish, I spoke up,

'But the solution is so simple! You trade your 200 horses for me now. It will take me a year at least to produce a son. Meanwhile, you can make enquiries of other monarchs about the remaining 600. If I am destined to be traded for horses, it matters little how many kings I am bedded down with! As long as you get your horses…!'

There was irony in my proposal. I had hoped that my mockery would shame him into a vehement protest! It is said that if you walk seven steps with someone, he becomes your friend, even if it be an animal from the forest. Well, I had walked more than a million steps with Rishi Galab over the last few days. Could I not expect at least a grain of sympathy from him? Was he so immune to a friend's heartrending anguish?

Not a shadow of pain crossed his face. He was ecstatic. And then dull again.

'Your proposal is good. But there is a snag in it.'

'Is that so?'

'You mean you really don't know?' Galab's surprise was evident. 'You are born into a royal family, don't you know that monarchs prefer virgins. What king will be prepared to accept you after a year spent with another one?'

Blessed be the mind of man! A woman on hire and a virgin housed in the self-same body?

Taking refuge in a simple subterfuge, I smiled,

'If that is all, that's no problem. Pleased with my devotion in my childhood, a sage well versed in the Vedas, had once blessed me with a strange boon, that my virginity would be renewed after each childbirth.'

'Nonsense! How can that be possible?'

'It is. You see, we women are at the mercy of men like you. You can grant us any boon you deem fit. As long as it suits your desires.'

For all his perusal of the shastras, how ignorant he was of the ways of the world, I thought. All his knowledge did not reveal to him the simple fact that a woman loses her chastity even by losing her heart to a man, leave alone her body!

In a fit of joy. Galab seized my hand,

'Daughter of Yayati, how can I thank you? You have saved me.'

'There is no need. Only give me your word that once your target is achieved, you will…'

'Of course, of course. Do you think I cannot appreciate how terrible it is for a woman to lead such a life?'

I was taken to the inner chambers of King Harshashwa's palace. Galab departed.

And thus began a new life for me. The life of a river that flowed and flowed without end.

Time passed. Only I knew what I went through. I was mated with three kings in quick succession. After Harshashwa, it was the turn of Divodasa, the King of Kashi, and then that of Bhojraj Ushinor. Each was great in his own way. The first known for his munificence, the second for his valour, Ushinor, for his pursuit of truth. But in one respect they were all alike. Not one of them was reluctant to enjoy a woman in return for his horses. Perhaps, there was some subtle religious satisfaction involved in all this.

Each one of them was however granted his heart's desire. I carried the seed of each in my womb according to the law of Nature, and gifted him with a son. Basumona was the son of Harshashwa, Pratardan in the palace of King Divodasa and Shibi, in Ushinor's. The news of each birth was ceremoniously conveyed to my father. I am told he was ecstatic about his grandsons.

Leaving each of these infants in the hands of a wet nurse, I was forced to resume my journey. On the first occasion, when Galab came to fetch me, my heart cried out for Basumona. How could I forsake this helpless infant? I had begged King Harshashwa to allow the boy to be with me for a while till he was a little older. He refused. How could his son be brought up in another's home? I had forgotten that unlike the animal kingdom, in the human world a child is never his mother's.

My mother's milk froze in anguish. Froze, festered with pus, congealed and dried up. Thrice!

I turned to Galab just outside Ushinor's palace:

'You still have 200 horses left to acquire. Where to, now?'

There was a look of melancholy on Galab's face.

'All my efforts have been in vain. All my labour has been wasted!' He confessed in despair.

His labour? I felt like laughing. Still I asked,

'Why, what's the matter?'

'I must confess I am in a terrible quandary. Garuda came to me yesterday with the news that all these rare horses had once belonged to

Maharshi Richak, who had secured them from the abode of Varuna. Richak had offered a thousand white horses as dowry for his daughter Satyavati's wedding to Gadhi, the King of Kanyakubja. The King had in turn gifted them to the Brahmins, from whom these three Kings, Harshashwa, Divodasa and Ushinar had bought two hundred each. The remaining four hundred were stolen on the way. That means I have no hope of getting more horses of this kind. Of course, Vishnusakha Garuda asked me to offer the six hundred I have already secured, to my Guru as *gurudakshina* and confess my inability to get the rest. He believes my Guru would be sure to appreciate the problem.'

For an instant the hope of liberation leapt up in my heart.

'Garuda seems to be right.' I said brightly.

'Daughter of Yayati, that is impossible. My learning at the feet of my Guru will remain incomplete without the *gurudakshina* being paid in full.'

Darting a sweeping look at me from head to foot, he said in a thoughtful voice,

'However, there is one thing that could still be done. I am not sure whether that will help.'

'What is that?' My voice shook.

'If I could have offered you up to my Guru instead of the remaining horses?... But that cannot be. Gurudev will be insulted. He has asked for horses. Would he be satisfied with a woman?'

The company of three kings had taught me a thing or two about the ways of the world. I knew that he would certainly be satisfied. I also knew that, rishi or not, he was a male.

Galab seized my hand,

'Once more, just once more, daughter of Yayati! You have to bear it just once more for my sake.'

I choked back the rising tears,

'Let us go.' I said.

'Let us go. Perhaps, he will agree to accept you, just out of compassion for me?'

Ironical, wasn't it? A heartless man pleading for compassion? And the definition of that compassion? Merely, whether another man would be satisfied with a beautiful woman instead of horses!

I was not mistaken. One glance at me was enough to excite the passions of the great sage.

'What a fool you are, Galab!' He said in a voice overwhelmed with emotion. 'You have such a beautiful woman in your possession, couldn't you have offered me this woman long ago? I am a forest-dweller. What use are horses to me? I merely wanted to put you to test because you pleaded for gurudakshina. What a waste of time! However, better late than never!'

My life thus underwent another change. I was forced to exchange the royal palaces for the *ashram* life. However, the result was the same, the same sexual exploitation continued. The outcome was a son, Ashtak, whose father's lust vanished with his birth. Perhaps, the sage busied himself with thoughts of the Parambrahman once more. After all, how long can you expect a sage to be pre-occupied with a mere mortal, that too, a woman?

I was sent back to Rishi Galab, battered and broken in mind and body. I was totally drained out, exhausted. The sight of the sage no longer aroused me. My first love had long since withered in my heart, a distant memory. What lingered on was a faint sense of relief. I was tired of flowing on and on. I had realized to my cost, that princess or otherwise, a woman could never have an independent existence or identity, nor even a choice of her own. If I could somehow force myself to spend my remaining days with Galab, I would be content.

Once again, I resumed my journey behind Galab, across mountains and forests, rivers and cities. One afternoon, we crossed a swift flowing stream and sat down to rest beneath a *shingshapa* tree. The place seemed familiar, wasn't this the place where we had sat beside each other on the first day? The same thought must have crossed Galab's mind too, for he looked around him at the riverside scene. In the heat of the month of Chaitra, the wind swirled in gusts. A cuckoo chirped away in the forest. The silent sage broke his silence,

'What are you thinking, daughter of Yayati?'

I merely shook my head in response. He smiled slightly,

'The last few years have taken a heavy toll of your life, haven't they?'

I remained silent. His observation was meaningless.

'Your self-sacrifice will not go in vain, you'll see. The fame of the sons you have borne will spread far and wide. Basumona will be known

for his generosity, Pratardan for his valour, Shibi, for his religiosity and
Ashtak, the son of my Guru, will be an ascetic. Well, are you happy now?'

For an instant, four infant faces flashed through my mind. I wondered
how they were faring. Did they cry for their mother? Did they even
remember their unfortunate mother? The next moment, my lips twisted
into a smile. Galab was blessing my sons, not their mother. No crumbs
of generosity could ever be expected to fall on a woman. Alas! This was
a typical man!

'How does my happiness matter?' I said tonelessly. 'Your purpose
has been served, that is all.'

The cuckoo's call struck a sharper note. Galab edged closer and put a
hand on my shoulder. He turned to look full into my eyes. Once my heart
had yearned for such a moment. Today, I did not experience any such
emotion. Yet, I was familiar with that look in a man's eyes, with that touch.

'Control yourself, Rishivar!' I said drily.

'Why?'

'Not here. Not in this way.'

'Why, what is wrong with this place?' said Galab as he drew me into
a fierce embrace.

'This is a beautiful spot,' he whispered, 'the perfect setting of the
river, of trees and Nature. We are alone together. Years ago you had
offered yourself to me here, don't you remember? Well that auspicious
moment has arrived in your life. Don't let it flitter away.'

My heart churned with revulsion. Never before, not with the three
kings, not even with Vishwamitra, had a man's touch so revolted me.

I thrust him aside roughly,

'What's the hurry? Your purpose has been served, I don't have to be
taken to anyone anymore. Let us go to your ashram, and then throughout
my life I can be yours…'

'Throughout my life? In my ashram? With you?' Galab leapt away
from me. 'Don't you know, you cannot be taken to the ashram? The
ashram is a place of utmost purity. To live there with a woman associated
with another, is unethical. I cannot take you there as my wife.'

For a moment I was dumbfounded. The next, I was calm again. Why,
this was a fitting response from a man like Galab. I should have anticipated
this.

But I was adamant,

'I am not a used woman. I have given birth, now I am a virgin again.'

'You, a virgin?' Galab roared with laughter. 'Surely, you do not expect me to believe that tall tale?'

Furious, I screamed recklessly,

'If you knew it was a tale, then why did you offer me up to those kings each time, as a virgin? Was that not unethical?'

'Daughter of Yayati, you really are a fool.' He said, 'Minor subterfuges are permissible for a greater cause, it is no sin to take shelter in any such.' He made an effort to draw me close to him once again. 'Come, let us be united. Do not be afraid. I will deliver you to your father.'

I thrust him aside,

'Leave me alone. Don't touch me.' I cried.

Galab did leave me alone. Perhaps, his ego was hurt. He departed forever. He left behind him a girl without a name or an identity in the palace of her father Yayati.

Well, that could well have been the end of my story. I could at least have been left to spend the rest of my days in a corner of my father's palace in peace, if not in happiness. Princesses do not have to worry about the next meal, surely.

But Fate willed otherwise. The virtuous King Yayati hovered around me, he could not bear to leave his daughter unmarried, he was spending sleepless nights. Worse, a daughter without a husband would never achieve salvation in the hereafter. A husband would have to be found. But a husband for the mother of four sons would surely make him the object of ridicule in royal circles.

The King deliberated long and hard with his five sons. He even managed to come up with a solution. I was ordered to prepare for a *swayamvar,* without further ado.

Horrified, I tried to protest. No one bothered to listen.

A *swayamvar sabha* had been arranged at the confluence of the Ganga and the Yamuna at Prayag. I was ordered to go. Why there? The spot was sacred, it would absolve me of my sins. What my father left unsaid was that some hapless victim, twice married or thrice, had to be trapped for me to find succour.

The day has dawned. I have been brought to the *ashram* at the pilgrimage site of Prayag. Here, the swayamvar sabha has been arranged. My father has not joined us. Urgent royal duties have kept him away. I have not tried to verify the claim. However, my brothers, Yadu and Puru have personally supervised all arrangements and decorations, adorning the ashram and the altar. The air is heavy with the fragrance of flowers. My father's minions and sentinels are everywhere, welcoming each royal entourage.

Strangely enough, there seems no dearth of kings ready to enter into wedlock with a mother of four sons. I am told that even the serpent kings and the *yakshas* and *gandharvas* are present. I wonder why? Because I am a princess or because my womb is an auspicious, proven one?

My handmaidens have dressed me in my bridal attire. The maidens of the hermitage have woven my wedding garland for me. All that remains to be done is to step into the *sabha* and garland the prince of my choice.

Whom should I choose? Which Harshashwa, Divodasa, Ushinor or Vishvamitra would he be? Or perhaps, a Galab? Today I have the option of choosing anyone of these or none at all. But that would mean an ignominious return to the male domain of my father's palace. After him, with my brothers, males too. Or, should I wait till my sons came of age and staked their claim on their mother. But by then each would have become a male chauvinist in his own right.

Is there no escape? None at all? Should I escape into the forest? Surely, the wild beasts could treat me no worse than these!

I am still lost in a dilemma. The flowers in my garland have withered.

Bengali original: 'Aami Madhobi'
Translated by Saumitra Chakravarty

Glossary

CLASSICAL AND MYTHOLOGICAL REFERENCES:

ashram—hermitage

brahmarishi—Brahmin saint

dwisho johi—control over envy, malice

gandharva—glendoveer, belonging to a class of demi-gods proficient in music and war

Garuda—king of birds in Hindu mythology on whom Lord Vishnu rides, also called Vishnusakha, friend of Vishnu

Jamadagni—son of sage Richaka and Satyavati

karma—one's destiny as determined by his actions, according to Hindu and Buddhist philosophy

Karma Yoga—a system of purifying oneself through action

Kubera—Hindu god of wealth

munivar—reverent form of address to a rishi

Nachiketa—son of Aaruni (Uddalaka); gained knowledge of the Supreme from Yama

Lakshmi—Hindu goddess of wealth

Raktabeeja—a demon, every drop of whose blood, as it fell to the ground, could raise another demon equal in potential

rishi—seer/sage

Sabari—female member of ancient hunting non-Aryan community who waited all her life for Rama

Sakti—cult of worship—powerful goddess

sankhya—a philosophical treatise written by Kapila, a system of philosophy

Shaktishel—deadly mythological missile

swayamvar—ancient Indian custom whereby a princess could choose her husband from an assembly of kings and princes

Swetaketu—son of Uddalaka; stipulated rules of conduct for men and women

Trishanku—mythological king who was accommodated after his death in the void between heaven and earth, having recourse to neither alternative

Upamanyu—one of the pupils of sage Dhoumya, a great devotee of Shiva

yaksha—a class of demi-gods in Hindu mythology, guardian of Kubera's underground hoard of wealth

yajnas—Vedic sacrifices

Yasho Dehi—a prayer for fame

FAMILY RELATIONSHIPS: (OR KINSHIP TERMS)

baba—father

bowdi, dada—elder brother's wife, elder brother

chorda—younger among the brothers elder to one

choto khuki—an affectionate name, 'choto' meaning young girl, 'khuki' meaning girl child

dadababu—respectful address by maid to master

didi, mejdi—elder sister, second among the sisters elder to one

mejo bowdi—wife of the second elder brother

Indir Thakurun—name immortalized by Bibhuti Bhushan Bandyopadhyay

Jamaibabu—husband of elder sister

jetha, jethima—father's elder brother, his wife

kakima—aunt, father's younger brother's wife

mama, mamima—maternal uncle, his wife

mashima—aunt, mother's sister

nutan ginni—mistress of the house, fourth in order of seniority

pishi, pishima—father's sister

sahib kaka—father's younger brother, called 'sahib' because he is settled abroad

thamma—childish diminutive for Thakurma, paternal grandmother

thakurpo—husband's younger brother is thus referred to, in conservative families

FESTIVALS, CEREMONIAL AND RITUAL ITEMS AND IMPLEMENTS:

Adhivas—ceremony of ritual purification on the eve of a ritual function

Alta—lac dye used by Hindu women to edge their feet, symbol of auspiciousness

Baisakhi—festival of New Year in Assam

Bihu—harvest festival of Assam

Bijoya Dashami—Dusshera, tenth day of the holy month after Durga Puja

Brahminkanya—daughter of a Brahmin and therefore to be treated with respect

Brahmo—member of monotheistic religious movement initiated in Bengal

Chhat—seasonal festival

daker shaaj—ornaments of pith and tinsel used to decorate an idol

dhenki—husking pedal

'Durga, Durga'—cry of benediction uttered at the time of departure, normally wishing the person a safe journey

gobar–gangajal—cow-dung and Ganges water used in ritual purification

gurubhai—co-disciple

gurudakshina—fee payable to guru on completion of education at the hermitage

habishya—food cooked without oil or spices, prepared by the chief mourners for consumption during a bereavement in the family, before the 'shraddha' or memorial service is held

kanyadaan—the giving away of a girl to her husband by her father during the wedding ceremony

kulo—bamboo platter for winnowing, lamps laid out on it to welcome a new bride into her husband's home

naivedya—offerings made to a deity

palloo—edge of the saree worn over the shoulder, drawn over to cover the head by married women

Panchami, Shashti, Saptami, Ashtami, Nabami—fifth, sixth, seventh, eighth, ninth lunar days of the holy month of Durga Puja

rangoli—ornamental patterns drawn on the floor for festive occasions

Rath yatra—annual festival of the drawing of the chariot of Lord Jagannath

Sandhi Puja—special puja at the juncture of the eighth and nineth lunar days during Durga Puja

sindoor—vermilion powder used by married women in the parting of their hair

FLOWERS AND TREES:

bakul—large ever-green flowering tree with sweet-scented white flowers

champaka—flowering tree of the magnolia variety

gulmohur—tree with red flowers

kash—tall species of grass of which brooms are made, bears feathery white flowers

kolke—yellow, bell-shaped flowers

palash—cotton tree with large red flowers

rangabaran—ixora

sandhyamalati—a kind of jasmine that flowers in the evening

shingshapa—the dulbergia tree

FOOD ITEMS:

aloo dum—spicy curry of boiled potatoes
bata—small silvery-white fresh water fish
chhatu—flour made of barley, pigeon-pea, maize
chira—flattened rice
dalmoot—spicy savoury item of fried chira, gram, etc.
ghugni—curry prepared with pigeon peas, potatoes, coconut and spices
gosht—meat of lamb or goat
khichuri, khijri—spicy preparation of rice and lentils boiled together
labra—mixed vegetable curry
laddoo—a sweet drop
lau-bori—bottle-gourd cooked with ground and sun-baked dumplings of lentils
lau-chingri—bottle-gourd cooked with shrimps
lau-shaker chharchari—dry curry made of bottle gourd leaves
luchi—rolled-out balls of dough, fried in ghee
makai—maize
mourala macher bati chharchari—curry of a kind of very small fish
patal-bhaja—fried vegetable of cylindrical shape
payesh—rice pudding of thickened milk
rohu—fresh water fish, trout

MONTHS OF THE BENGALI CALENDER:

Aasarh—third month, from mid-June to mid-July
Aaswin—sixth month, from mid-September to mid-October
Baisakh—first month, from mid-April to mid-May
Bhadra—fifth month, mid-August to mid-September
Chaitra—last month, from mid-March to mid-April
Falgun—fifth month, from mid-February to mid-March

MUSICAL INSTRUMENTS AND TERMS:

alaap—to sing a tune faithfully and in perfect detail
keertans—songs sung in praise of god
khol—a musical instrument of percussion resembling a longish tom-tom
mejraph—a kind of wire thimble used by instrumentalists
mridanga—percussion instrument similar to the khol
pakhwaj—similar percussion instrument
tabla—a kind of tabour played mainly as accompaniment

tanpura—stringed musical instrument that helps the singer maintain perfect tune

saraswati veena—a kind of musical heptachord

sloka—couplet, distich, verse

surbahar—stringed musical instrument akin to the veena

MISCELLANEOUS:

akbari mohurs—an obsolete gold coin of India and Persia of the time of Akbar

akhara—gymnasium

andar-mahal—inner chambers reserved for women

Bagdi—a lowly Hindu caste

baraat—bridegroom's party coming to the bride's house for the wedding

bhadramahila—a gentlewoman

deota—devata, term of respect for Brahmin

Dhaniakhali—variety of Bengal cotton saree, named after the place where they are woven

dhouli—literally 'one who is fair'

dibri—open flame in a small container

dusad, ganju, dhobi—lower castes

durwan—security guard

gouna—going to live with husband after puberty

jatra—open-air opera or dramatic performance

jotedar—owner of a proprietary agricultural farm

kabi—poet, kabir larai—poetic duels

kutcherry—a feudal lord's court and office

lota—metal pot

machan—platform

mahajan—usurer

manashi—woman as envisaged within the mind

manushi— woman in actual life

maulvi—a Mohammedan scholar

nautanki—folk theatre

nikah—re-marriage of divorced or widowed women in Muslim custom

randi—ironically used for both a widow and a prostitute

sarkar—master

tuntuni—species of small, warbling bird, tailor bird

vyayam samiti—place for physical exercise, gymnasium

zilla pradhan—chief of a district

Note on Translators

Dhouli
Sarmistha Dutta Gupta is a translator and editor based in Kolkata. She has co-edited and translated *The Stream Within* (Calcutta: Stree, 1999), a volume of short stories by contemporary Bengali women writers.

The Divorce, Love Story
Vikram Iyengar, a Kathak dancer based in Kolkata, is also involved in experimental theatre and research in performing arts.

And the Rains Came Again
Krishna Sen is Professor of English at the University of Calcutta. Her publications include *Negotiating Modernity: Myth in the Theatre of Eliot, O'Neill and Sartre* (Minerva), *Critical Essays on 'The Guide' with an Introduction to Narayan's Fiction* (Orient Longman), the contributions on Amitav Ghosh and Amit Chaudhury in the *Dictionary of Literary Biography (South Asian Writers)*, and several scholarly articles in national and international journals. She has edited Ibsen's *A Doll's House* (Penguin India) and Amitav Ghosh's *The Calcutta Chromosome* (Orient Longman), and is a contributor to the forthcoming *A Companion to James Joyce* (Basil Blackwell).

Stories by Bani Basu, Ashapurna Devi and Suchitra Bhattacharya
Saumitra Chakravarty is a gold medalist from Calcutta University. Her Ph.D. thesis was on 'The Search for Identity in Contemporary British Fiction (1950–70)'. She has published a volume of poems, entitled *The Silent Cry* and co-authored a volume of critical essays entitled *The Endangered Self*. Her critical articles and research papers have been published in books like *Images of Women in Indian Writing in English* and in journals like *The Literary Criterion, The Critical Endeavour, The Atlantic Review* and in the *Il Bianco e*

Il Nero. Her poems have been translated into Spanish and published in *Bells*, the *Journal of the University of Barcelona*. She has presented papers at many regional, national and international seminars. She has worked as co-coordinator of a British Council Project on Translations and is currently working on a project on 'Partnership Discourse in World Literatures Written in English' with the University of Udine, Italy. She is Professor and Head of Department of English at VVS College, Bangalore.

The Aftermath
Ahitagni Chakraborty is a consultant in creative solutions and media/ advertising, based in Bangalore.